*THEY STUDIED* **Man**

CHARLES DARWIN

HERBERT SPENCER

EDWARD TYLOR

JAMES FRAZER

EMILE DURKHEIM

FRANZ BOAS

BRONISLAW MALINOWSKI

ALFRED KROEBER

RUTH BENEDICT

SIGMUND FREUD

*ABRAM KARDINER*

*and* *EDWARD PREBLE*

# THEY STUDIED

# MAN

THE WORLD PUBLISHING COMPANY

CLEVELAND AND NEW YORK

PUBLISHED BY *The World Publishing Company*
2231 West 110th Street, Cleveland 2, Ohio

PUBLISHED SIMULTANEOUSLY IN CANADA BY
Nelson, Foster & Scott Ltd.

*Library of Congress Catalog Card Number: 61-5808*

FIRST EDITION

# CONTENTS

CONTENTS

## ILLUSTRATIONS

*(following page 128)*

Charles Darwin (Courtesy American Museum of Natural History)

Herbert Spencer (New York Public Library Picture Collection)

Edward Tylor (National Portrait Gallery, London)

James Frazer (Lafayette, Ltd., London)

Emile Durkheim

Franz Boas (Columbia University)

Bronislaw Malinowski

Alfred Kroeber (Columbia University)

Ruth Benedict (New York Public Library Picture Collection)

Sigmund Freud (The Bettmann Archive)

THE LABORS involved in writing this book were unevenly divided. The plan of the book was conceived by Abram Kardiner, but Edward Preble did the major part of the work. Kardiner must take special responsibility for the final section of the work. Most honorable mention must go to Mr. Arthur Cohen for his persistence and determination in bolstering the courage of the authors, and for his valuable editorial assistance.

A collaboration of this kind can be compared to the focusing of binoculars with individual eye focus, where joined but independent views are slowly integrated. Introduce now the hand of a third party on the binoculars' housing and the analogy is complete.

We are grateful to Helene Boas Yampolsky, daughter of Franz Boas, and to Jozefa Malinowska Stuart, daughter of Bronislaw Malinowski, for valuable biographical information and for generous co-operation and hospitality.

William Duncan Strong, Columbia University, read part of the manuscript and made comments which are greatly appreciated.

We are indebted to James Dunbar Pickering, Gettysburg College, for simplifying unnecessary complications; and to James J. Walsh, Columbia University, for complicating misleading simplifications.

Maytee Preble typed the original manuscript in the peanut butter-and-jelly sandwich factory that constitutes her kitchen, and in this setting was prompted to make spon-

taneous and penetrating comments on the central issue in
this book—human adaptation.

ABRAM KARDINER
EDWARD PREBLE

PART 1

*THE NEW DIMENSION:* **Culture**

## INTRODUCTION

THIS BOOK is an experiment in the description of an episode in cultural change. It takes as its text a segment of the cultural history of the nineteenth and twentieth centuries, the period in which, from nebulous origins, cultural anthropology developed into a scientific discipline.

The authors have not attempted to write a history of anthropology, for they are neither qualified nor interested in such an enterprise. Rather, they have attempted to relate the seminal hypotheses of the few great innovators in the development of a "science of man" to the ethos of the times and to the specific lives of these innovators. By using this method of treatment, the birth and growth of this scientific tradition can be presented within an adaptational framework. On the cultural level the hypotheses, theories, and techniques of these scientists are portrayed as creations responsive to the collective interests and needs of the time. On the individual level, these creations are seen as the products of idiosyncrasy and genius. Adaptation and genius are not, as some people like to believe, incompatible. Human genius is not altogether a whimsical phenomenon; it derives from an acute sense of relevancy. Scientific hypotheses in any field lose their usefulness sooner or later and are replaced by others that are more relevant to the constantly changing conditions of human life. Our selection of anthropologists was decided by the judgment that each one invented either a seminal hypothesis or a new technique for the study of man. There will be disagreements concerning

13

our judgment in this selection, but we are emboldened by the fact that there is no way of telling how historians a century from now will evaluate the achievements of the anthropologists of this period.

Along with the account of a succession of ideas and techniques in the study of man, we have attempted to describe something about the dynamics of the transitions. The replacement of one hypothesis or technique for another is not due to fatigue, boredom, or rebellion. It occurs when the particular hypothesis or technique exhausts its ability to yield new knowledge, or when the conditions of the new ethos of a succeeding generation disqualify what passed for *truth* in the preceding one. In some instances the stimulus for new knowledge comes from another discipline. In the final chapter we attempt to demonstrate that the interest in the two disciplines with which we are mainly concerned— anthropology and psychology—had its roots in the vast social changes that took place in Western society between 1770 and 1850. We suggest that the new social machinery created by these changes gave a new direction to human needs and aspiration.

The story of the seminal ideas in cultural anthropology and their vicissitudes is relatively simple. The first organizing principle was furnished by the theory of evolution. This idea was conceived and implemented in such a way that after fifty years it ground to a halt insofar as it was capable of yielding new knowledge or even the kind of knowledge that would satisfy those who were living in the throes of the new social ferment that preceded the First World War. The original techniques and theoretical outlook of evolutionary anthropology were altered by two men, Emile Durkheim and Franz Boas. Durkheim brought to anthropology some ideas and attitudes from the germinating discipline of sociology, and Boas brought with him the precision and discipline of the natural sciences. This new school of functionalism was still concerned with institutions —accepted as the basic unit of anthropology—but it was now concerned with more complete and accurate observations, and with new organizing principles dealing with the relations of institutions to each other. There was much difference of opinion about how institutions relate to each other; Durkheim, Boas, Malinowski, Benedict, and Kroeber all represent different points of view on this question.

In the thirties a new dimension was introduced into anthropology. The original stimulus came from Freud. His first attempt to account for some aspects of man's social life (in *Totem and Taboo*) was completely rejected by anthropologists, and justifiably so. He had gone to the literature of evolutionary anthropology for confirmation of his psychological theory of human development. Specifically, he was looking for evidence that the experiences of primitive man were constitutional determinants in the life of modern man. This Lamarckian bias of Freud and most of his followers, and the devastating criticism of evolutionary anthropology by Boas, Goldenweiser, and Kroeber, disqualified the use of Freudian ideas in anthropology. Later attempts to introduce into anthropology an adaptational psychodynamics based on revisions of Freudian theory were, except for a limited and brief acceptance, rejected by anthropologists. The effort, however, is still being made to bring to anthropology an empirically based knowledge of the impact of social patterning on human development, and of the resulting effects on social change.

It is not the intention of the authors to engage in polemics concerning the fate of the psychological disciplines in their contact with anthropology. We only want to present some of the evidence for the belief that social institutions and social change are incomprehensible without a knowledge of human ontogenetic development, human motivation, and the inner workings of the mind. It is our contention that Freud, in spite of his blundering with Lamarckian oversimplifications, came upon a number of basic discoveries on which can be erected a sound psychology of adaptation; one that is capable of empirical derivation and confirmation, susceptible of correction and revision in the face of new evidence, and capable of widening the ambit of knowledge about man's personal and social adaptation.

A knowledge of the impact of institutions and of cultural

change on the human mind is of paramount importance in the twentieth century, because alterations in social patterning constitute the dominant issue of our time the world over. We must develop techniques for measuring the effect of these changes on man, lest we overlook the indication of individual and, consequently, social failure. Only with some advance warning can we introduce remedial measures. The science of man has acquired responsibilities it cannot at present meet. It cannot afford to ignore a promising technique, while debating irrelevancies. The techniques of a science of man must become more than the subject matter for academic virtuosity. They must be developed into instruments of human welfare and survival.

# CHARLES DARWIN

*A SECOND LIFE*

ON ANY WHITMONDAY between 1850 and 1880 the members of the Coal and Friendly Club of the little village of Down, in Kent, England, would march with band and banner to the house of Charles and Emma Darwin, a quarter of a mile away. Here the group of villagers would parade upon the green in front of the house until the treasurer of the club, Charles Darwin, emerged. Darwin would give a warm and individual greeting to the club members and then make a little speech, sprinkled with a few worn jokes, regarding the financial condition of their charity organization. The ceremony over, the Friendly Club would close its ranks and march back to the village, its three-piece band playing and its banner waving. Darwin, the man who had convinced the world that "From death, famine, rapine and the concealed war of nature . . . the highest good . . . has directly come," would turn and walk into the house.

Charles Darwin's personality is important for an understanding of his work and influence. Darwin was famous for his modesty and his ability to remain aloof from the condemnations and eulogies that poured in upon him for

17

twenty-two years, yet his personal writings reveal an amazing self-concern, expressed with wonderful naïveté and candor. His fiancée considered him ". . . the most open, transparent man I ever saw. . . ."

Charles Robert Darwin was born at Shrewsbury, England, in 1809. His paternal grandfather, Erasmus Darwin, was a versatile genius. He was a highly successful physician whose patients came to him from all over England and the Continent. He was also a poet, a man of letters, and a bold speculator in science and philosophy. His ruminations on the origin of species, written in verse, established him as an evolutionist who fully anticipated the views of the great Lamarck. Charles Darwin's maternal grandfather was the famous potter, Josiah Wedgwood—a man of imagination and of resolute independence and courage. Charles Darwin's father, Robert Waring Darwin, was the second son of Erasmus Darwin. Charles was to make the most of his hereditary potential for genius.

Robert Darwin followed his father into the medical profession and became a prosperous physician in Shrewsbury. A commanding figure in bulk and personality, he erected a paternal empire, dominating family, friends, and patients. "The Tide," as he was called by his daughter-in-law, played a crucial role in his son's life and work. Charles' mother, Susannah Wedgwood, had six children, Charles being the fifth-born. She died when Charles was but eight years old and he retained thereafter only the faintest memory of her.

For the first twenty-two years of his life Darwin seemed well on the way to fulfilling the prophecy of his father that "You care for nothing but shooting, dogs and rat-catching, and you will be a disgrace to yourself and your family." He "learnt absolutely nothing" at Dr. Butler's school at Shrewsbury, withdrew from the study of medicine at Edinburgh, and was only a mediocre theological student at Christ's College, Cambridge. His only real interests during these years were collecting insects and shooting. At Cambridge, however, his attractive personality introduced him not only into the sporting set but also into the company of several distinguished faculty members, notably Professor

John Henslow, whose botany lectures aroused Darwin's interest in natural history. It was through Henslow that Darwin was elected as a naturalist for the around-the-world voyage of the H.M.S. *Beagle*.

At the prospect of this voyage Darwin wrote: "My second life will then commence, and it shall be as a birthday for the rest of my life." It was, in fact, a "birthday" for the entire world. Darwin's experiences on the voyage of the *Beagle* inaugurated a chain of events which was to end in the public acceptance of the most revolutionary doctrine in the history of man's attempt to find his place in nature. But the "second life" barely missed being stillborn. Darwin's father was against the plan, and, although Charles was twenty-two years old and ecstatic at the prospect of going, he submitted meekly to his father's wish after a feeble protest. It was only through the gratuitous intervention of a respected uncle that the father reluctantly gave his approval. Darwin was overjoyed, but never completely recovered from the feeling that perhaps he should have followed his father's advice.

The Commander of the *Beagle*, Captain Robert Fitz-Roy, was convinced that through science ". . . sooner or later the truth of every statement in the Bible would be proved." Darwin, the man whom Fitz-Roy had taken aboard the *Beagle* partly in the hope that he would help establish this proof, began his undermining of one of the Bible's greatest doctrines—the separate creation and immutability of species—before the voyage was even completed.

In 1836, after five years of exploration, the *Beagle* returned to England. The next year Darwin started his first notebook on the transmutation of species; and in the following year he ". . . got a theory by which to work . . ." from a reading of Malthus' *Essay on Population*. The theory, under Darwin's extension, became the key to organic evolution: Natural Selection.

Darwin married his cousin, Emma Wedgwood, in 1839, and in the same year published the first of his many works. In 1842 the Darwins moved to Down House near the village of Down, where it was hoped that Charles would find some relief from the unidentified illness which was to plague him all his life. It was in the same year that Darwin wrote the first brief sketch of his theory of species. This hurriedly penciled and almost illegible essay contained, with one exception, all the essential theoretical points later elaborated in the *Origin of Species*. This sketch was further enlarged in 1844, but remained unpublished. To only a few friends, such as Charles Lyell, Joseph Hooker, and Asa Gray, did he hint at the development of his monumental theory.

Fate, however, was to interfere with Darwin's diffidence. On June 18, 1858, Darwin received in the morning post the few sheets of a hastily written essay which stated, in abstract form, Darwin's entire theory regarding the origin of species. The modest author of the essay, Alfred Wallace, had sent the paper to Darwin in the hope that Darwin would deem it of sufficient interest to send it to the great geologist, Charles Lyell. Darwin's reaction to this threat to his priority in a theory he had arrived at twenty years earlier is revealing. He has often been represented as having given no thought to his own reputation in the field and of refusing, in deference to Wallace, to make his own views public until his friends took the matter out of his hands and publicized his twenty years of work on the subject. But Darwin was not so saintly, and unhuman, as these romantic versions suggest. His own correspondence reveals a man tortured and overwhelmed at this stroke of fate. To Lyell, who had urged him in 1856 to publish his views on species, he wrote, "Your words have come true with a vengeance— that I should be forestalled"; and in the same letter, "So all my originality, whatever it may amount to, will be smashed. . . ." And in a second letter to Lyell he states: "There is nothing in Wallace's sketch which is not written out much fuller in my sketch, copied out in 1844. . . ." But, then, a few sentences later: "I would far rather burn my whole book, than that he [Wallace] or any other man should think I behaved in a paltry manner." He then leaves the door open for Lyell and Hooker to do whatever they would think honorable. There could have been no doubt in his mind as to what they would do.

On July 1, Lyell and Hooker presented before the Linnean Society a joint paper by Darwin and Wallace on the theory of evolution by natural selection. Darwin's previous work was briefly, but clearly, accounted for, and it is Darwin's name that has served to epitomize the theory ever since. This, of course, is as it should be and was so recognized without hesitation by Wallace himelf.

In his short, sixty-page *Autobiography*, written in 1876, Darwin says nothing about the Wallace incident which would indicate that it had produced any emotional crisis. He does, however, recall a hunting experience in 1826 which he relates in enthusiastic detail: "One day when shooting at Woodhouse with Captain Owen . . . and Major Hill . . . I thought myself shamefully used, for every time after I had fired and thought that I had killed a bird, one of the two acted as if loading his gun, and cried out, 'You must not count that bird, for I fired at the same time,' and the gamekeeper, perceiving the joke, backed them up." Darwin was angry at this beclouding of his priority in a shooting match, and it remained an indelible experience which he could recount with great feeling fifty years later. About the Wallace incident, a question of priority involving his life's work, he stated simply and without emotion, "I cared very little whether men attributed most originality to me or to Wallace . . ." It was fortunate for Darwin that he had exciting hobbies, such as shooting.

In 1859 Darwin published an abridged version of the work he had been preparing on the origin of species. The title of the published work was *On the Origin of Species by Means of Natural Selection, or the Preservation of Favoured Races in the Struggle for Life*. He never did complete the larger work, and the book of 1859 has since carried the burden of the argument. Although considered a mere sketch by Darwin, its pages are filled with a hundred facts to support every essential point in the theoretical argument. Darwin's extreme reticence to make his views public until he could marshal overwhelming evidence played a large part in their early acceptance and enormous influence. Another factor in their success is to be found in Darwin's inordinate self-effacement. He seldom expressed a positive notion without first citing, and often exaggerating, the evidence against it and ending with an apology or a dismissal of the idea as irresponsible. He referred frequently to his own "moderate abilities" while extolling the genius of other workers. Those who were not won over by the weight of his evidence and the beauty of his theory were simply disarmed. It was difficult to attack a man who put his head on the block and provided his opponents with an axe. Of course, there was some bitter criticism—from science and religion; but, considering the radical implications of the theory, it is truly remarkable that there was so little.

Darwin was relieved of the task of defending his views against lay and clerical critics by his loyal friend Thomas H. Huxley, who became known as "Darwin's Bulldog." Huxley, a famous scientist, loved to fight, and he wrote to Darwin after the publication of the *Origin of Species:* "I trust you will not allow yourself to be in any way disgusted or annoyed by the considerable abuse and misrepresentation which, unless I greatly mistake, is in store for you . . . And as to the curs which will bark and yelp, you must recollect that some of your friends, at any rate, are endowed with an amount of combativeness which (though you have often and justly rebuked it) may stand you in good stead.

"I am sharpening up my claws and beak in readiness."

Darwin confined his efforts in behalf of his work to the scientific community. In the same spirit as he had once kept track of the birds he shot by tying knots in a string attached to a buttonhole, he now entered every new scientific "convert," as he called them, on a list so that he could tell at a glance how the battle was going. He rejoiced in every capture and fretted over the dissenters and the undecided.

By 1865 Charles Kingsley, a minister, could write to F. D. Maurice, "Darwin is conquering, and rushing on like a flood, by the mere force of truth and fact." Encouraged, often ecstatic, at the reception of his work, Darwin continued the deluge of facts and speculation.

*The Variation of Animals and Plants Under Domestication* was published in 1868. It was an extensive elaboration of material that had appeared in the relatively condensed arguments of the *Origin of Species*.

Darwin had believed since 1837 that man himself is subject to the law of "mutable productions." Encouraged by the general acceptance by naturalists of the theory of evolution, after thirty-five years of note-taking and three year of writing, he produced *The Descent of Man* in 1871.

His last major work, *The Expression of the Emotions in Man and Animals*, was published in 1872. He continued to work hard, when his health permitted, for ten more years. He died at Down House in 1882 and was buried in Westminster Abbey, a few feet from Sir Isaac Newton.

*The Descent of Man* (1871) contained Darwin's application of natural and sexual selection to the biological and social evolution of man; but the *Origin of Species* (1859) set the stage for the later work and is of greater historical significance. In establishing the doctrine of organic evolution, Darwin fathered one of the greatest ideological revolutions in history.

Although "one of the oldest guessings of human thought," as Höffding has put it, the idea of evolution could not gain acceptance until sufficient factual evidence in support of the idea and a plausible theory to account for the facts were presented. Darwin finally produced the evidence and the theory that placed the doctrine of evolution on solid ground, susceptible of the tests of science and common sense.

There are two important features to Darwin's *Origin of Species:* the presentation of the evidence for evolution, and the explication of the process by which it has occurred; the *what* and the *why* that must be present in any scientific explanation.

The first evidence for evolution that impressed Darwin emerged from his notebooks of the *Beagle* voyage. Two sets of observations especially impressed him as he read his own *Journal of Researches*, the published account of his travels on the *Beagle*. First, there was the observation that each separate island of the Galápagos had species of animals and plants which, though distinct from those on neighboring islands, had counterparts on all the islands and on the adjoining continent. The other observation was that the fossils of extinct forms of life that he had discovered resembled in a striking way the living species of the area. It dawned on Darwin that these puzzling sets of facts could be explained by a simple but heretical assumption: these similar species were blood relatives with a common descent. Species, in a word, are not immutable; the Judaic-Christian doctrine of creation must be wrong. For Darwin, a devout Christian, this realization was like "confessing a murder."

Darwin did not hesitate. He amassed evidence from the breeders of domestic animals on the modification of species. Breeders had for years modified animals by selecting for reproduction those animals that possessed in the highest degree the traits they wanted to exaggerate. If man can modify species by this form of imposed selection, perhaps, reasoned Darwin, there is a force in nature which produces similar change.

The great clue came when Darwin read Malthus' *Essay on Population*, which maintained that the rate of procreation among animals surpasses the means of subsistence, and that the weak must perish in the competition for survival. Malthus' work became the cornerstone for Darwin's theory of "natural selection"; the theory that would account for the evidence for evolution that Darwin had discovered.

The theory of natural selection ranks with Newton's laws as a great explanatory idea. Its comprehensive simplicity made the world of living things intelligible for the first time. It can be stated briefly:

Since all organisms reproduce at a rate which exceeds by many times the available means of subsistence, only a favored few of those born are destined to survive and perpetuate their kind. Only those individuals whose natural deviations place them at an advantage in the life-and-death competition for the means of life will survive. The greater the competition, the greater the significance of the smallest differences between individuals. The traits that insured the success of the survivors will be passed on to the next generation, where the selective process begins all over again. The cumulative effects of this process over many generations can result in a radical departure from the original form. The form the departures take will be determined by the specific problems of survival in a given environment. A different environment will result in modifications correlated with the different problems of adaptation. Thus, the different islands of the Galápagos are inhabited by similar but different species of plants and animals, the differences corresponding to the problems of adaptation peculiar to each island. In a world of almost unlimited diversity of living conditions, with a scale of time measured by geological epochs, the theory of natural selection can account for both the perfection and the diversity of living things without recourse to supernatural "explanation."

At the end of the *Origin of Species* Darwin stated that from that work, "Much light will be thrown on the origin of man and his history." He continued this task himself in *The Descent of Man*, published in 1871.

Darwin begins *The Descent of Man* by noting the similarity of body structure in all the higher animals, including man. He argues, as he did in the *Origin*, that such a similarity is unintelligible unless explained by a theory of modification through descent from a common ancestor. In any other view, the analogous structures, say, of the hand of a man or a monkey, the foot of a horse, the flipper of a seal, and the wing of a bat are inexplicable. Added to this great class of facts are the facts of comparative embryology, which reveal the almost identical development at a certain stage of the embryos of man, dog, seal, bat, reptile, and so on. And further, there is the universal existence of rudimentary organs which can only have come from ancestors who possessed the organs in a perfect state. "He who regrets with scorn," says Darwin, "that the shape of his own canines, and their occasional great development in other men, are due to our early forefathers having been provided with these formidable weapons, will probably reveal, by sneering, the line of his descent." Man has evolved with the vertebrates, and his long pedigree runs from an animal related to the sea squirt, through the fishes, amphibians, reptiles, birds, mammals, and Old World monkeys. He is, in Darwin's historic words, descended from "a hairy, tailed quadruped, probably arboreal in its habits, and an inhabitant of the Old World."

After establishing man as a product of the evolutionary process, Darwin sets out to show how natural selection has probably worked in the physical, intellectual, moral, and social development of man. That man has evolved under the action of natural selection is a necessary conclusion from the assumption that, like all animals, man tends to multiply at a rate beyond the means of subsistence and is therefore subject to a struggle for existence.

Darwin makes it clear that although man's intellectual and social powers are of great importance in his development, it would be a mistake to overlook or minimize the importance of a modified bodily structure to his success. The free use of the hands and arms, which is made possible by an erect posture, must have been a great advantage to the progenitor of man. With the free use of his hands and arms he had an advantage in both defense and attack in his ability to use clubs, stones, and other weapons. An increased dexterity and sensitivity of the hand necessary for the production of weapons and tools was made possible by the freeing of the hands from the rigors of locomotion and bodily support. Many changes in bodily structure were necessary in man's development as a biped, such as the flattening of the feet, the broadening of the pelvis, the special curving of the spine, and the altering of the position of the head.

Darwin believed that most of the distinctive bodily characteristics of man have been acquired either directly or indirectly through natural selection, but he attributed some modifications to the inherited effects of the use and disuse of certain parts of the body (the basis of Lamarck's evolutionary theory) and some to the direct action of changed conditions in the environment (the basis of Buffon's evolutionary theory). He held that all these means of modification co-operated in a way which made it very difficult to single out the operation of any one factor in the development of a given trait.

In concluding the chapter on man's bodily development Darwin meets the criticism that man's physical weakness, compared to that of other animals, would have made it impossible for him to survive in a struggle such as was postulated in the idea of evolution through natural selection. Darwin turns the argument around and conceives of man's biological weakness as probably his greatest asset, because it necessitated a highly co-operative relationship among individuals and thus led to the formation of human society —the main source of man's adaptive success.

Turning to man's "mental powers," under which Darwin discussed the aesthetic and the emotional as well as the intellectual, Darwin argues by detailed comparison that the differences in these areas between man and the lower animals are of degree and not of kind. "There is a much wider interval," says Darwin, " in mental power between one of the lowest fishes, as a lamprey or lancelet, and one of the higher apes, than between an ape and man; yet this interval is filled up by numberless gradations." All the higher animals exhibit traits usually attributed only to man, such as reason, imagination, curiosity, abstraction, emotion, imitation, and speech. However, the main difference between man and the other higher animals in these respects is that man makes his mental associations faster.

Darwin also believed that the higher animals share with man a sense and appreciation of the "beautiful." He thought, however, that the sense of the beautiful in animals was confined to the attractions of the opposite sex. The elaborate display of colors, especially in birds, for the benefit of the opposite sex was a common example.

If "religion" includes the belief in spiritual agencies, then, Darwin insisted, animals share this attribute with man. He gives examples of animals having been disturbed by the occurrence of some event where the familiar agent was absent—for example, the movement of a parasol by a breeze—and attributes the animals' disturbance to the belief that some strange, unseen living agent is the cause of the event. A belief that natural objects are animated by living, unseen agents was held by Darwin to be universal among the less civilized races, and he believed that a natural extension of this belief resulted in the "creation" of one or more gods whose attributes mirrored the ideas, values, and attitudes of the societies. The complex elements of religious devotion, such as love, submission to an exalted power, a sense of dependence, fear, reverence, gratitude, and hope, have their origin in man's experience in his physical and social environment. And again Darwin points to man's relationship with the lower animals by finding the same elements of devotion in the relationship, say, of a dog to its master.

Darwin passes to the "moral sense" in man which, although not absent in the lower animals, serves as the highest distinction between man and the lower animals. The moral sense arises from the "social instincts," which are common to many animals and are probably an extension of the parental and filial affections which are necessary for survival in those animals having a long period of dependency. The social instincts may be observed operating in certain animal species where sentinels are posted to warn the community of danger, and the individuals act in concert to defend the community or to attack their enemies or their prey.

Darwin believed that as soon as any animal endowed with the social instincts arrived at the intellectual level of man, it could not help but achieve a moral sense, or "conscience." He made it clear that the moral sense would take a form dictated by the problems of adaptation presented by the environment and would not necessarily reflect man's moral sense: "If, to take an extreme case, men were reared under precisely the same conditions as hive-bees, there can hardly be a doubt that our unmarried females would, like the worker bees, think it a social duty to kill their female daughters; and no one would think of interfering." A feeling of right and wrong, while not agreeing with ours, would exist and operate in circumstances related to the welfare of the community.

Among primitive peoples in general the social virtues would be essential to the survival of the group. Only those peoples who had, by natural selection, developed special instincts for aiding their fellow men would survive in a hostile environment.[1] While admitting that man's protection of the weak and helpless tends to propagate their defective traits, to the injury of the race of man as a whole, Darwin held that man cannot check his sympathy for them ". . . even at the urging of hard reason, without deterioration in the noblest part of his nature," and that ". . . if we were intentionally to neglect the weak and helpless, it could only be for a contingent benefit, with an overwhelming present evil."

According to Darwin, the social virtues first developed among the savages only as they obviously (for the savage) affected the welfare of the tribe. Thus, one of the chief causes of the "low morality" of savages—their "intemperance," "licentiousness," and "unnatural crimes"—is their ignorance of how the "self-regarding virtues" affect the welfare of the tribe. The beneficial effects of these virtues are too far removed to be recognized by a shortsighted mentality. Darwin believed, however, that ". . . as soon as marriage, whether polygamous, or monogamous, becomes common, jealousy will lead to the inculcation of female virtue; and this, being honoured, will tend to spread to the unmarried females"—and, slowly, to the males. "With increased experience and reason, man perceives the more remote consequences of his actions, and the self-re-

---

[1] It is worth noting that in promoting the "jungle philosophy" of progress, the social philosophers of the propertied, industrial classes in the late nineteenth century and early twentieth, found their justification in Darwin's account of the success of the predatory, rather than of the social animals. Darwin himself believed that the Golden Rule lies at the foundation of human morality and that it has evolved out of the social instincts of the higher animals.

garding virtues, such as temperance, chastity, etc., which during early times are . . . utterly disregarded, come to be highly esteemed or even held sacred. . . . Ultimately our moral sense or conscience becomes a highly complex sentiment—originating in the social instincts . . . largely guided by the approbation of our fellow men, ruled by reason, self-interest, and in later times by deep religious feelings, and confirmed by instruction and habit."

Darwin believed that as soon as man had reached an intellectual and social level which gave him the means to improve his position in the environment—through the use of tools, weapons, clothing, shelter, fire, and so on—natural selection would cease to operate in the modification of bodily structure. "Man," he says, "is enabled through his mental faculties 'to keep with an unchanged body in harmony with the changing universe.'" But natural selection continues to operate on man's intellectual, moral, and social behavior. It is no longer the excellence of bodily structure but the excellence of the intellect and social cooperation which has the survival value. The evidences of extinct or forgotten tribes of men are found over a great part of the earth and throughout all of history. Their failure must have been due to their intellectual and social inadequacy.

Darwin argues that a selfish, unco-operative, and contentious people will lack the means for the united effort which is necessary for continued social existence and will disappear or become replaced by more co-operative peoples. But if this be granted, it can still be asked how, in the beginning, enough individuals in whom the predominant traits were benevolence, courage, selflessness, and altruism survived in a tribe. These are the very individuals whom one would expect to perish first in an individual struggle for survival, and to leave no descendants to perpetuate their characters. Darwin has two answers to this objection:

In the first place, as reason and foresight developed in man he would come to realize that aid to his fellow man would be returned in kind, with an advantage to both— "From this low motive he might acquire the habit of aiding his fellows; and the habit of performing benevolent actions certainly strengthens the feeling of sympathy which gives the first impulse to benevolent actions." Darwin believed that such habits would probably tend to be inherited. A second and more important answer to the objection is man's susceptibility to the praise and blame of his peers. The instinct of sympathy, probably acquired by natural selection, is the basis for man's bestowal of praise and blame on his fellow men. Darwin is not very clear as to the factors responsible for the "selection" of the sympathetic instinct but is inclined to attribute it to the gradual realization that kindness to others is returned in the form of aid and co-operation, leading to a better adaptation for all. The concern for social approbation probably emerged at a remote period in primeval man, since it can be seen operating in the lower animals and in the "rudest savages" today.

On a narrow interpretation of natural selection, where the only issue is whether or not an individual survives and begets offspring which inherit his character, Darwin's explanation of the rise of sympathetic and co-operative individuals seems merely to assume what was to be explained. But Darwin held a more complex and subtle view on the workings of natural selection than is usually attributed to him. His concluding remark on the perpetuation of the social virtues, although not very helpful, at least indicates a readiness on his part to consider supplementary ideas: "A man who was not impelled by any deep, instinctive feeling, to sacrifice his life for the good of others, yet was roused to such actions by a sense of glory, would by his example excite the same wish for glory in other men, and would strengthen by exercise the noble feeling of admiration. He might thus do more good to his tribe than by begetting offspring with a tendency to inherit his own high character." Of course, one can still ask how the "sense of glory" originated.

The foregoing ideas concerned the advancement of man from a semi-human state to that of the contemporary savage. Darwin thought the action of natural selection in the development of civilized societies to be a very complicated, and to a large extent, an unfathomable process. He insisted that progress in human society is not an invariable rule: Some societies arise, achieve a highly civilized stage, and spread out successfully over a larger and larger area; other societies remain fixed at a rude state of development; whereas others undergo a deterioration from a relatively advanced stage and, in many cases, perish altogether. Natural selection, in societal development as much as in plant and animal development, acts only tentatively. Many concurrent favorable conditions are necessary for any advance in adaptation, and these conditions are always related to the given environment and the fortuitous changes that occur. In general, progress in human societies will depend upon ". . . an increase in the actual number of the population, in the number of men endowed with high intellectual and moral faculties, as well as on their standard of excellence." The "self-regarding virtues" are highly important and necessary acquisitions in the movement toward a civilized state because they involve an awareness of the remote consequences of man's actions. As noted above, these virtues are inculcated largely through the marriage institution, which promotes jealousy and places a premium on such virtues as chastity. Darwin did not identify the "remote consequences" of the self-regulating virtues—probably because he assumed them to be obvious to his readers—except to say that they promoted a high degree of self-command.

By far, the greater part of *The Descent of Man* is devoted to an account of the development of the secondary sexual characteristics and other external traits not directly related to individual survival. The problem was to account for the existence in animals of such characteristics as bright colors, loud and beautiful voices, the cockscomb, and the horns of the stag beetle; such traits, that is, which are useless or even a handicap in the struggle for existence and cannot, therefore, have evolved under the action of natural selection. A supplementary theory, "sexual selection," was introduced by Darwin to account for these phenomena.

According to the theory of sexual selection, there exists

among most animals a strong competition among the males for possession of the available females. In these circumstances the female has the power of choice and selects those males who are best equipped to meet her material, aesthetic, and sexual requirements. A great variety of traits are selected in this way, such as hunting prowess, bright coloration, pleasing voices, arrangement of hair, dancing ability, and special virility. Another order of traits is associated with the ability of the male to win and defend the female in battle with other males; and yet another with the ability to pursue and secure the female.

The perpetuation and exaggeration of the characteristics favored by sexual selection does not depend on the extinction of the losers in the competition for the females, but rather on the fact that only the winners would engage in sexual activity and propagate their kind. Sexual selection, then, "depends on the advantage which certain individuals have over others of the same sex and species solely in respect of reproduction." That the male is usually the aggressor in sexual activity is attributed by Darwin to the fact that the male has "stronger passions" than the coy, relatively passive female.

Darwin takes ten chapters to trace the evolution of the secondary sex characteristics through the animal kingdom, from the mollusk to the moose, and finally comes to man. He observes that, in general, men delight in competition and are more ambitious and selfish than women, whose maternal instincts have made them more tender, sympathetic, and passive. The possession of desirable women has always been a potent cause of strife between men, and men would have therefore come under the action of sexual selection, at least in the early stages of human evolution. Sexual selection would have ceased to operate when, by the loss of instinctive behavior and a gain in foresight in intelligence, men introduced, for economic advantage, such institutions as female infanticide, infant betrothals, and the subjugation of women. These practices would, of course, interfere with the workings of sexual selection, which must have a "free market" in which to operate. Although he is very cautious about it, Darwin believes sexual selection to have been the most efficient cause of the racial differences in man and, to some extent, the cause of certain differences between man and the lower animals.

Although the sexual selection theory of Darwin's has been almost completely rejected—especially since the advances in knowledge about heredity and the endocrine glands and their connection with the secondary sex characters—there are ideas and observations connected with it which have an independent interest. There is, for example, his emphasis on the importance of the marriage institution, whether monogamous or polygamous, as a means of promoting the social virtues which are necessary for social co-operation.[2] Then there was Darwin's insistence on the adaptive value of female infanticide for primitive peoples. This practice was overlooked or minimized by most of Darwin's contemporaries. His emphasis on the parent-child relationship as a source of the social affections was another important observation.

Darwin did not make of these observations what the social scientist of today might want to make of them, but if they are of any value, Darwin was justified in saying that ". . . false views, if supported by some evidence, do little harm, for every one takes a salutary pleasure in proving their falseness; and when this is done, the path towards error is closed and the road to truth is often at the same time opened."

Man, then, has suffered from the same physical evils as the lower animals and has been subjected to natural and sexual selection, at first in his bodily and instinctual equipment and eventually in his social characteristics. It must be acknowledged, Darwin concludes, ". . . that man with all his noble qualities, with sympathy which feels for the most debased, with benevolence which extends not only to other men but to the humblest living creature, with his god-like intellect which penetrated into the movements and constitution of the solar system—with all these exalted

---

[2] Jealousy, a trait disturbing for today's parents to find in their children, was for Darwin the basis for marriage and therefore a pillar in the construction of society.

powers—man still bears in his bodily frame the indelible stamp of his lowly origin."

Darwin's position in the history of anthropology is in dispute. For the most part, his importance to the development of anthropology is either minimized or ignored by professional anthropologists. Of the historians of anthropology, only Pennington and Haddon, both countrymen of Darwin, rank him among the great contributors to anthropology.

Although it is generally agreed that evolutionary theory is at the foundation of modern anthropology, it is pointed out that the idea of evolution and progress had a history independent of Darwin and biology. In cultural history Turgot and Condorcet in the eighteenth century reconstructed human history according to theories which emphasized man's progress through successively higher stages of development. Early in the next century (1830) Comte extended the idea of progress as a key to the understanding of cultural history. In archaeology the stone, bronze, and iron age sequence in civilization was established by various workers from 1800 to 1850. The antiquity of man had been suggested by Boucher de Perthes as early as 1836; his views had become generally accepted by the time of the publication of the *Origin of Species.* In geology Charles Lyell, Darwin's teacher and friend, had established the theory of geological evolution. His work had made a great impression on Darwin during the *Beagle* voyage.

In anthropology proper the first anthropological societies go back to 1840. By 1860 anthropology was considered an academic discipline, although the nature of its subject matter, its methods, and its goals were in doubt. There was only a general understanding that anthropology had to do with the study of primitive peoples. In 1843 J. C. Prichard (1786-1848) published *The Natural History of Man,* in which he described many primitive races, both as to physical and cultural traits. Gustav Klemm (1802-1867) collected a great amount of data on primitive peoples and made a good try at a definition of culture in 1854. He also proposed an evolutionary theory of human history, which outlined three progressive stages of cultural development: savagery, tameness, and freedom. Theodor Waitz (1821-1864) introduced a critical note, urging caution and a scientific approach to the literary sources of anthropology. He was interested especially in primitive mentality.

The early classical works in anthropology were written after the publication of the *Origin of Species*. Henry Maine, the founder of the study of comparative law, published his works in 1861, 1871, 1875, and 1883. J. J. Bachofen's pioneer work on matrilineal descent, *Das Mutterrecht*, was written in 1861. J. F. McLennan's *Primitive Marriage* was published in 1865. E. B. Tylor's great work, *Primitive Culture*, appeared in 1871. Lewis H. Morgan's classic works on social organization were published in 1871 and 1877.

To what extent these founders of modern anthropology were indebted to Darwin is difficult to say. Tylor specifically denies having profited from Darwin's work. The fact remains, however, that the idea of evolution was the dominating cultural idea of the nineteenth century, and anthropological theories, as well as the theories in almost every other field, were cast in its mold. And there can be no doubt that it was Darwin's work which justified the acceptance of evolution as a guiding and integrating concept.

For the most part, nineteenth-century anthropology used the idea of evolution in two ways: to reconstruct and compare the "stages" of human development, and to trace human history through a study of "survivals"—the quaint, anachronistic traits and artifacts of contemporary people that were viewed as vestiges of ancient and primitive life. In their enthusiasm for applying the idea of evolution to reconstruction, they overlooked the most applicable revelation in Darwin's work: the capacity of living things, including man, to adapt to varying environmental conditions.

Anthropological investigation, guided by the concepts of function and adaptation, was delayed for many years. Only recently has anthropology shown signs of making the most of Darwin's revolutionary ideas.

# HERBERT SPENCER

## *THE BINDING PIN*

HERBERT SPENCER was one of the tidiest men who ever lived. He could not tolerate an inefficient saltcellar any more than he could abide a disorderly universe. His life was obsessed with the need to fit all of nature—the inorganic, the organic, and the "super-organic"—into a neat, perfectly axiomatized system. His great intellect focused on the most insignificant details of daily life at the same time that it explored the phenomena of nature which have stimulated the creations of artists, philosophers, and scientists through the centuries. William James could write of him in *Memories and Studies*, that "Greatness and smallness surely never lived so closely in one skin together."

In 1860, at the age of forty, Spencer published his *First Principles*, an outline of universal knowledge, which he planned to develop in the succeeding years with all the relevant material on life, mind, and society. It was designed to reveal the orderly structure and workings of nature, from the evolution of galaxies to the evolution of the human emotions. By this act Spencer made himself a hostage of the future, and history has inevitably sacrificed him.

37

Herbert Spencer was born at Derby, England, in 1820. He was the eldest and only surviving child of nine born to William George and Harriet Spencer. His brothers and sisters each died within a few days of birth, with the exception of one sister who lived for only two years.

Spencer's father became a teacher at seventeen and taught as long as he could afford to. The elder Spencer antedated the now popular conviction that teachers should not hold any opinions—least of all radical ones; he was a determined nonconformist in his social, political, and religious views. A product of the Age of Reason, with its insistence on the dignity of man and man's ability to understand and conform to the universal laws of nature, he was impatient to get about reforming the world. He carried this passion for reform into all of his relationships. He refused, for example, to take off his hat to anyone, no matter what his rank, and addressed everyone, whether statesman or bishop, as "Mister." Improvement through self-help was his creed, and he demanded this in an exacting manner of all with whom he came in contact.

Spencer's mother, on the contrary, was a quiet, gentle woman who patiently conformed to the demands that were made of her. She was quietly orthodox in her religious beliefs and showed no interest in nature or in the scientific ideas that occupied her husband, and later, her son. A woman of very ordinary intelligence, she confined her reading to short stories and articles of popular information. In all these respects she was a great disappointment to her husband. He could not reconcile himself to her mediocrity, and all of his life he was unkind to her. It was the one great drawback that the son, Herbert, admitted of his father. In his *Autobiography* he described the relationship of his parents as one of chronic alienation.

Spencer admired his father greatly and came under his influence at an early age. The father encouraged him to take an interest in science, and Spencer applied himself to natural history, chemistry, and physics to the almost complete exclusion of history and the classics. This imbalance persisted throughout his life and was a chief cause of both the success and downfall of his great "Synthetic Philosophy." As a child he was fascinated by all natural phenomena and was forever seeking the natural causes which he felt must lie behind every event. He had few contacts with other children and spent many of his hours daydreaming. His own recollection of this habit, described in his *Autobiography*, is interesting: "In early days the habit was such that on going to bed, it was a source of satisfaction to me to think I should be able to lie for a length of time and dwell on the fancies which at the time occupied me; and frequently next morning, on awakening, I was vexed with myself because I had gone to sleep before I had revelled in my imaginations as much as I had intended. Often these dreams, becoming literally daydreams, quite filled my consciousness when walking. Even in the streets my state of abstraction was such that I occasionally talked aloud as I went along: a fact which I was from time to time made aware by people who turned to look at me." This inordinate tendency to daydream persisted in one form or another throughout Spencer's life.

Thus there was manifest in Spencer's boyhood that combination of traits which was to shape his life and work— a keen sense of observation, a speculative mind searching out natural causes, and a synthesizing imagination.

Spencer's first employment, at seventeen, was with the railroad as a construction engineer. He rose rapidly in position and reputation. His aggressiveness and ingenuity, although at times bringing him into conflicts with his superiors, insured his success as an engineer. He quit, however, in 1841 and for the next few years did some political writing, served as a subeditor for a radical paper, and produced a miscellany of mechanical inventions, including a sort of flying machine. The only invention which made any money for him at this time was a binding-pin which served to bind loose sheets of paper. This invention was symbolic of Spencer's future work, which can be pictured as one great binding-pin designed to tie together all the loose ends of nature, once and for all.

Spencer had refused the offer of an uncle to send him

to Cambridge for a university career, and experienced the disadvantages—and advantages—of a lack of academic direction and discipline. He would put aside the classics in history, literature, and philosophy as soon as he disagreed with the authors, a disagreement which usually occurred early in his reading. His persistent interest was in the natural sciences, a predilection that was to be favored by the intellectual developments of the nineteenth century.

In 1840 he purchased a copy of Lyell's *Principles of Geology* in which Lyell devoted a chapter to the refutation of Lamarck's theory on the origin of species. Lamarck's theory, based on the inheritance of acquired characteristics, offered a naturalistic interpretation of the creation of species which was at least plausible and which denied supernatural intervention. "Hence," says Spencer, "when my attention was drawn to the question whether organic forms have been specially created, or whether they have arisen by progressive modifications, physically caused and inherited, I adopted the last supposition; inadequate as was the evidence, and great as were the difficulties in the way." From this beginning Spencer became one of the leading champions of the theory of cosmic evolution.

Between 1848 and 1857 Spencer wrote numerous essays on society and government in which he stressed the adaptive capacities of the individual to the external conditions of physical and social life. Leave man alone, said Spencer in *Social Statics*, and he cannot fail to move in the direction of perfect adjustment. The external conditions to which any organism must adapt if it is to survive are the very causes of the modifications which make the adjustment possible: "Progress, therefore, is not an accident, but a necessity."

In 1852, seven years before Darwin's publication of the *Origin of Species*, Spencer published a paper entitled "Development Hypothesis" which, as he put it later, ". . . struck the keynote of all that was to follow." It was a brilliant defense of the theory of organic evolution and came close to identifying the struggle for existence as the key to evolution.

Although the general idea of evolution had impressed Spencer since 1840, it came into dramatic focus for him in 1857 as he was rereading his essays preparatory to publishing them in a collected volume. Running through all of the essays was the assumption of evolution based on Baer's physiological law concerning the development of organic material from a homogeneous to a heterogeneous state; that is, from a uniform structure, such as the initial embryonic cell carrying on all of the life functions, to the finished organism with its great variety of structure and function. It occurred to Spencer that here was a universal law applicable to all orders of phenomena: "Whether it be in the development of the Earth, in the development of Life upon its surface, in the development of Society, of Government, of Manufacturers, of Commerce, of Language, Literature, Science, Art, this same evolution of the simple into the complex, through successive differentiations, holds throughout. From the earliest traceable cosmical changes down to the latest results of civilization, we shall find that the transformation of the homogeneous into the heterogeneous is that in which progress essentially exists." With this law Spencer did his greatest castle building.

In attempting to account for the assumed principle of increasing homogeneity he was led to the then familiar concept of the Conservation of Force, which stated that the various kinds of force exhibited in nature are but manifestations of one constant force which cannot be increased or decreased, the result being a constant redistribution of matter and motion. He quickly conceived of the "persistence of force," as he called it, and the laws deducible from it as being applicable to all organizations of matter: "Clearly the astronomic, geologic, biologic, psychologic, and sociologic groups of phenomena, form a connected aggregate of phenomena: the successive parts having arisen one out of another by insensible gradations, and admitting only of conventional separations. Clearly, too, they are unified by exhibiting in common the law of transformation and the causes of transformation. And clearly, therefore, they should be arranged into a coherent body of doctrine, held together by the fundamental kinships."

And clearly, Herbert Spencer was the man to do it. By the time of his death in 1903, the enormous project known as "Synthetic Philosophy" was, except for the volumes on astronomy and geology, completed. Spencer had excluded these volumes, which would logically come first, not because they did not fit into the system, but because he was afraid that ill health might cause him to postpone developing the more important interpretation of organic phenomena.

Parts of the work were published from time to time as units were completed. The "Synthetic Philosophy" included, along with *First Principles*, volumes on biology, psychology, sociology, and morality. When the final volume was completed in 1896 Spencer was internationally famous and was one of the great influences of the nineteenth century. His synthesis of the phenomena of nature into one harmonious order, expressed in language understood by the layman, captured the popular imagination and elevated Spencer, in some eyes, to an almost supernatural status. The *Christian Spectator* in England expressed one reaction: "Like Moses, when he came down from the Mount, this positive philosophy comes with a veil over its face, that its too divine radiance may be hidden for a time. This is Science that has been conversing with God, and brings in her hand His law written on stone."

Specialists in the fields of history, science, and philosophy were not so easily impressed, however, and although he won the support of many influential men, such as Charles Darwin and Thomas Huxley, there was still critical opposition from many responsible quarters. In general, the opposition struck at Spencer's "deductive" method. Spencer inferred many subtle laws from vague first principles, such as the persistence of force, and then proceeded to illustrate his system of laws with material aptly selected from the literature in the various fields. Never having been more than an accomplished amateur in the sciences, and having little knowledge of history, he was regarded with suspicion in many places. Even Darwin, who once expressed the thought that Spencer might be equal to any English philosopher that had ever lived, reflected later that, although Spencer impressed him with his "inexhaustible wealth of suggestion," he never "convinced" him. And his sympathetic but impartial friend, Thomas Huxley, summed up Spencer's chief deficiency in characteristic fashion by stating that "Spencer's definition of a tragedy was the spectacle of a deduction killed by a fact."[1]

The first volume of *Principles of Sociology* was published in 1874 and dealt with the "Data of Sociology," "The Inductions of Sociology," and "The Domestic Relations," in that order. This ordering of the material suggests an adherence to the Baconian ideal of science, where empirical generalizations arise out of a careful collection and tabulation of all the relevant data. Spencer gives the impression that he was following just this method; it is, in fact, the order in which he presented all of the works of the "Synthetic Philosophy": data, inductive generalizations, and deductive elaboration. It might be asked, therefore, why it is that Spencer's greatest weakness is generally ascribed to his penchant for what is loosely termed "deductive reasoning," where the generalizations come first, usually from so-called self-evident principles. A simple example suggests the answer: A principal generalization in the "Inductions of Sociology" is the conception of society as an organism. The genesis of this concept is not found in any data, but in the *Social Statics*, published in 1850, twenty-four years earlier. The idea is further refined in the essay "The Social Organism," published in 1860, and then appears as an inductive generalization in the *Principles of Sociology* in 1874. The deliberate collation of data for the *Sociology* was not begun until 1867, when Spencer assigned an assistant, David Duncan, to the collection and tabulation of material from the literature on "uncivilized races" and classical civilization.

A discussion of scientific methodology is out of place here; suffice it to say that both induction and deduction have a

[1] Quoted in William James, *Memories and Studies.*

role in the establishing of valid scientific generalizations, and that they are complementary rather than antithetical. The purpose of citing the above example of Spencer's method is to distinguish what Spencer says he is doing from what he actually does—and to focus attention on the latter. To simply carp at Spencer for not going into his investigations with an open mind serves no purpose and can be misleading as to the nature of scientific inquiry. Contrary to the views expressed in many science textbooks, it is not an *open* but a *biased* mind which is essential in scientific discovery. But Spencer was so sure of his analogies and generalizations that their verification was to him merely a time-consuming routine. He prepared a system of investigation designed to support his generalizations and sent assistants to the anthropological and classical literatures to select the appropriate data.

Bergson aptly pointed out that Spencer's evolutionism posits in advance that which is to be explained and likened his method to the activity of a child when he pastes a picture on a card, cuts the card into many pieces, and fits them together again with a conviction of having *produced* something.[2]

There was, however, a positive side to the picture which Spencer's critics tended to overlook. It consisted in Spencer's having directed attention to the ancient, but vague and neglected, notion that the institutions of a society and the human units in that society evolve along lines which are dictated by the problems of survival. Spencer made *adaptation* the central theme in his work. Beginning as early as 1843, in the essay "The Proper Sphere of Government," he urged people to drop their "educational blinkers" and ". . . recognize things lying off the beaten track, and to see their relative importance. . . . To have before us,

---

[2] Josiah Royce, in *Herbert Spencer,* quotes Bergson: "He [Spencer] takes reality in its present form; he breaks it to pieces, he scatters it in fragments which he throws to the winds; then he 'integrates' these fragments and 'dissipates their movement.' Having *imitated* the Whole by a work of mosaic he imagines he has retraced the design of it, and made the genesis."

in manageable form, evidence proving the correlations which everywhere exist between great militant activity and the degradation of women, between a despotic form of government and elaborate ceremonial in social intercourse, between relatively peaceful social activities and the relaxation of coercive institutions, promises furtherance of human welfare in a much greater degree than does learning whether the story of Alfred and the cakes is a fact or a myth, whether Queen Elizabeth intrigued with Essex or not, where Prince Charles hid himself, and what were the details of this battle or the other siege—pieces of historical gossip which cannot in the least affect men's conceptions of the ways in which social phenomena hang together, or aid them in shaping their public conduct." The validity of the correlations which Spencer "proved" can be questioned, but his advice on where to look for sociological correlations is as pertinent today as it has ever been.

Before examining the specific correlations and generalizations which are set forth in Spencer's *Principles of Sociology*, it is necessary to summarize briefly the laws of evolution which he deduced from the "persistence of force" and the constant redistribution of matter and motion in nature.

For Spencer, evolution proceeds through three main stages: (1) The simplest form is the gradual concentration of scattered, moving elements into a coherent aggregate, with a concomitant loss of motion in the elements; (2) The intermediate form arises within the coherent aggregate when minor concentrations of matter take place within it. These changes slowly transform the homogeneous mass into a heterogeneous one, with divisions and subdivisions down to the most minute; (3) The highest form of evolution is established when the forces of the differentiated parts balance the forces to which the entire aggregate is exposed. This "equilibration" can never become static because the forces upon the aggregate are constantly changing, thus giving rise to a countertendency toward dissolution. The result must be a moving equilibrium in which there is a constant internal adjustment to the changing forces. These laws operate in the evolution of every conceivable organization of force and matter: in stellar systems, in plant and animal organisms, and in human societies. The *Principles of Sociology* takes up these three stages in the evolution of human societies.

According to Spencer, human society includes ". . . all those processes and products which imply the co-ordinated actions of many individuals—co-ordinated actions which achieve results exceeding in extent and complexity those achievable by individual actions." The important point to be noted here is that the products of co-ordinated actions exceed those of individual action, and therefore constitute a distinct order of phenomena: the "super-organic." The institutions of a society—its language, industrial techniques, religion, and government—are beyond the power of any single individual to create. They originate in the co-operative efforts of the individuals to adapt to the external environment. Once institutionalized, they constitute another set of conditions which poses additional problems of adaptation and initiates further change. And so it goes in an endless spiral, where the social institutions are now the *products* and now the *springs* of evolution.

The first step in social evolution occurred when men were brought together by the exigencies of the physical environment. A lone man could not survive for long in a hostile environment where he had to combat the beasts and the elements in the struggle for survival. His biological weakness demanded that he unite with other men for protection, shelter, and the quest for food.

At this early stage primitive man was impulsive and not co-operative beyond the minimum necessary for survival. But the necessary company of other men awakened in him the desire for signs of approval from his associates. The desire for approbation is a natural trait, which can be observed even in animals who, according to Spencer, ". . . show themselves gratified by applause after achievement." From this early expression of egoism the way was prepared for man's eventual submission to tribal opinion and the social regulation of conduct. A "council of emotions" emerged from the subordination of individual passions and made social co-operation possible.

Spencer illustrates the evolution of the social emotions by citing the emotional development of a child: "That the child of the civilized man is impulsive, is improvident, is in infancy without the love of applause but shows this early in childhood, and only afterwards begins to exhibit a sense of justice, are facts which verify the above inferences respecting the emotional nature of the Primitive man." Anyone who has lived closely with children will admit the pertinence of Spencer's parallel and can supply his own illustrations.

True social development is impossible, as in the case of the Mantras of the Malay peninsula, where "intolerance of restraint is joined with want of sociability." When the Mantras dispute, they separate; and this ". . . cause of dispersion is not checked by a cause of aggregation." This citation is a good example of how neatly Spencer fits the data into his evolutionary scheme: the concentration of elements into an aggregate means progress, their dispersion brings dissolution.

Opposed to man's inherent egoism is his altruistic instinct. Altruism, originating in the animal's love and protection of the helpless, is best exemplified in the parental instinct. According to Spencer, it has to be a universal phenomenon in the weaker animals, including man, ". . . since deficient endowment of it must ever be followed by disappearance of the species or variety." From the reconciliation of the primitive instincts of egoism and altruism arise the complex institutions which enforce the subordination of the individual to the interest of a common struggle for survival. The institutionalized pressures responsible for individual submission and co-operation in a given society appear in many forms; for example, admiration or fear of natural or supernatural power; dread of penalties, present or future; and the love of social relationships.

Turning to the primitive intellect, Spencer finds two predominant qualities: the inability to generalize and a strong tendency to imitate. After citing numerous examples to support this conclusion, Spencer makes the following observation: " 'The eccentricity of genius' is a current phrase implying the common experience that men of original powers are men prone to act in ways unlike the ordinary ways. To do what the world does, is to guide behavior by imitation. To deviate from the usages of the world, is to decline imitation. And the noticeable fact is that a smaller tendency to imitate goes along with a greater tendency to evolve new ideas."[3]

Spencer takes up next his theory of animism: the belief in spiritual agents. According to Spencer the primitive emotions and the primitive intellect combine in the production of basic primitive ideas. Dominating the system of primitive ideas are the religious beliefs which are derived from ancestor-worship. Primitive man is keenly aware of the changes that go on around him. Things come into being and pass away. The sun rises, sets, and rises again; clouds form, disperse, and re-form; the moon grows big, wanes, and becomes full again; comets, meteors, rainbows, and lightning appear and disappear. All of these changes suggest to primitive man a basic duality in nature—a visible and invisible existence of things. Sooner or later it occurs to man that he has two selves, one visible and one invisible. Experiences of dreams, swoons, and apoplexy suggest or reinforce this idea. In these unconscious states the individual goes some place and does things. But on regaining consciousness

---

[3] This quotation from *Principles of Sociology* suggests how closely, almost literally, Spencer's personality is infused in his work. All of his life Spencer conscientiously avoided acceptance of the honors that were accorded him. He rarely attended social functions of any kind and, except for association with a few close friends, remained aloof from society. He refused, that is, "to do what the world does." That he was a great generalizer and considered himself a genius is clear. He believed that his *Principles of Psychology* would ultimately stand beside Newton's *Principia*. In the "Social Organism" he observes that "Those who regard the histories of societies as the histories of their great men, and think that these great men shape the facts of their societies, overlook the truth that such great men are the products of their societies." But there is little evidence that Spencer considered *himself* a product of society. It is a temptation to believe that Spencer's self-imposed alienation from society and his studied ignorance of history were employed as antiseptics against cultural contamination and the loss of perspective that he thought went with it.

he is assured by witnesses that his body has not moved; then another, invisible self must have had these experiences. The conception of death as a temporary absence from the body is a natural extension of this duality. Spencer points out that the care and protection of the body after death is to a practical end, for when the individual resumes his existence in the body he should be put to as little trouble as possible in getting it running again. This concern of primitive peoples for the bodies of the dead is responsible, for example, for the complicated embalming process to prevent putrefaction. A mutilated body or no body at all would be apt to discourage any ambitions of reanimation an ancestral spirit might have.

Spencer cites a large number of practices which are related to the primitive beliefs in reanimation: the construction of mounds to protect the body (the pyramids being an extreme development); the provision of food, weapons, clothing and, in some cases, animals, slaves, and wives to accompany the dead man in his burial place; the removal of uncomfortable pressures and impediments to breathing; and sometimes the inclusion of fire for warmth and cooking.

As society evolves and individual resurrection is indefinitely postponed, the concept of the second self becomes less immediate and realistic, until finally its existence may be wholly ethereal and undefined. The concept of soul has evolved. For if the dead do not come back to this world, they must inhabit another world—the soul and the other world make religion possible.

In the primitive mind there emerges, according to Spencer, a corollary to this world of ancestral spirits. The spirits are the invisible agents of change in the environment. As the spirits of the dead accumulate, they form a community of invisible but active agents which extends everywhere. As man's curiosity about natural events grows and becomes more sophisticated, he looks for "causes." The active and omnipresent ancestral spirits are a logical choice. The circle is completed in Spencer's account: from a naive acceptance of change arose a belief in spirits; and finally, as society evolved, these spirits were posited as the causes of change.

The offspring has become the parent of its own progenitor.

Primitive man, then, has a vested interest in the deified dead. His behavior is influenced by the prevailing ideas concerning the deities, and religion becomes a means of social leverage. Religion joins tribal government as the basis for social cohesion, with fear, in the broadest sense, underlying both. As Spencer sums it up in the *Principles of Sociology:* "While the *fear of the living* becomes the root of the political control, the *fear of the dead* becomes the root of the religious control."

The ghost-agents must be reckoned with. They hold the power of good or evil for man. They can bring health or disease, wealth or poverty, rain or drought, pleasure or pain. Having a human character, they have human needs and vanities; hence, they can be influenced by propitiation, prayer, flattery, and offerings of food and human companions. This is the beginning of worship with its ritual and ceremony; the spirits have become deified. Worship requires medicine men and priests, who are the specialists in the art of ritual. They may even assume supernatural properties themselves, as witnessed in the practice of exorcism and sorcery, and the performance of miracles.

A society, for Spencer, is like an organism. It grows; it becomes differentiated both in structure and function, with an increasing mutual dependence of the parts; and as a unit, it is quite unlike its separate parts. The only significant difference between an organism and a society is that in the former the seat of consciousness is located in a small part of the aggregate and in the latter it is diffused almost equally throughout the individual units. The evolution of the homogeneous ovum into the heterogeneous individual is a process of multiplication in size and complexity. So it is with social evolution. In order to grow, a society must develop more efficient ways of utilizing the environment for the support of the increasing number of individuals. This task can only be accomplished by division of labor according to specialized talents, both natural and learned; the best shoemaker makes all the shoes, the fastest runner carries all the messages, and so on. Increased specialization make the functioning of one part essential to the existence of all the parts, as the heart is to all the other organs of the body. Growth, complexity, and interdependence add up to greater efficiency and adaptive power in the organism and in society, and therefore provide the factors necessary to evolution.

The second important generalization that Spencer projected is the classification of societies into two great divisions: the predominantly *militant* and the predominantly *industrial*. The militant society is founded on *compulsory* co-operation, with status as the basis of social relationships. The industrial society is founded on *voluntary* co-operation, where contract regulates social relationships. As in the individual organism, where the outer organs are completely regulated by a central nervous system, the individuals in a militant society are completely subject to a central governmental power. The industrial society, on the other hand, is decentralized and is sustained by the free transactions between individuals which occur in the market place. These two classes of society emerge because of the adaptive value of each in dealing with the peoples within them, accordingly as those peoples are predominantly warlike or peaceful.[4]

Spencer's comparative analysis of primitive man in his environment convinced him that there is a general order of societal development, of "co-existence and sequence," in all of human society. Therefore social phenomena, like physical phenomena, ". . . form the subject-matter of a science reducible, in some measure at least, to the deductive form."

Armed with the law of evolution and the subordinate generalization of social movement from militarism to in-

[4] It may be noted in passing that the many hours of close-order drill familiar to any soldier are designed to replace his preservative instincts with automatic responses to given signals. If a private has for months been executing *By-the-left-flank!* and *By-the-right-flank!* maneuvers on command, it is believed that he will be more disposed to charge a machine-gun nest on command before weighing the advantages and disadvantages. This disciplined, automatic response has an adaptive value for the nation, if not for the individual. There is a persuasion in Spencer's generalizations which invites such illustrations and makes his exposition plausible.

dustrialism, Spencer makes his great synthesis of social institutions. He describes these institutions under the headings of the domestic, ceremonial, political, ecclesiastical, professional, and industrial and brings them all into perfect harmony with his general laws. For Spencer, the awesome complexity of man—his body, his genius, and his passions—in his natural and social environment was reducible to simple, universal laws. He, Spencer, had done for man what Newton had done for the heavens—brought order and harmony out of chaos and darkness. When asked about the remarkable absence of lines on his forehead, Spencer replied, "I suppose it is because I am never puzzled." In the future, as a consequence of the "Synthetic Philosophy," lines on the brow of man would be the vestigial remains of a pre-Spencerian age!

There is a fundamental conflict in Spencer's work which he makes no clear attempt to resolve: There is his belief in the *necessity* of progress in the evolutionary process and, on the other hand, there is the realization that local conditions shape the adaptive patterns which further evolution in any given setting. The first conviction has been far more publicized than the second, partly because of the dramatic deductions Spencer made from it, and partly because of its usefulness in whetting the axes Spencer's critics happened to be grinding.

Spencer made the necessity of progress the rationale for his intolerant advocacy of complete individual freedom, short of interference with another's freedom, in social relationships. In *Social Statics* he argued that individuals should be allowed to make avoidable fatal mistakes, for then the stupid and inefficient would be gradually eliminated and the human species would be that much improved. If an individual is so ignorant as to entrust his health to a "quack" instead of a qualified physician, and dies as a result, the species has been improved by his removal. The government, therefore, has a moral obligation *not* to interfere by passing laws to protect the individual from misrepresentation and malpractice in medicine. "Inconvenience," he states in *Social Statics*, "suffering and death are the penalties attached by Nature to ignorance, as well as to incompetence—are also the means of remedying these. Partly by weeding out those of lowest development, and partly by subjecting those who remain to the never-ceasing discipline of experience, Nature secures the growth of a race who shall both understand the conditions of existence, and be able to act up to them. It is impossible in any degree to suspend this discipline by stepping in between ignorance and its consequences, without to a corresponding degree, suspending the progress. If to be ignorant were as safe as to be wise, no one would become wise. And all measures which tend to put ignorance upon a par with wisdom, inevitably check the growth of wisdom." If not interfered with, nature will soon claim the imperfectly organized— the consumptive, the crippled, the ignorant, and the blind —and keep the species strong: "A sad population of imbeciles would our schemers fill the world with, could their plans last. A sorry kind of human constitution would they make for us—a constitution continually going wrong, and needing to be set right again—a constitution ever tending to self-destruction. Why the whole effort of Nature is to get rid of such—to clear the world of them and make room for better," says Spencer. He is probably the most energetic opponent of socialism, creeping or running, in history.

But Spencer also insisted that the immediate conditions of a given environment determine the course of evolution in that place. Unless there is some progressive universal evolution of *conditions* going on, including those of climate and terrain, for example, social evolution does not necessarily imply progress. In the *Principles of Sociology*, Spencer makes the point very clearly: "Evolution is commonly conceived to imply in everything an *intrinsic* tendency to become something higher; but this is an erroneous conception of it. In all cases it is determined by the co-operation of inner and outer factors." Despite such passages in Spencer, most critics are content to present him as an unqualified advocate of "progressive" evolution. They quote mainly from the *Social Statics* (1850) and disregard subsequent writings, thus illustrating very well the fallacy of selection of which they correctly accuse Spencer. It is true that Spencer remained to the last a bitter champion of individual freedom and noninterference by government, but he shifted the ground for his belief considerably from the time of the *Social Statics*. Later, he dwelt more on the inefficiency of and oppression by bureaucracy than on the necessity of progress through evolution.

Spencer made some attempt at reconciling organic evolution and individual independence by maintaining that the entire range of evolution might be considered as approaching perfect equilibrium, but only in indefinite time. This conception, however, he thought to transcend human thought: "That which persists unchanging in quantity, but ever-changing in form, under these sensible appearances which the universe presents to us, transcends human knowledge and conception—is an unknown and unknowable power, which we are obliged to recognize as without limit in space and without beginning or end in time."

Professional anthropologists in this country do not credit Spencer with any significant contribution to their field. In *The History of Ethnological Theory* Robert H. Lowie does not even mention Spencer. The British social anthropologists are somewhat more generous. Evans-Pritchard regards Spencer, along with Emile Durkheim, as having "directed the attention of social anthropologists towards functional analysis. . . ." An estimation of Spencer's importance to anthropology will be determined by one's conception of what anthropology is, or should be.

Spencer was always concerned with discovering how social phenomena "hang together." He was not satisfied with merely collecting and classifying data on primitive peoples; he wanted to make some sense out of the evidence, to discover what it was about the particular arrangement of institutions in a society that kept the society in equilibrium. As an evolutionist, he saw adaptation as the central problem in social analysis. He was willing to go "off the beaten track," as he put it, to discover what mattered to people in their daily lives, and what relationship that had to the development of social institutions. This has proved a fruitful method of inquiry for those anthropologists, such as Malinowski, who have used it.

Above all, Spencer believed that human behavior, as expressed in social structure and process, is susceptible of scientific inquiry, and he wanted to reduce social phenomena to general laws. His hopes for establishing an axiomatized science of man were not realized. He oversimplified the complexities of human life, and his conclusions have failed to stand the test of time. He erred on the side of optimism, but that failure seems preferable to the cynicism of much of modern anthropology with respect to the possibility of establishing a science of man.

An estimation of Spencer's over-all contribution must rest with the estimator's attitude toward history. If his criterion for greatness is the longevity of a man's work as a relevant body of doctrine, then Spencer does not belong with the great. Spencer was not a pioneer whose ideas had to be caught up with by society. He took the prevailing social conceptions—of social progress and the perfectability of man—and gave them a cosmic justification in a synthesis of the scientific knowledge of the day. As those social conceptions changed and scientific knowledge increased, Spencer was bound to be left behind. His relevancy was for the present, not the future.

But if another view be admitted, the view that an age is served by the activities of a man who devotes his life to giving the people of that age an understandable synthesis of current knowledge and speculation by which their imaginations are set free, then Spencer must be ranked much higher than he has been. He was for his time, as William James tells us in *Memories and Studies*, the philosopher whom those who had no other philosopher could appreciate. The thoughtful laymen of every age can use such a man.

# EDWARD TYLOR

## MR. TYLOR'S SCIENCE

A BUTCHER IS HANDED a Tasmanian skin-scraper and asked to test it on a side of beef; a children's street game is interrupted for the benefit of a bystander who wants the rules explained; gamblers, busy at their trade, are the uneasy objects of quiet, intensive scrutiny. In studying such cases of everyday work and play, Edward Burnett Tylor, the founder of modern anthropology, had been at work patiently reconstructing the past from observations of the present.

As modern highways are often laid upon remains of ancient tracks of barbaric roads, so, thought Tylor, was modern thought and behavior following the courses of primitive existence. To a university man, steeped in the traditions of academic learning, the commonplaces and trivia of daily life might seem a strange place to look for the origins and development of cultural history. To Tylor, who was denied a university career, it seemed natural to study the living for knowledge of the dead.

Tylor was born at Camberwell, England, October 2, 1832, the third son of Joseph Tylor and Harriet Skipper. The father ran a prosperous brass foundry, which belonged to the family. Both parents were Quakers, and Tylor was to make the most of his inheritance of freedom from religious formality. This independence cost him a classical education, however, because he could not pass the tests of religious orthodoxy which were then required for admission to the universities. He received, instead, a brief and informal education at a school maintained by the Society of Friends.

He entered the family business at the age of sixteen and worked there for seven years. In 1855, at the age of twenty-three, his health showed signs of breaking down, and he was advised to quit work and indulge his health by leisurely travel.

He spent almost a year traveling in the United States, and in the spring of 1856 was in Cuba. Here his Quaker affiliations provided the chance opportunity that so often gives direction to a man's life. While on a Havana bus he overheard a passenger use the pronoun "thou," which at that time identified the speaker as a Quaker. Tylor approached the stranger and introduced himself as a fellow Quaker. The man happened to be Henry Christy, a prosperous businessman, who had become an archaeologist and ethnologist of considerable reputation. He was one of the archaeologists who later made the important confirmation of the validity of Boucher de Perthes' discoveries concerning the antiquity of man. The two men took an immediate liking to each other, and Christy persuaded Tylor to accompany him on an archaeological expedition to Mexico. Tylor turned out to be one of Christy's greatest "finds" for anthropology.

Under Christy's expert and mature guidance (he was twenty years Tylor's senior), Tylor's curiosity and natural capacity for careful observation and balanced judgment were turned to good account in the reconstruction of the pre-history of Mexico. He was especially interested in the problem of the development of society, which was suggested by the material remains of culture discovered by the two travelers, as well as by the antiquities of popular rites, customs, beliefs, and legends which were to be observed among the contemporary peoples of Mexico. He observed that many extant customs were similar or identical to the customs of ancient peoples. He noticed, for example, the practice of Mexican penitents scourging themselves at church under the fierce exhortations of a monk, and was reminded of the identical rite at the Egyptian festival of Isis. This early interest in the survival of ancient customs in civilized societies was the starting point of one of Tylor's most important achievements in anthropology: the formulation of the "doctrine of survivals."

Another problem that interested Tylor on the Mexican expedition was that of the independent origin or diffusion of cultural institutions. This question was to become a crucial one in anthropology, with important implications for social, political, and religious thought. After considering a specific problem in this area, Tylor employed a caution which characterized much of his subsequent works: "Set the difficulties on one side of the question against those on the other, and they will nearly balance. We must wait for further evidence."

Although it was of much shorter duration (six months), Tylor's expedition in Mexico played the same role in his career that the *Beagle* voyage played for Darwin: it shaped once and for all the course of his life's work. His life was henceforth to be devoted to the founding of a science of culture.

Tylor is everywhere described as a commanding, benevolent figure. He was tall, well-built, and extremely handsome. His simplicity, patience, and quiet humor made him popular as a teacher and organizer, and contributed to an easy, persuasive style which won a wide audience for his writings. His writings were always free of jargon or pretension of any kind, a consequence, perhaps, of the fact that he was taken from school at sixteen and never again became a "student" in the academic sense.

His life, as much as his work, exemplified what Lowie has called Tylor's "sense of fitness." His relationship to Anna Fox, whom he married in 1858, was regarded as a model of marital life. They lived together quietly and happily for fifty-nine years, until Tylor's death in 1917. It is said that Lady Tylor always attended a certain series of her husband's lectures, and that on one occasion, before a large audience, Tylor turned toward his wife after a lengthy exposition and said absent-mindedly, "And so my dear Anna, we observe. . . ."

In 1861 Tylor published *Anahuac*, an account of the Mexican expedition with Christy. His *Researches in the Early History of Mankind* was published in 1865, and it immediately established him as a leading figure in anthropology. His professional maturity came at a time when several lines of inquiry and speculation were converging toward a point which would radically alter man's conception of himself and his place in nature.

In geology Charles Lyell, building on the work of James Hutton, had successfully challenged the cataclysmic theories required by Biblical cosmology, and had shown the earth to have evolved over many millions of years instead of the few thousand required by scriptural authority. With the doctrine of "uniform causes," which assumed that the processes of geological change in the past were similar to those observable in the present, it was possible to block out an approximate chronological series for earthly formations.

In archaeology the confirmation in 1858 of Boucher de Perthes' discoveries of fashioned implements of great antiquity climaxed almost three centuries of fragmentary discoveries and speculations about man's ancient past; the existence of paleolithic man was definitely established.

In biology Darwin's work established the evolutionary view of nature as a key to the general problem of origin and development.

These developments in the mid-nineteenth century constituted a challenge of survival to religious orthodoxy. One of the many heresies the ecclesiastics had to combat was the idea that man had gradually evolved, not only from the lower animals, but, what was perhaps even worse, from a primitive state of humanity comparable to existing savages. The savage with his naked body, many wives, and pagan gods was regarded as a poor representative of

Christian morality and hardly worthy of God's initial human creation.

To combat this particular heresy, the "degeneration (or degradation) theory" was advanced as an alternative to the evolutionary theory. According to this doctrine, man was created in a highly civilized, moral condition, but had, in some cases, degenerated to a savage state—become "outcasts of the human race," as the Duke of Argyll put it.

The degeneration theory became a popular alternative to the developmental (evolutionary) theory and was defended by such influential men as Richard Whately, Archbishop of Dublin, and the Duke of Argyll, among others. But while this theory established the glory of man's beginning, it suggested a dim view of his future. To those who had inherited the optimism of the eighteenth century regarding man's capacity for self-improvement, the degeneration theory was intolerable and had to be smothered. Sir John Lubbock (Lord Avebury) complained that "if the past history of man has been one of deterioration, we have but groundless expectation of future improvement." Lubbock, along with Lyell and others, carried on a spirited debate over the question with the clerics and their supporters. The following is a typical exchange: The Duke of Argyll was explaining why the highland Eskimos do not have any weapons or any idea of war: "No wonder, poor people! They have been driven into regions where no stronger race could desire to follow them. But that the fathers had once known what war and violence meant there is no more conclusive proof than the dwelling place of their children." Lubbock responds: "It is perhaps natural that the leader of a great highland clan [Argyll] should regard with pity a people who, having 'once known what war and violence meant,' have no longer any neighbors to pillage or to fight, but a Lowlander can hardly be expected seriously to regard such a change as one calculated to excite pity, or as any evidence of degradation."

Tylor, a freethinking Quaker and firm believer in man's rationality and capacity for improvement, plunged into the very middle of this controversy. There is little doubt

that he considered the implications of the degeneration
theory to be a serious threat to man's confidence in himself
and his future. The developmental theory of civilization
had to be established beyond all doubt if the faith in progress was to be sustained.

Two general premises were necessary for the establishment of a progressive theory of cultural development: (1)
the basic similarity of human minds and, (2) the priority
of Primitive Man in the chronological series. Tylor's second
book, *Researches Into the Early History of Mankind*
(1865), dealt largely with the first question (among other
things), and his third book, *Primitive Culture* (1871),
completed the argument by establishing the second.

That Tylor's aims had a missionary quality to them is
suggested by these stanzas which he contributed anony-
mously to Andrew Lang's "Double Ballade Of A Primitive Man":

> *From a status like that of the Cres,*
> *Our society's fabric arose,—*
> *Develop'd, evolved, if you please,*
> *But deluded chronologists chose,*
> *In a fancied accordance with Mos-*
> *es, 4000 B.C. for the span*
> *When he rushed on the world and its woes,—*
>
> *But the mild anthropologist,—he's*
> *Not recent inclined to suppose*
> *Flints Palaeolithic like these,*
> *Quaternary bones such as those,*
> *In Rhinoceros, Mammouth and CO.s,*
> *First Epoch, the Human Began,*
> *Theologians all to expose,—*
> *'Tis the mission of Primitive Man.*

Tylor was the first serious student of culture to embrace
the entire field of man and his environment. For him, the
scope of anthropology should include man's body, his
physical and cultural environment, and his soul.

Tylor was not a field worker, but, as Lowie has insisted,
he was far from being an "armchair anthropologist." He

studied culture wherever he happened to be—in a junk store of a big city; at a school for the deaf and dumb (where he worked out important features of his work on gesture-language); at a knitting mill; a butcher shop; and at festivals and religious ceremonies. The greater part of his time was spent with the literature which dealt in any way with the history of civilizations and institutions, artifacts, beliefs, and customs of primitive peoples. He became, as has been said, a "circumnavigator of books," and his knowledge of the literature was both wide and profound.

Not being a field worker, Tylor had to rely largely on material gathered from the accounts and publications of travelers, missionaries, adventurers, colonists, sailors, and the like. These reports were largely fragmentary, uncritical, biased, and generally unreliable. The facile use of this kind of material by other workers had resulted in confusion and contradictions. Practically any assertion about primitive cultures could be supported by citations from the literature.

Tylor was very much aware of this problem and set about constructing canons of "internal evidence" which could be applied to the sifting out of reliable data from the mass of testimony. His main tool here was the "test of recurrence," or "undesigned coincidence," by which statements were evaluated according to their frequency in other accounts, the most unique statements being assigned the highest probability. Lowie has said that "The student of Tylor in 1890 could profit from a vast mass of thoroughly sifted and authenticated material, interpreted from a unifying evolutionary point of view, tempered with sanity."

After he had established anthropology as a discipline at Oxford, Tylor was able to send students all over the world, as "the field naturalists of human nature." They went into the field with precise instructions and techniques for gathering data and for organizing the material so that it would yield useful relationships and generalizations.

Most impressive of all was the actual bulk of material

that Tylor collected and employed. A reviewer of the French translation of *Primitive Culture* commented: "What one notes above all is the abundance of documents. One finds them by piles, by heaps, by mountains, and when these are cleared there are still others."

Tylor is famous for the caution and tentativeness with which he advanced his theories and ideas. Many references are made to his "infinite respect for facts," his "great patience in eliciting the universal from a multitude of particulars," and his patience in allowing the facts themselves to "crystallize into generalizations." Tylor's obituary in the *London Times* praised this aspect of his work: "he [Tylor] held that the enumeration of facts must form the staple of the argument, and that the limit of needful detail was reached only when each group of facts so displayed its general law that fresh ones came to range themselves in their proper riches as new instances of an already established rule."

It should be noted, however, that it was the fashion in the early development of the social sciences to emulate the attitudes and techniques that had been so successful in the rapid advance of the physical science in the seventeenth and eighteenth centuries. The Baconian ideal of perfect induction in science was considered the only reliable method for arriving at scientific generalizations, and even a verbal adherence to this ideal was impressive. It has been seen how Herbert Spencer, one of the most "deductive" minds in the social sciences, claimed and believed that his was a completely inductive work. Tylor was undoubtedly more careful and thorough than Spencer, but it would be a mistake to picture him as a man without definite preconceptions and vested interests in the work he was doing. His early work, especially, is boldly speculative and, in fact, owes much of its greatness to a zealous, partisan point of view.

Tylor approached his main subject—primitive man— with a sense of cultural relativity unusual for his time. "Measuring other people's corn by one's own bushel," was a cardinal mistake, according to Tylor, and had to be guarded against at all times. And although he is not completely free from censure on this point, he succeeded better than most of his contemporaries.

Above all, Tylor believed that the "inner springs of human behavior," the beliefs and attitudes that underlie institutions, comprise the most reliable evidence of man's history and development. Myth, folklore, religion, and custom were the sources for such information and must be studied along with written materials and artifacts if a reliable reconstruction is to be made. Tylor erred in certain of his emphases, but he exposed a whole new dimension for the study of culture.

Tylor was a thoroughgoing Darwinian in his biological views, but he specifically denied any direct influence from Darwin's work. He states in the preface to the second edition of *Primitive Culture:* "It may have struck some readers as an omission, that in a work on civilization insisting so strenuously on a theory of development on evolution, mention should scarcely have been made of Mr. Darwin and Mr. Spencer, whose influence on the whole course of modern thought on such subjects should not be left without formal recognition. This absence of particular reference is accounted for by the present work, arranged on its own lines, coming scarcely into contact or detail with the previous works of these eminent philosophers." Many of to-day's anthropologists, such as Lowie, Herskovits, and Kroeber, have expressed the same judgment regarding the influence of Darwin on Tylor and on the development of anthropology in general. It is a question which can be argued with authority from either side. Tylor, though not a strict unilinear evolutionist (one who believed that every society must pass through the same definite stages), employed many concepts which paralleled the methods and ideas employed in the Darwinian reconstruction of organic evolution.

One of Tylor's problems was to establish the essential similarity of human minds; the "psychic unity of mankind," as it was called. Similarities of artifacts, customs, and beliefs between past and present cultures had been pointed out by many workers already, but Tylor saw that where there was a chance of cultural contact and the transmission of culture traits (which he always admitted according to the evidence), similarities did not require an independent development. What had to be shown was that under like conditions men's minds would work in like ways. The argument here would have to rest more on psychological than on historical data, because the history of a given culture trait could seldom rule out the possibility of cultural borrowing. It would be essential that the traits selected for study be those which have not, as Tylor says "travelled far from their causes." A great variety of cultural traits had resulted from generations of cumulative training and no longer reflected initial mental and environmental conditions. In certain areas, however, there had been little change, such as in picture-writing and gesture-language; games, proverbs, and riddles; myth, legend, folklore, and religion. Such traits represent more directly the untrained mental processes and provide for a safer reconstruction of the human mind, as such. Accordingly, in the *Researches* (1865), Tylor chose to offer a history of civilization based primarily on an examination of language, myths, rites, customs, and beliefs.

The similarities of gesture-language in societies separated in time and place were convincing evidence to Tylor "that the mind of uncultured men works in much the same way at all times and everywhere." The history of magic everywhere pointed to one underlying phenomenon: the outward projection on to material reality of the inner processeses of individual thought. In the lengthy, detailed treatment of mythology, Tylor identifies eight mythological themes which commonly occur in North and South America, and in Asia: World-Tortoise, Man Swallowed by Fish, Sun Catcher, Accent of Heaven by the Tree, Bridge of Dead, Fountain of Youth, Tail-Fisher, Diable Boiteux. Here again was telling evidence for the fundamental similarity of the human mind.

With the assumption of psychic unity established, Tylor was in a position to accept the evidence of either diffusion or independent development. They both appeared to be due to the similarity of the human mind: in the first case, the transfer of traits seemed to be made possible by the similarity of the inventing and the borrowing mind; and in the second, a parallel development seemed to be due to the action of like minds working under like conditions.

The *Researches*, then, proved a landmark in anthropology on two counts: it advanced the developmental theory by its treatment of the problem of similarities, and it made theoretical use of an important and neglected body of cultural material.

Having established the psychic unity of man, the next step for Tylor was to establish a cultural reconstruction which would show a progressive development from primitive to civilized man. He accomplished this in the publication of *Primitive Culture* (1871), an anthropological classic which marks the beginning of the scientific study of culture. Two major contributions to cultural anthropology emerged from this work: The "doctrine of survivals" and the theory of "animism."

Tylor considered two methods of evolutionary reconstruction which suggested the method of survivals to him. One was the reconstruction of material culture by the archaeologists and geologists on the basis of the discoveries of material relics (artifacts) in the geological strata. The archaeologist, working with the geologist, could establish from a few surviving artifacts (such as fragments of weapons, implements, pottery) a general picture of the material culture of an ancient society, and its approximate place in a chronological series. The three well-known stages (stone, bronze, iron) of material culture had been established in this way. The other suggestion for a method may have come from the use the biologists made of rudimentary (vestigial) organs in the reconstruction of organic evolution, where nonfunctional parts of the body were considered as survivals from ancestral forms in which they had a functional role.

In brief, Tylor's doctrine of survivals considered the quaint and nonfunctional customs and beliefs of civilized peoples as ancient "artifacts," or "vestigial remains." As stated previously, Tylor was interested as early as 1856 in the existence of quaint and unrealistic customs and beliefs in modern civilization. What are these, asked Tylor, but the relics of a cultural past, which have been preserved in the "strata" of human behavior.

With the assumption of man's essential rationality within a given environmental context, these "survivals" become trustworthy clues to man's cultural past: "When in the process of time there has come general change in the condition of a people, it is usual, notwithstanding, to find much that manifestly has not its origin in the new state of things, but has simply lasted on into it. On the strength of these survivals, it becomes possible to declare that the civilization of the people they are observed among must have been derived from an earlier state in which the proper home and meaning of these things are to be found; and thus collections of such facts are to be worked as mines of historical knowledge." They exist in our midst, Tylor continues, as the "primeval monuments of barbaric thought and life."

The doctrine of survivals added utility and prestige to the "comparative method" as the key to ethnological research; Tylor, in fact, is often referred to as the founder of "comparative ethnology." The comparative method had rested on the almost gratuitous assumption that contemporary savage peoples represented earlier stages of cultural development which had been traversed by civilized peoples. By the study of survivals (material and nonmaterial) in modern societies, it was now possible, according to Tylor, to find the actual traces of these stages in modern society: "Look at the modern European peasant," says Tylor, "using his hatchet and his hoe, see his food boiling or roasting over the log-fire, observe the exact place which beer holds in his calculation of happiness, hear his tale of the ghost in the nearest haunted house, and of the farmer's niece who was bewitched with knots in her inside till she fell into fits and died. If we choose out in this way things which have altered little in a long course of centuries we may draw a picture where there shall be scarce a hand's breadth difference between an English ploughman and a Negro of Central Africa. . . . We have continued reason to be thankful for fools. . . . It is quite wonderful . . . to see how large a share stupidity and impractical conservatism and dogged superstition have had in preserving for us traces of the history of our race, which practical utilitarianism would have remorselessly swept away."

Tylor's doctrine of survivals became the most valuable tool of the evolutionary anthropologists and resulted in a growing body of valuable ethnological material, which can be summed up under the general heading of "folklore."

Before taking up Tylor's influential theory of animism it may be useful to consider his approach to myth in general, because it paves the way for his exposition of animism.

Tylor believed that myth originated in the human intellect when it was in a childlike state. Myths represented for Tylor the crude but essentially rational attempts of childlike peoples to make sense out of their environment and experiences. "Legend," he states, ". . . is only telling the perennial story of the world's daily life." He believed that in myth and legend one had access to the primitive philosophy of nature and life. The following Polynesian nature-myth is an example of the kind of evidence on which Tylor founded his "primitive philosopher" idea:

Sky (father) and Earth (mother) created all things in nature. But at first there was no light because Sky and Earth still cleaved to each other. The children counseled with one another on whether to slay the parents or rend them apart so as to admit the light. The "father of the forests" advised that the parents be separated, the sky to become a "stranger" and the earth a nursing mother. Several of the children tried and failed to separate Sky and Earth and finally the father of the forests tried. He placed his head against the earth, his feet against the sky, and sundered them as they cried, groaned, and shrieked aloud. The father of wind and storms had not consented to the plan of his brothers, and followed his father into the heavens. He then waged war on his brothers by sending wind and storms to stir up the sea, break down the forests, and destroy the plant and animal life. In the course of the battle the reptiles fled from the sea to seek safety in the woods. The Earth caught up the gods of the plants and animals and hid them from the storm god. Finally the storm god attacked the "father of fierce men," the one who had planned the destruction of the parents; but the storm god could not shake him, and man remained erect and unshaken upon the bosom of mother Earth. Man was furious at having been deserted by his brethren in the battle and has exploited them for his benefit ever since. He conquered all but the storm god who still attacks him periodically with tempest and hurricane. And until this time Sky and Earth have remained separated, but their love continues. The warm sighs of the Earth's bosom (the mists) are directed to the parted spouse, and the Sky drops frequent tears (dew-drops) on his beloved Earth.

Tylor says of this myth that there is "scarcely a thought that is not still transparent, scarcely even a word that has lost its meaning to us." He means, of course, that it is a realistic, if childlike, interpretation of natural phenomena. This is characteristic of Tylor's rationalistic approach to all folklore, and it underlies his entire theory of animism.

Tylor called the belief in spiritual beings animism and considered it to be the minimum definition of religion. Tylor's animism in fact is a comprehensive theory of the origin and development of religious systems everywhere, and it served to illustrate the kind of reconstruction that can be made with a developmental theory. Animism rests on one very simple idea: that where men dream by night, have phantasms by day, and die, the belief in spiritual beings will arise. He divided the animism of primitive peoples into two principal ideas: the concept of the *soul* and the derivative belief in *other spirits*.

The idea of the soul Tylor thought to be a crude but reasonable inference on the part of primitive man. The savage, like every man, is confronted daily with the dual nature of existence. At death certain phenomena disappear—breath, pulse, consciousness, and the capacity for voluntary movement. The body remains, but that complex of phenomena known as "life" has disappeared, "passed away," as we say today. Life, or soul, has left the body.

Dreams and phantasms suggest a related duality. Here, human shapes appear which are images of individuals who may be some distance away, or even dead. The savage reasonably concludes that man's body has a phantom copy which may leave the body and have independent experiences.

According to Tylor, the primitive mentality makes a natural connection between these two separable attributes of the body—the phantom copy and the soul—and brings them together in an apparitional-soul, or ghost-soul. It is the ghost-soul which accounts for death as well as dreams, visions, sleep, swoons, illness, coma, and the like; conditions, that is, where life processes are impaired, distorted, or destroyed. It is the key to the entire psycho-biology of primitive man: "It is a thin unsubstantial human image, in its nature a sort of vapour, film, or shadow; the cause of life and thought in the individual it animates; independently possessing the personal consciousness and volition of its corporeal owner, past or present; capable of leaving the body far behind, to flash swiftly from place to place; mostly impalpable and invisible, yet also manifesting physical power, and especially appearing to men waking or asleep as a phantasm separate from the body of which it bears the likeness; continuing to exist and appear to men after death of that body; able to enter into, possess, and act in the bodies of other men, of animals, and even things."

The next stage in the development of animism is the natural extension of souls and phantom-copies to animals, there being only a small distinction in the primitive mind between man and the other animals. Animals appear in dreams, and they die; hence the ghost-soul can account for animal as well as human existence. To support this theory, Tylor cites many examples of animal sacrifice which are made at human burials—the idea being that the ghost-soul of the sacrificed animal will accompany the ghost-soul of the individual and serve him in the next world as it did in this. Dogs, for example, are buried with children in some primitive cultures, to lead them to the land of souls. Horses are led to a warrior's grave, killed and thrown in the grave with their master. Tylor found a case of this kind occurring as late as 1781 in Europe and stated that it was still practiced in Asia.

The next extension of the ghost-soul is to non-living objects. Things also appear in dreams and must have phantom-copies. Unlike animals, they do not "die," but this requirement is probably overlooked on the ground that where one (the phantom) is evident, the other (the soul) can be assumed. Evidence for this idea is found in the common practice of sending objects, such as weapons, implements, pottery, and so on, along with the dead man in his grave, for his use in the next life.

Three general beliefs concerning the existence of ghost-souls after death are derived from these early stages of animism: (1) the conviction that the ghost-souls hover around the earth and take an interest in the living—sometimes visiting their former homes, (2) the belief in metempsychosis—the transmigration of souls into other human beings, or even into animals, plants, and things, (3) the idea of a special residence in another world, such as the Western Islands, the Underworld, the Mountains, and Heaven. This last kind of belief falls into one of two categories, which Tylor calls the "continuance theory" and the "retribution theory." In the first, a life similar to earthly life is carried on, and in the second, the ghost-souls are rewarded or punished according to the deeds of their earthly life. The second theory would, of course, have a special effect on the social behavior of the people who adopted the belief.

The general idea of the primitive ghost-soul animating men, animals, plants, and things naturally leads to the belief in another order of spiritual beings which are on a higher level. These are called "manes," which are souls in origin but which acquire a special quality raising them to the level of demons or deities. This development resulted in one of the great branches of religion: Manes-Worship.

Manes are souls of individuals who, in real life, were in a position of authority with respect to the worshiper. This will often be a parent, hence ancestor-worship becomes a common form of Manes-Worship. But it might also be the soul of a tribal-chief, a tribal-hero, or any other powerful person. He can have been a power for good or evil, and thus become either a deity or a demon.

Regarding Manes-Worship, Tylor says: "Its principles are not difficult to understand, for they plainly keep up the social relations of the living world. The dead ancestor, now passed into a deity, simply goes on protecting his own family and receiving suit and service from them as of old; the dead chief still watches over his own tribe, still holds his authority by helping friends and harming enemies, still rewards the right and sharply punishes the wrong."

Manes-Worship was especially instructive for Tylor in the reconstruction of animism, because he saw it as intermediate in the hierarchy of the spiritual world, standing between ordinary souls and superhuman demons and deities. It was clear evidence for Tylor of the modeling of superior spirits on the human soul. He cites the worship of saints in modern religion as a clear case of Manes-Worship, being as it is the worship of dead men and women who form a class of inferior deities.

Another important feature in the development of primitive religion is the general idea of the *embodiment* of spirits. As the soul may be in or out of the body, so are spirits free to run in and out of objects—living and non-living. This idea serves two important purposes in lower animism: As a theory of "demoniacal possession," it explains all forms of human disease and derangement. Tylor gives a particularly vivid account of this phenomenon:

> As in normal conditions, the man's soul, inhabiting his body, is held to give it life, to think, speak, and act through it, so an adaptation of the self-same principle explains abnormal conditions of body or mind, by considering the new symptoms as due to the operation of a second soul-like being, a strange spirit. The possessed man, tossed and

shaken in fever, pained and wrenched as though some live
creature were tearing or twisting him within, pining as
though it were devouring his vitals day by day, rationally
finds a personal spiritual cause for his sufferings. In hideous
dreams he may even sometimes see the very ghost or night-
mare-fiend that plagues him. Especially when the mysterious
unseen power throws him helpless to the ground, jerks and
writhes him in convulsions, makes him leap upon the by-
standers with a giant's strength and a wild beast's ferocity,
impels him, with distorted face and frantic gesture, and
voice not his own nor seemingly human, to pour forth with
incoherent raving, or with thought and eloquence beyond his
sober faculties to command, to counsel, to foretell—such a
one seems to those who watch him, and even to himself, to
have become the mere instrument of a spirit which has
seized him or entered into him, a possessing demon in whose
personality the patient believes so implicitly that he often
imagines a personal name for it, which it can declare when
it speaks in its own voice and character through his organs
of speech; at last, quitting the medium's spent and jaded
body, the intruding spirit departs as it came.

The practice of exorcism emerges as the therapeutic device
for dealing with the invading demon spirits. The exorcist
removes the spirit by cajolery, bribes, threats, or by per-
suading or driving it to another abode.

Related to the "possession theory" (above), is the next
important application of the Embodiment idea, known as
fetishism. As the savage may "lay" a demon spirit in a
foreign body, so may he manipulate a useful spirit to his
advantage. It may be carried around in an object to fend
off enemies and disease, or it may be set up as a deity in a
material object, for propitiation and worship.[1]

Fetishism merges into idolatry when a fetish object is
altered in some material way by the worshiper so as to indi-

---

[1] It may be noted here that for Comte, to whom Tylor was consciously
indebted for many ideas, fetishism was used to designate primitive religion in general. Tylor used the term to indicate a subordinate department of animism, and restricted its use for spirits embodied in, or related
to material objects, living or non-living.

cate its special function as the abode for a spirit. A few scratches on a dab of paint may serve to construct an idol, or a more elaborate job may be done in the construction of a definite image, as in a statue or picture. The important thing is that the idol takes on a "personality," or soul, which is absent in the pure fetish. An idol, for Tylor, must thus combine the characteristics of portrait (no matter how crude) and fetish. The connection between souls and other spirits—the crucial factor in Tylor's theory—is further reinforced by this view of Idolatry: soul and spirit are both embodied in the idol, just as they are both embodied in human bodies, at least on occasions.

The next stage in animism occurs when the primitive mind draws the analogy between human behavior and the behavior of nature at large. As the human body functions by virtue of its inhabiting ghost-soul, so does nature in general appear to be animated by analogous agents. Thus animism, beginning as a philosophy of human life, becomes a comprehensive philosophy of all nature. The "causes" of all natural phenomena are nature-spirits. They cause the wind to blow, the sky to rain, the rivers to move, the volcanoes to erupt.

Beginning, most likely, from very particular spirits for particular events, the idea of nature-spirits becomes generalized, and there arise the species-deities: the gods of Forest, Heaven, Earth, Water, Sun and Moon. Next, invisible species-deities emerge: the gods of Agriculture, War, Peace, Good, and Evil. This is the great stage of polytheism.

And finally, the concept of one Supreme Deity arrives. Above the souls, manes, nature-spirits, and species-deities of class and element—one deity is elevated to divine supremacy. Monotheism, the great belief of civilized peoples, has evolved from the primitive past. A developmental theory can adequately account for monotheism and the entire history of religion; there is no need of Divine Revelation. Tylor has answered the clerics who would defend the degeneration theory—and on their own ground.

Lowie has said of Tylor's method of "adhesions" that

"nothing that Tylor ever did serves so decisively to lift him above the throng of his fellow-workers." Briefly, the method involved the application of statistical methods of probability to ethnological data. The method aimed at discovering the causal relationships, if any, between culture traits; whether, for example, the customs of residence are related to, or are independent of, customs of avoidance. If relationships, or adhesions, can be discovered, then, thought Tylor, inferences of cultural causality can be made over the whole range of mankind; "social arithmetic" could be employed to disclose the course of social history. His attempt, according to Lowie, was to "substitute the mathematical concept of function for the metaphysical concept of cause."

Tylor employed the method in the following way: He was interested, for example, in the cultural laws of marriage and descent and had data on these customs from over 300 peoples, from "savage hordes" to "cultured nations." All customs related to the subject were tabulated and classified. By consulting the tables, the investigator could easily determine what customs accompanied other customs, such as teknonymy (the term invented by Tylor for the custom of naming parents after children) and matrilocal residence. If the recurrence of the given coincidence in the tables exceeded significantly the number that could be expected on a chance distribution, then a causal relationship could be assumed. In the above example—teknonymy and residence —the "reckoning of the adhesions" showed a connection between teknonymy and matrilocal residence in twenty-two cases, where accidental distribution would yield eleven. Teknonymy was even more closely related to avoidance, fourteen cases occurring, with a chance expectation of four. Taking the three customs together—teknonymy, matrilocal residence, and avoidance—they would appear by chance only once or twice among all the peoples studied; they actually appear together eleven times, giving odds of about six to one for a causal relationship.

Tylor realized that many refinements must be made before this method could be applied with complete confidence, but his experience so far with it made it clear to him "that the rules of human conduct are amenable to classification in compact masses, so as to show by strict numerical treatment their relations to one another."

Except for a few detractors, such as G. Elliot Smith and other extreme diffusionists, and those who incorrectly place Tylor among the uncritical unilinear evolutionists, Tylor is rated among the very greatest in anthropology. He is considered the founder of cultural anthropology and has had enormous influence. Sir James Frazer, to name one individual, was greatly indebted to Tylor for his work. Max Müller referred consistently to ethnology as "Mr. Tylor's Science"; Andrew Lang stated, in 1907, that Tylor, along with Lubbock, "towered above all British Anthropologists, like Saul above his people"; Lowie states that "the lapse of time has merely confirmed the earlier judgment of his greatness."

The most common and obvious criticism of Tylor's work centers around his extreme rationalistic interpretations of ethnological data. His "sense of probability," as Lowie called it, was carried to the extreme in conceiving of all human beings as relatively sophisticated philosophers. Tylor recognizes this one-sidedness in some places, as where, after the exposition of animism, he states that "the intellectual rather than the emotional side of religion has been kept in view." And then he goes on: "Even in the life of the rudest savages, religious belief is associated with intense emotion, with awful reverence, with agonizing terror, with rapt ecstasy when sense and thought utterly transcend the common level of daily life." But he justifies the exclusion of a treatment of these emotional factors on the ground that they represent divergencies from his main purpose of showing the transmission of certain main features of cultural history, in this case animism.

Probably part of Tylor's rationalistic emphasis can be attributed to his conscious polemic against the clerics, who would create an impassable gulf between civilized man and his primitive ancestors. Tylor had to show that the "rude savage" was potentially an English gentleman, with the capacities for rational inference within his limited historical sphere. There is no mistaking the delight with which Tylor directs the attention of theologians to the beginnings and transmission of their noble doctrines and beliefs. "Theologians all to expose," was "the *mission* of primitive man," as Tylor could say in poetry.

Probably most important, as far as his influence is concerned, was Tylor's justification of the evolutionary method as a technique of investigation and interpretation in the social sciences. It may be said that many of the followers of this method lacked Tylor's relatively critical and sophisticated use of it, and finally brought it into general discredit; but in one form or another it has continued to exert great influence to the present day.

Finally, the general influence of Tylor's personality may be mentioned again. With Tylor, as with Darwin, a quiet but shrewd geniality helped pave the way for the early acceptance of ideas and methods which were loaded with explosive implications for contemporary thought and society.

# JAMES FRAZER

## *LABOR DISGUISED IN EASE*

S IR JAMES FRAZER was the dutiful, obedient son of extremely pious parents. As a child he never misbehaved
or dreamed of questioning parental or religious authority.
As a man, however, he spent over sixty years in the libraries
of Trinity College, Cambridge, undermining the belief in
a literal acceptance of the Bible and publicizing the fascinating "misbehavior" of primitive peoples. His quiet,
persistent, and unconscious rebellion, effected through
scholarship, produced *The Golden Bough*, one of the
world's great anthropological odysseys.

Frazer's father and mother were staunch Presbyterians
and strictly orthodox in the Calvinist tradition. They were
extremely religious people whose home life centered around
daily worship and good reading. His father, Daniel Frazer,
had an excellent library of English literature and had written two small works, one on local history.

The entire family—parents and children—knew the
*Shorter Catechism* by heart and accepted it as the orthodox
statement of religion.[1]

[1] The *Shorter Catechism* was the third of the Reformation Catechisms—
the Luther and the Heidelberg Catechisms were the other two—and pre-

On Sundays the family did not leave the house except to go to church; the day was given over to quiet worship, hymn-singing, and reading. The central importance of religion and piety in Frazer's early life was always a source of pleasant association for him: "I look back to those peaceful Sabbath days with something like fond regret, and the sound of Sabbath bells, even in a foreign land, still touches a deep chord in my heart." According to Frazer, the parents never tried to indoctrinate the children with their religious views; the subject was "too sacred for common conversation" and was simply accepted without question.

This was characteristic of the way Frazer accepted the authority of his parents in all matters. He states that none of the children were ever punished and goes on to say: "Indeed they had no occasion to punish us, for we were dutiful and obedient children who never dreamed of questioning their authority or thwarting their wishes."

Frazer summed up his father's personality and character with such language as "sterling character," "strictest integrity," "respected by all," "courteous to everyone without distinction of rank or station," and "devout Christian." The father accepted the Bible in its literal sense as the inspired and infallible word of God.

Although everyone "respected" his father, Frazer states that everyone "loved" his mother: "She endeared herself to all by her sweet, gentle, and truly womanly nature." She was a gentle, sociable, and cheerful woman who enjoyed the simple pleasures of domestic life and the companionship of family and friends. But, Frazer points out, "With all her gentleness she was by no means destitute of spirit: she told me that whenever she heard military music she felt moved to 'rush out and plunge into the fray'!" She shared what Frazer called his father's "childlike faith in religion." She was devoted to her family and died with her arms resting on one of Frazer's classical studies, *Pausanias*, the publication of which she had eagerly awaited for many years.

---

sented the Calvinistic interpretation. It is known for its exceptional clarity of expression and its precise, almost mathematical analysis of the then current controversies in religion.

Frazer always showed the greatest respect and affection toward his early life with his family and attributed whatever success he had attained to "wise and tender upbringing" by his parents. He always spoke of them with great love and affection.

Although one of the chief consequences of Frazer's lifelong work was the undermining of the literal validity of the Scriptures—the unquestioned belief of his parents—he never outwardly expressed anything like the anti-clericalism of Spencer, or even Tylor. If he was in rebellion at religious orthodoxy, he was never conscious of it. He says of the Bible: "This may not be science and history, but it is at least an impressive pageant, a stately drama: without metaphor, it is noble literature, and like all noble literature it is fitted to delight, to elevate, and to console." It was through this kind of appreciation of the Scriptures that Frazer believed a reconciliation could be made between the old and the new thought.

Frazer was born January 1, 1854, at Glasgow, Scotland. He was one of four children (two boys and two girls) born to Daniel Frazer and the former Katherine Brown. The father was the leading partner of a prosperous drug and chemical firm in Glasgow, and the mother was the daughter of a prosperous merchant.

Unlike Darwin, Spencer, and Tylor, Frazer's education followed the usual pattern of the times for one in his position. He began his schooling with a "red-faced dominie of the old school" and recollected nothing of the experience. He attended Springfield Academy for a short time and then passed to Larchfield Academy, where he spent his happiest school days and received the foundation and inspiration for much of his later work. It was here, under the instruction of Alexander Mackenzie, that he learned the rudiments of Latin and Greek which were to play such a large part in his later studies. In 1869, at the age of fifteen, he matriculated at Glasgow University, where the foundation of his subsequent career was firmly laid.

Frazer found the rigid requirements of Glasgow for the Master's degree very congenial: "In my time," he said in

1932, "no option whatever was allowed to a student preparing for the Master's degree. Every one without exception had to study and satisfy the examiners in precisely the same subjects, which were Greek and Latin, Mathematics, Natural Philosophy (which meant Physics), Logic and Metaphysics, Moral Philosophy, and English Literature. It was an excellent scheme of a sound and liberal education, and I very much doubt if it could have been improved upon by being left to the choice of raw youths in their teens, as were many, if not most, of the students of those days. Certainly, for myself, I have always been glad that in my sixteenth year I was allowed no discretion, but was shepherded into the fold of knowledge by wiser and more experienced heads than my own."

At Glasgow Frazer worked under three men whose influence can be traced throughout his life's work: G. G. Ramsay, John Veitch, and Sir William Thomson (later Lord Kelvin). Under Ramsay, Frazer acquired a lasting interest and competence in the classics. "To him more than to anyone else," said Frazer, "I owe the powerful impulse which directed the main current of my thought for many years to the classics of antiquity." Frazer regarded the study of Greek and Roman civilization as the "best preparation for a general study of man." He dedicated his six-volume work, *Pausanias*, to Ramsay, and Ramsay called the dedication his "greatest honor." John Veitch was Professor of Logic and Metaphysics at Glasgow and he made a profound impression on Frazer, one that was reflected in Frazer's thought and style. He stated that Veitch and his predecessors among Scotland's philosophers (such as Hume and Hutcheson), "wrote like gentlemen in the language of polished society, and not like pedants in the uncouth jargon of the schools." From Lord Kelvin, the great physicist, Frazer acquired a belief in the rational and intelligible order of nature. This conception of the universe as being "regulated by exact and absolutely unvarying laws of nature expressible in mathematical formulas" remained a settled belief throughout his life. He remained intolerant of the "new physics" with its relativity and indeterminancy because it implied for him the denial of a rational explanation of nature.

While at Glasgow Frazer thought of competing for a scholarship at Oxford, but his father, mistrusting the High Church tendencies of Oxford, decided that he should go to Cambridge instead, and Frazer entered Trinity College on a scholarship in 1873. There he remained the rest of his life, his Fellowship being renewed three times and finally for life.

At Cambridge Frazer continued his work in classical literature and philosophy and also studied law. The philosopher James Ward soon directed Frazer's attention to Tylor's *Primitive Culture*, and it was this work which stimulated Frazer's interest in anthropology. Frazer states that it "marked an epoch in my life." It was William Robertson Smith, however, who fired Frazer with a lasting enthusiasm for anthropology. Smith, a minister, had been expelled from his teaching position at Free Church College at Aberdeen on grounds of heresy connected with his work in comparative religion. He was welcomed at Cambridge, however, where he favored Frazer with his interest and friendship. But for Smith, said Frazer, "my interest in the subject [anthropology] might have remained purely passive and inert."[2]

Smith, being engaged as editor of the ninth edition of the *Encyclopaedia Britannica* and knowing of Frazer's interest in anthropology, assigned to Frazer the writing of the articles "Taboo" and "Totemism." For Frazer, these articles "were the beginning of a systematic application to anthropology and especially to a study of the backward races of men whom we call savages and barbarians." Frazer gave his reasons for concentrating on savagery rather than on civilization as follows: "Civilization is extremely complex; savagery is comparatively simple, and moreover it is undoubtedly the source from which all civilization has been ultimately derived by a slow process of evolution. It

[2] Malinowski has called Smith the "spiritual father" of the "sociological theories of culture movement" and holds that he was the first to see that religion must be accounted for by its social nature.

seemed to me therefore that if we are to understand the complex product we must begin by studying the simple elements out of which it has been gradually compounded; in other words, we must try to understand savagery before we can hope fully to comprehend civilization."

Frazer's monastic devotion to the "drama of human existence" is summed up in the eighty-four pages of the published bibliography of his works. Although isolated from the drama by choice, he read and wrote of it with insatiable passion.

In 1885 Frazer read one of his first anthropological papers, "On Certain Burial Customs as Illustrative of the Primitive Theory of the Soul," before the Anthropological Institute. Tylor's influence was clearly shown in this paper. Tylor himself heard the paper and remarked that "its original and ingenious treatment of the evidence must materially advance the study of animistic funeral customs." Tylor also noted "the excellent results of Mr. Frazer's study of classical authors, not as mere ancient texts, but as repertories of real facts full of anthropological value."

His articles, "Taboo" and "Totemism," for the *Encyclopaedia Britannica* appeared in 1888. These early papers reveal a general idea about social origins which became a guiding principle for much of Frazer's work; namely, that from irrational beginnings systems of great adaptive value for society are evolved. In "Taboo" Frazer remarks: ". . . we shall scarcely err in believing that even in advanced societies the moral sentiments, in so far as they are merely sentiments and are not based on an induction from experience, derive much of their force from an original system of taboo. Thus on the taboo were grafted the golden fruits of law and morality, while the parent stem dwindled slowly into the sour crabs and empty husks of popular superstition on which the swine of modern society are still content to feed."

The first edition of *The Golden Bough* was published in two volumes in 1890; the second edition (three volumes) in 1900; and the third edition (twelve volumes) between 1911 and 1915. It is Frazer's most famous work and has had an enormous influence. Frazer defined the purpose of *The Golden Bough* as follows: "The cycle of *The Golden Bough* depicts, in its sinuous outline, in its play of alternate light and shadow, the long evolution by which the thoughts and efforts of man have passed through the successive stages of Magic, Religion and Science. It is, in some measure, an epic of humanity which, starting from magic, attains to science in its ripe age, and will find there, perhaps, its death. . . . The cycle of *The Golden Bough* treats principally, almost completely, with the past. The sacrifice of the Divine King, put to death for the good of his people, is studied at length in its pages: that episode, so important in Christian theology, is like the symbolized epitome of the lugubrious history of humanity."

Frazer's most important classical study came out in 1898, after nine years of study. It was a translation of and a commentary on Pausanias' *Description of Greece*, and its six volumes constituted a great summary of the knowledge of classical Greece.

*Psyche's Task* was first published in 1909; in 1928 it appeared, with the addition of one paper, as *The Devil's Advocate*. It is one of the most speculative of Frazer's works, and amounts to "A Plea for Superstition" (the subtitle of *The Devil's Advocate*). Frazer argued that although superstition has often been an evil, it has also had a positive value for mankind "in promoting respect for authority and abstention from many forms of violence." It is *Psyche's* task to separate the true from the false; but this may not always be a gain from the point of view of accepted ethical standards and social behavior. Marett has said of this work that "One sees here the rationalist who, confronted with the unreason manifest in so much of the actual policy that has swayed mankind, must shrug his shoulders and admit that, pragmatically at all events, such foolishness has answered well enough."

The four-volume *Totemism and Exogamy* was published in 1910. Here, the idea was advanced that after totems had become hereditary, exogamy developed as a means for preventing inbreeding.

*The Belief in Immortality and the Worship of the Dead* was published in three volumes, between 1913 and 1924. This work employed Tylor's idea of polytheism as originating in personified causes, or nature spirits. According to Frazer, scientific theories eventually replace nature spirits as explanations for a given class of events, but the idea of deity is retained as the one great "cause."

*Folk-Lore in the Old Testament* was published in three volumes in 1918. In this work Frazer treated the Old Testament as a body of folklore, which he defined as "the whole body of a people's traditionary beliefs and customs, so far as they appear to be due to the collective action of the multitude and cannot be traced to the individual influence of great men." Frazer insisted that "Despite the high moral and religious development of the ancient Hebrews, there is no reason to suppose that they formed an exception to this general law." He then proceeded to present the many prior and parallel legends which were similar to those found in the Old Testament.

*The Worship of Nature* was published in 1926 and presented the now familiar thesis that religion is based on the human personification of nature.

Frazer's remaining works included *The Gorgon's Head* (1927), containing literary essays, articles, and translations, in prose and verse; The *Fasti* of Ovid (1929), which started out to be a translation but developed, characteristically, into a five-volume treatise on Roman history and mythology; and *Aftermath* (1937), a supplement to *The Golden Bough*.

Frazer's one venture outside the libraries was in a teaching position at Liverpool University, where he was appointed Professor of Social Anthropology. He resigned after one year, convinced that he should never have left the library. Unwelcome respite from his work occurred on those occasions when he journeyed to accept the many academic honors and awards that were bestowed upon him. He was an original Fellow of the British Academy, was knighted in 1914, elected a member of the Order of Merit (1924), elected to the Royal Society (1920), and received high recognition from France, being made an associate member of the Institut de France and a Commander of the Legion of Honor. In 1921 the Frazer Lectureship in Social Anthropology was founded in his honor at the Universities of Oxford, Cambridge, Glasgow, and Liverpool.

Frazer was not tall, but carried himself erectly. He was quick and agile. The most conspicuous feature of Frazer's appearance was his eyes; they were a piercing, sapphire blue and are startling even in a photograph. A picture of Frazer taken in 1933, when he was seventy-nine years old, reveals hardly a wrinkle in his face. He had a short, neatly pointed beard which covered little more than his chin. A visitor to Frazer in 1935 wrote: "His look of close application, his short, white beard, and his tightened lids behind his glasses suggest someone who is more accustomed to taking a patient's pulse than to exploring those primitive abysses in which the gods of man slowly come to life."[3]

Frazer spent his life in libraries and studies: Marett has called him "a veritable athlete of the study, never out of training and as true and tough as steel." At forty-two he married Lily Grove, a French writer, and it was agreed at the outset that he would continue to devote practically all his time to his work. He spent at least as much, if not more, time in the libraries after his marriage as before, and his wife devoted herself completely to the advancement of his work and reputation, especially in France.

Frazer was an extremely modest, polite, and courtly man who would probably have been more at home in the eighteenth century, according to his secretary and biographer, R. Angus Downie. He seemed little interested in public opinion and stayed out of the controversies that centered around his work. R. R. Marett, a friend of Frazer, has said: ". . . he was no speech-maker or verbal duelist, and, when present at some heated debate, as might by a rare chance happen, was wont to maintain a sublime silence, such as might suggest a timid suspension of judgment to

[3] Jaloux, Edward, "A Visit to Sir James Frazer," *Living Age*, 348:135-39, 1935.

those who did not realize how boldly and firmly he thought for himself. Yet he was, in fact, the very embodiment of intellectual, as reinforced by moral, courage."

Sarah Campion, the British author and daughter of the well-known medievalist G. G. Coulton, wrote an interesting portrait of Sir James and Lady Frazer in 1951. She was employed by the Frazers for a few months in 1940, the year before their death. Miss Campion was especially fascinated by Lady Frazer; she says: "I have never met anyone who more thoroughly knew what she wanted, or more ruthlessly set about getting it. . . . She had no other thought in life, no other purpose in living, than to prolong by any means in her power the tenuous life and contentment of her famous husband. I dare say this battle for contentment was the only one she ever lost: for, as far as I could see, they were neither of them happy." In the last years of their lives, Lady Frazer was deaf and Sir James, blind. Lady Frazer hovered over her husband, forcing food, "forkful by forkful into his protesting mouth," according to Miss Campion. Even at this time, when Frazer had received almost every conceivable recognition, Lady Frazer spent hours pouring over *Who's Who* to find sources of more honors for her husband. As for Frazer himself in these days, he maintained a quiet, courtly concern for the physical comfort of those around him and submitted to the overpowering care of his wife. Miss Campion says: "I think of them now in some Elysian field, seated near the entrance so that she can tell him who is coming in or going out: seated on twin thrones, the sightless and the deaf, while her right hand is laid possessingly, maternally, over his. I think of them both often, and always with affection: for they were, in their utterly different ways, a most memorable and lovable pair." Lady Frazer died a few hours after her husband.

With his wife and his Fellowships at Cambridge to isolate him from the practical demands of life, Frazer lived and worked in a great world of fantasy and folklore. These last four stanzas of his "June in Cambridge" seem to epitomize very well the kind of life he lived:

*Still, still I con old pages*
*And through great volumes wade,*
*While life's brief summer passes,*
*And youth's brief roses fade.*

*Ah yes! Through these dull pages*
*A glimmering vista opes,*
*Where fairer flowers are blooming*
*Than bloom on earthly slopes.*

*The dreamland world of fancy!*
*There is my own true home,*
*There are the purple mountains*
*And blue seas fringed with foam.*

*And there the deathless garlands*
*That crown the chosen head,*
*When youth's brief June is over.*
*And youth's brief roses dead.*

One can suspect that Frazer meant to include himself when he observed in *The Golden Bough* that "the height of heroism is reached in men who renounce the pleasures of life and even life itself for the sake of keeping or winning for others, perhaps in distant ages, the blessings of freedom and truth."

Malinowski knew Frazer for over thirty years and speaks of the "paradox" of Frazer's life and thought. He refers to Frazer as "one of the world's greatest masters and teachers," in spite of the fact that in his personal contacts Frazer was completely ill at ease and inept. This was especially true in any situation where Frazer was called upon to defend a position extempore. He avoided, whenever he could, the give and take of even friendly controversy. Although he was always ready to revise or discard a theory in his work, he would not tolerate personal contradiction and would not engage in argument. After Andrew Lang wrote a critical review of *The Golden Bough* in which he referred to Frazer's work as the "vegetable" or "Covent Garden" school of Anthropology, Frazer became so upset he had to interrupt his work for several months—the greatest possible sacrifice for him. After this incident he refused to ever read an adverse review of his work.

Malinowski also seems to corroborate Sarah Campion's opinion of Lady Frazer. He says: "Lady Frazer was unquestionably a puzzling element to most of Frazer's friends as well as in his position in the academic world." He refers to her as a "somewhat redoubtable life companion of Frazer. . . ."

There are some hints in Frazer's work which tempt one to look further into the relationship of his personality to his life's work. He was always fascinated and delighted by the "misbehavior" of his savages. Malinowski says: "With an almost maternal attitude of concern, he delighted in their pranks and pleasures, while regretting their naughtiness." And Marett, in describing the experience of reading *The Golden Bough,* says: "We are children again as we study these childish doings of the peasant or the savage. No doubt, they behave as naughty children sometimes. But who shall say that he was never a naughty child, or that it is not human to derive satisfaction from the story of one's infant peccadilloes?" To Marett's rhetorical question, one may answer that Frazer himself never behaved as a "naughty child," if we are to take his word for it.

There is another parallel which is suggested by Frazer's over-all account of the progression of man through the phases of magic, religion, and science. At first, man believes that he can magically control all external events. Then, if he is astute, he becomes aware of his impotence and prostrates himself before the arbitrary powers of a divine will. This is religion, which, as Frazer always insists, "affects only those higher intelligences." Finally man arrives at science, which in a way represents the realization of the dreams of the initial stage of magic. But here Frazer grows pessimistic and speaks of the "dark shadow which lies athwart the end of this fair prospect" and the "great forces which seem to be making silently but relentlessly for the destruction of all this starry universe in which our earth swims as a speck or mote." In the end man's puny hands will not have strength "to speed afresh our slackening

planet in its orbit or rekindle the dying fire of the sun."
And *The Golden Bough* ends with the ringing of church
bells and the sound of the *Ave Maria*. It would seem that
Calvin and Frazer's parents had the last word after all.

FRAZER was not a field worker; he never laid eyes upon a
real "savage." He relied, as did Tylor, on the field reports
of other workers and travelers and on his vast knowledge
of classical literature. He knew Greek, Latin, French, German, Spanish, Italian, and Dutch, and so was able to read
much of his material in the original language. Before he
had taken his first degree at Cambridge he had read all of
Plato in the original Greek. As Frazer read through his
sources—which he did from twelve to fifteen hours a day—
he would note the passages he might be able to use and
later copied them out into notebooks. In this way he amassed
great mounds of material, most of which, one suspects,
were included in his publications. His works contain page
after page and volume after volume of detailed descriptions
culled from his documents. This was the familiar inductive
method that characterized so much of the work of Spencer
and Tylor.

Frazer did not employ any canons of internal evidence
for evaluating field material, as did Tylor, but he is supposed to have examined the credentials of any reporter very
carefully. He also published and circulated a pamphlet,
"Questions on the Manners, Customs, Religions, Superstitions, etc., of Uncivilized or Semi-Civilized Peoples,"
which was designed to guide field workers and travelers in
eliciting useful information from primitive societies for
him. As a result of this pamphlet Frazer carried on a large
and steady correspondence with informants from all over
the world. He was always much more interested in reports
of direct observation than in speculative ideas concerning
primitive cultures.

Frazer was never very interested in theories, including
his own. He says in the third edition of *The Golden Bough*:
". . . it is the fate of theories to be washed away . . . and

I am not so presumptuous as to expect or desire for mine an exemption from the common lot. I hold them all very lightly, and have used them chiefly as convenient pegs on which to hang my collection of facts." Malinowski said that "He [Frazer] loved additions to his live world: the drama of human existence. He disliked any surgery done upon this world by the theoretical criticism." Malinowski went on to claim that ethnological field work was under the spell of Frazer's suggestions for fifty years. In a letter to Sir Baldwin Spencer, the great field worker of Central Australia, Frazer wrote: "Works such as yours . . . will have a permanent value . . . Books like mine, merely speculative, will be superseded sooner or later (the sooner the better for the sake of truth) by better inductions based on fuller knowledge; books like yours, containing records of observations, will never be superseded."

The one great generalization that emerged for Frazer from his masses of documents was "the essential similarity in the working of the less developed human mind among all races, which corresponds to the essential similarity in their bodily frame and anatomy." In one place (in *Spirits of the Corn and of the Wild*), Frazer attributes certain resemblances between the religions of East and West to "similar causes acting alike on the similar constitution of the human mind in different countries under different skins." This adherence to the principle of "psychic unity" brought Frazer right into line with the comparative school of evolutionists, and he became one of its most famous advocates. His close agreement with Tylor is evident in the following passage: "modern researches into the early history of man, conducted on different lines, have converged with almost irresistible force on the conclusion that all civilized races have at some period or other emerged from a state of savagery resembling more or less closely the state in which many backward races have continued to the present time and that, long after the majority of men in a community have ceased to think and act like savages, not a few traces of the old ruder modes of life and thought survive in the habits and institutions of the people." Like

Tylor, Frazer was not a slave to the idea of independent origins of culture traits and admitted the possibility of diffusion. Downie heard him say once: "No one pretends that Christianity originated in Scotland: it reached there by diffusion." On the whole, however, Frazer built his theories on psychological rather than on historical material, and he remained a determined evolutionist throughout.

Frazer was not, however, a slavish follower of Tylor. His most significant deviation from Tylor was his denial of primitive man's rationality—a fundamental idea in Tylor's work. Frazer says: ". . . primitive man looks at the world from such a totally different point of view from us, that what seems simple and obvious to us almost certainly did not seem so to him; and *vice versa* what seems simple and obvious to him is almost always so entirely remote from our ways of thought that we should never have dreamed of it. Accordingly, any explanations of the origin of religion or society which commend themselves to us as entirely agreeable to reason and probability ought always, in my opinion, to be regarded with the greatest distrust. Their inherent probability (from our point of view) is a strong presumption against them." Frazer's picture of primitive man was much different from Tylor's "primitive philosopher," who, given a premise, could make rational deductions. Superstition was the guiding force in Frazer's primitive man.

Frazer's two most important anthropological works are *The Golden Bough* and *Totemism and Exogamy*. Of these, the first is the better known and has had the most far-reaching influence. Malinowski has called it "perhaps the greatest scientific Odyssey in modern humanism"; Marett has named it "that golden treasury of stories for grown-up children" and states that *The Golden Bough* has become "part of what every schoolboy knows, and what every gentleman must at least have forgotten."

Since Frazer had little regard for theoretical formulations, many of his specific theories concerning the Golden Bough myth are quite naive. One gets the impression that Frazer did not care whether they were taken seriously or not. As for his general theoretical orientation, Frazer was, of course, an evolutionist and a firm believer in the comparative method. He accepted the assumptions and implications of the theory and method of evolution with few reservations and did not even trouble to state his theoretical or methodological position in any definite way.

By the time of the third edition of *The Golden Bough* Frazer admitted what was obvious all along: that his explication of the Golden Bough myth was just a dramatic device for setting forth all the information he had gathered on primitive thought and culture. He says (in the third edition) of the priest of Nemi, the central figure in the myth, that "he, too, for all the quaint garb he wears and the gravity with which he stalks across the stage, is merely a puppet, and it is time to unmask him." Nevertheless, it would seem to have been impossible to present the ideas in *The Golden Bough* outside of the framework of the myth.

The myth to be explained concerned the rule of priestly succession at the sacred grove of Diana at Nemi, in the Alban hills of Italy. The lake (Nemi) and the grove were sometimes known as the lake and grove of Aricia, after a town some three miles away. The Priest-King of this sacred grove spent his time with drawn sword around a certain tree in the grove, constantly on guard. He had succeeded to his title by murdering his predecessor with a sprig of the mistletoe bough which grew high up on the tree, and he, in turn, was destined to be murdered by a successful challenger in the same manner. He defended himself successfully only so long as his powers of awareness, skill, and strength suffered no deterioration; as soon as he started to slip, he was murdered and the murderer reigned in his place.

Frazer became fascinated by this myth and set out to answer two questions: "first, why had Diana's priest at Nemi, the King of the Wood, to slay his predecessor? second, why before doing so had he to pluck the branch of a certain tree which the public opinion of the ancients identified with Virgil's Golden Bough?"

*The Golden Bough* answers these questions under seven main headings, taking up twelve volumes.

In the first part, *The Magic Art and the Evolution of Kings*, Frazer makes his famous distinction between magic and religion, a distinction which glorified man's capacity for self-effacement.

According to Frazer, magic is a kind of pseudo-science and pseudo-art by which primitive man attempts to manipulate nature. It is founded on his recognition of the uniformity of nature, in which he is right; and on his interpretation of this uniformity as being due to the similarity of causes and effects, in which he is wrong. Frazer called this principle of magic the Law of Similarity. The other principle of magic on which primitive man relies may be called the Law of Contact or Contagion. It is based on the idea that things which have once been in contact will continue to act on each other at a distance. Frazer included both of these principles of magic under the heading of "Sympathetic Magic," because they both assume that things act on each other at a distance through a "secret sympathy" transmitted through an invisible medium by means of an impulse.[4] All magical rites are applications of these magical principles: primitive man believes that the rules of his magical art (which are based on his own association of ideas) are identical with the laws of nature and that his performance of a certain act will result in the connected event in nature. Thus the savage believes that he may destroy or injure another person by constructing an image of him and destroying or injuring the image.

All magical ceremonies, rites, and spells are based on the principles of Sympathetic Magic. In its unadulterated form magic—and the magician—is the sovereign over nature: "He supplicates no higher power: he sues the favour of no fickle and wayward being: he abases himself before no awful deity." He alone wields the power to control the world; but he must conform rigidly to the rules; no mis-

[4] As un unshaken supporter of Newtonian mechanics, Frazer had here a convenient analogy in modern science. Here was primitive man unconsciously anticipating the scientific revolution of the seventeenth century.

take is allowed. The order of nature must be followed precisely.

The practice of magic in primitive cultures would naturally have important social consequences. The balance of social power would shift from the many to the one as certain exceptional individuals assumed the role of tribal magician, and eventually, king. Here, Frazer believed, were the beginnings of social supremacy and individual claims—a necessary development in the evolution of man. The change, says Tylor, "was on the whole very beneficial. For the rise of monarchy appears to be an essential condition of the emergence of mankind from savagery." The blessing was a mixed one, but necessary: "The general result is that at this stage of social evolution the supreme power tends to fall into the hands of men of the keenest intelligence and the most unscrupulous character. If we could balance the harm they do by their knavery against the benefits they confer by their superior sagacity, it might well be found that the good greatly outweighed the evil. Far more mischief has probably been wrought in the world by honest fools in high places than by intelligent rascals."

Religion is based on an entirely different, in fact, opposite, idea from magic. "By religion," Frazer says, "I understand a propitiation or conciliation of powers superior to man which are believed to direct and control the course of nature and human life." In religion the scientific conception of the uniformity of nature is abolished: the controlling powers can be propitiated, entreated, persuaded, bribed, and intimidated to alter the course of natural and human events. According to Frazer, religion could emerge only after man had advanced to a state of higher intelligence in which he would be able to recognize his own impotence. Thus, religion must have succeeded magic in man's evolution.

As the idea of powers superior to man evolved (in religion) there arose sacred leaders, or kings, who were endowed by the people with divine powers. Very often they were identified with the forces of nature, such as vegetation and fertility; or with the objects of nature, such as the sun, the moon, the forest. According to Frazer, the Priest-King at Nemi and the Goddess Diana were nature deities of this order. As King and Queen of the wood, they were responsible for the welfare of the people, and their union was particularly essential for the fertility of earth, beast, and man.

Since, as Frazer puts it, the worshipers of the Priest-King "have far too great a stake in his life to allow him to play fast and loose with it," they take elaborate precautions for his safety and good health. These precautions are expressed largely in the form of taboos, the subject of part two of *The Golden Bough*, entitled *Taboo and the Perils of the Soul*.

The main object of taboos being to preserve the life of the divine king, the taboos enacted must be based on a definite conception of life and death. Frazer follows Tylor here and features the soul, or mannikin, as the principle of life for primitive man. The following quote from Frazer shows how closely, almost literally, he followed Tylor's theory of the primitive soul: "This mannikin is of a thin, unsubstantial nature, though not so impalpable but that it may cause displacement on entering a physical object, and it can flit quickly from place to place; it is temporarily absent from the body in sleep, trance and disease, and permanently absent after death." The taboos which protected the life, or soul, of the god-man were also effective for the ordinary man. But for the ordinary man the observance of taboos is left to his choice; while for the god-man, the taboos are enforced under the penalty of his dismissal or even death. The entire community depends on the god-man for its health and survival and makes every effort to postpone his deterioration and death.

The elaborate concern for the well-being of the Priest-King of Nemi appears, at first glance, to conflict with the demand that the King must be murdered by his successor. In *The Dying God*, part three of *The Golden Bough*, Frazer shows that these two directives are complementary.

He discovered from his study of primitive societies that

in many cases, the king was put to death by his people or ended his own life, according to fixed custom. This usually occurred as the king was getting old and beginning to lose his powers. A common symptom of his failing was found in reduced sexual power. If, as Frazer believed, the prosperity of the people of a society was seen by them to be tied, by "sympathy," to the power and, especially, the virility of the king, then his enfeeblement would affect them all. The cattle would grow sick and fail to reproduce, the crops would fail, and men would perish of hunger and disease. By slaying the king at the moment before he began to fail, his soul could be liberated at the time of its greatest power and could pass, by descent or transmission, to a successor. This, Frazer thought, was the idea behind the scheme of priestly succession at Nemi.

*Adonis, Attis, Osiris* constituted the fourth part of *The Golden Bough,* and it was an especially eloquent elaboration and documentation of most of the preceding ideas which were mainly from the mythology, folklore, and religious literature of the Eastern Mediterranean. It attempted to trace the development of man's attempt to understand and control nature, first through magic and then through the worship of gods and goddesses whose lives were thought to be associated with the forces of nature. The importance of vegetation and the change of seasons was the key to most of this worship. Adonis, Attis, and Osiris were seen as great gods of vegetation whose deaths and resurrections were connected with the change of seasons and the concomitant growth and decay of vegetation.

In part five, *Spirits of the Corn and of the Wild,* Frazer pursued the general theme of the preceding part (the identification of the deaths and resurrections of deities with the phases of vegetation) among other religions and peoples. An emphasis was placed on the similarity of custom between East and West; the similarity being attributed to similar causes acting on the similar constitution of the human mind.

*The Scapegoat,* part six, is a sequel to *The Dying God.* It finds the origin of the scapegoat phenomenon in the primitive belief that evil spirits can be transferred from the suffering body to other objects, animate and inanimate. This is the familiar Embodiment theory of Tylor's. Frazer saw an extension of this idea in the belief of primitive peoples that the evils of an entire community could be transferred to an individual, whose sacrificial death would then relieve the community of its accumulated distress. It would be natural, and economical, thought Frazer, for people to slay the "Dying God" for this purpose as well as for the preservation of his positive powers through the release of his soul.

In *Balder the Beautiful*, the concluding section, Frazer brings together the arguments of the preceding sections for a final interpretation of the Golden Bough myth. (Balder was a Scandinavian god who was invulnerable to destruction, except by the bough of mistletoe with which he was finally slain.) In Frazer's hypothesis, the sacred oak tree represented Balder, and the evergreen mistletoe represented his soul. That the mistletoe was the seat of life for the oak was rendered credible by the fact that when the oak sheds its leaves, the mistletoe retains its fresh, green foliage. It was necessary, therefore, that the mistletoe be removed from the oak before the god the tree oak represented could die, fulfilling the role of both the Dying God and the Scapegoat. Frazer believed that the King of the Wood at Nemi presented a parallel to Balder the Beautiful and that he was the human embodiment of the great Italian sky-god, Jupiter, who came down from the sky to dwell in the mistletoe bough of the sacred oak in the wood of Diana, the sky-queen and wife of Jupiter. The King of the Wood is thus charged with the protection of Jupiter's life as well as his own, and must be sacrificed when his powers begin to fail.

The explanation of the Golden Bough myth was, as has been stated, only incidental to the meaning and value of the entire work. It served as a convenient scaffold on which to reconstruct the evolution of human thought and custom. That evolution showed a gradual development through ages of magic, religion, and science; science being a return to the magical stage—only this time equipped with the correct premises and techniques.

As to the benefits, present and future, of civilized man's science, Frazer seems undecided. In one place he says: "It is probably not too much to say that the hope of progress —moral and intellectual as well as material—in the future is bound up with the fortunes of science, and that every obstacle placed in the way of scientific discovery is a wrong to humanity." In other places he stresses the relentless destruction overtaking man and the impotence of his "puny hands" to do anything about it. And yet in other places he evinces a wistful concern over the demise of religion: "Bred in a philosophy which strips nature of personality and reduces it to the unknown cause of an orderly series of impressions on our senses, we find it hard to put ourselves in the place of the savage, to whom the same impressions appear in the guise of spirits or the handiwork of spirits. For ages the army of spirits, once so near, has been receding farther and farther from us, banished by the magic wand of science from hearth and home, from ruined cell and ivied tower, from haunted glade and lonely mere, from the riven murky cloud that belches forth the lightning, and from those fairer clouds that pillow the silvery moon or fret with flakes of burning red the golden eve. The spirits are gone even from their last stronghold in the sky, whose blue arch no longer passes, except with children, for the screen that hides from mortal eyes the glories of the celestial world. Only in poets' dreams or impassioned flights of oratory is it given to catch a glimpse of the last flutter of the standards of the retreating host, to hear the beat of their invisible wings, the sound of their mocking laughter, or the swell of angel music dying away in the distance."

In four large volumes Frazer also turned his attention to the institutions of totemism and exogamy. Totemism is a kinship organization based on identification with a particular type of natural or artificial object—usually a plant or animal—and exogamy is a social prescription to marry outside one's social group.

Prior to the publication of *Totemism and Exogamy* (1910) Frazer had regarded totemism as genetically related to exogamy. He discards the idea in this work and states that although they often appear together, they have an independent origin. His emphasis, however, is on the cases where they do appear together, whatever their ultimate origins.

Frazer defines totemism as "an intimate relation which is supposed to exist between a group of kindred people on the one side and a species of natural or artificial objects on the other side, which objects are called the totems of the human group." Frazer insisted that the relation of an individual to his totem was always one of friendship and kinship, where equality and/or identification were complete. Thus totemism, in its pure form, should not be interpreted as a religion, since religion always implies the relationship of an individual to a superior power, or powers. Frazer had previously identified totemism with religion and warned his readers not to repeat the error. Although totemism had, in some cases, developed into religion, because of the worship of anthropomorphic deities with animals and plants as their attributes, Frazer warned against assuming that this was normally or necessarily the case. The chief function of totemism, says Frazer, has been to knit men together in social groups so that collective action and responsibility are made possible. He considered this an important service to the "cause of civilization," where progress depends "on the cordial co-operation of men in society, on their mutual trust and good-will, and on their readiness to subordinate their personal interests to the interests of the community."

Frazer advanced, at one time or another, three distinct theories regarding the origin of totemism. As a believer in the "psychic unity of mankind," he was convinced that totemism must have arisen substantially in the same way among all peoples and that therefore a satisfactory explanation of its origin in one place could be asserted universally. His first theory supposed that the totem arose when an individual deposited his soul in some object, such as a plant or animal, for safe-keeping. Losing track of which particular plant or animal held his soul, the individual would have an investment in the entire species and tend to become identified with it. Subsequent evidence convinced Frazer that the theory was untenable. His second theory, which was suggested by the work of Baldwin Spencer and F. J. Gillen in Australia, supposed that totemism was consciously designed as a magical implementation of economic life. A tribe was thought to be organized into totemic clans, where each clan was responsible, through magical manipulation, for insuring a good supply of its species for the consumption of the community. Frazer eventually rejected this theory as implying rational motivations beyond the grasp of primitive man.

Frazer's third and final theory, known as the "conceptional theory of totemism," held that the totemic membership of a child was determined by the fancies of the mother at the moment she felt the first movement of the child within her. It rested on the assumption that, being ignorant of the causes of childbirth, the mother believed that the child entered her body at the time its presence was first felt. In looking for an external cause of the entrance of the child, the mother was likely to fasten onto something which she had seen or felt immediately before "conception." This could, of course, be an animal, a plant, a stone, or whatever. This object was then believed to have been the residence of the spirit of the child. This, according to Frazer, was the actual belief of all the peoples of Central and Northern Australia who had been studied. For Frazer this theory accounted very well for the individual's complete identification with the totem (the essence of totemism for Frazer) because, as Frazer explains, the individual "believed himself to be the very thing, whether an animal, a plant, or what not, which had entered his mother's womb at conception and had issued from it at childbirth." Thus, the ultimate source of totemism was to be found in the primitive's ignorance of paternity and a natural curiosity about the subject. Originally, then, the totem was an individual acquirement; later, for probably several reasons, it tended to become hereditary.

J. F. McLennan, a disputatious and boldly speculative Scottish lawyer, was the first to draw attention to the importance of both totemism and exogamy. He advanced no theory of the origin of totemism, but he had a definite idea about the origin of exogamy. He believed that it originated in the practice of bride-capture, which was made necessary by the scarcity of women in some tribes due to female infanticide. The practice of female infanticide was attributed to the fact that, being unable to support all of its children, a tribe would kill the females because of their inferiority in providing food and fighting hostile tribes. The scarcity of women would lead to either polyandry in one's own tribe or exogamy, through bride-capture from other tribes. Frazer rejected this theory on the ground that female infanticide occured chiefly among advanced tribes, much further along the evolutionary scale than exogamy. Frazer also argued that a consistent preponderance of males over females, for whatever reason, could not be shown.

Frazer turned to the theory of Edward Westermarck, who held that exogamy originated out of an instinctive aversion to marriage and sexual intercourse between individuals who had lived together from youth, and who were usually, but not necessarily, closely related in kin. Westermarck explained this aversion as one resulting from the processes of natural selection, which eliminated the issue of consanguineous marriages because of their supposed genetic weakness. According to J. F. McLennan, the primitive people were, of course, unaware of this process and their instinct could not differentiate between kinship relations and local relations. Frazer asked at this point how it came about that this local exogamy developed into kinship exogamy, and found no answer.

Frazer finally subscribed to the theory of L. H. Morgan, the famous evolutionist and founder of the science of kinship. Frazer states that "Unlike the other writers, whose hypotheses have been set forth, Morgan lived for many years on intimate terms with savages who still practiced both totemism and exogamy; and in approaching the problem his practical familiarity with exogamous communities gave him a decided advantage over enquirers who had no such first-hand knowledge of the institution they discussed."

Morgan's theory rested on one of his basic postulates: the sexual promiscuity of primitive man. "Primitive promiscuity," as it came to be known, had not been observed among any contemporary primitive peoples, and was admittedly only an inference.[5] Morgan, a morally righteous and devout Christian, believed that sexual promiscuity was the first conceivable stage of human society. Exogamy, according to Morgan, was instituted "as a reformatory movement to break up the inter-marriage of blood relatives, and particularly of brothers and sisters, by compelling them to marry out of the tribe. . . ." Frazer believed this to be "the true key to the whole system of exogamy." He went on to show, by reference to the Australian aborigines, the increasing complexity of exogamy, ranging from an original bisection (the "two-class system") through two more bisections (the "four-class" and "eight-class systems"). The first would prevent the marriage of siblings, the second the marriage of parents and children, and the third the marriage of certain first cousins. Frazer believed these bisections were deliberately instituted to prevent the marriage of near kin. He says: "no other human institution bears the impress of deliberate design stamped on it more clearly than the exogamous classes of the Australian Aborigines." He even employs Paley's familiar argument here by adding that "To suppose that they have originated through a series of undesigned coincidences . . . is to tax our credulity almost as heavily as it would be to suppose that the complex machinery of a watch has come together without human design by a mere fortuitous concourse of atoms. . . ." It

[5] Frazer always insisted against assuming that in contemporary primitive peoples we necessarily have examples of the earliest primitive life. He states in *Totemism and Exogamy*: "indeed in all these respects the chasm which divides the modern from the ancient savage may very well be much deeper and wider than that which divides the lowest modern savage from a Shakespeare or a Newton."

should be noted, however, that Frazer says in other places that, for example, "in human affairs it too often happens that the effects which an institution really brings about are by no means those which it was designed to accomplish."

Frazer believed that group marriages commonly followed the institution of two exogamous classes and gradually evolved into individual marriages: "Thus the history of exogamy may be compared to a series of concentric rings placed successively one within the other, each of lesser circumference than its predecessor and each consequently circumscribing within narrower bonds the freedom of the individuals whom it encloses. The outermost ring includes all the women of the tribe; the innermost ring includes one woman only. The first ring represents promiscuity; the last ring represents monogamy."

As for the postulated aversion to incestuous sex relations—the basic premise of the entire argument—Frazer offers no satisfactory explanation. He says, "We do not know and it is difficult even to guess." He does go on to do some guessing about the real or imagined effects on sterility of such unions, but does not seem at all satisfied with the explanation. He concludes by saying, "What they abhorred was really evil; what they preferred was really good," even though it was based on some superstitious or crude notion of causation.

IT IS not easy to determine Frazer's reputation in the history of anthropology. Estimates of his work range all the way from "learned nonsense" (G. E. Smith) to "the greatest anthropologist of our age" (B. Malinowski). Everyone is agreed, however, on the great influence, for good or bad, that he has had on the layman's interest in anthropology. His humor, clarity and eloquent style, always free of jargon, had much to do with the wide audience he gained for his writings. The following excerpt is a good example of the way in which Frazer won the interest of so many people: "In North Germany, if a ghost persistently intrudes on your premises, you can get rid of him very simply. You have only to throw a sack over him, and having thus bagged him to walk off with your sack to some other place and there empty it out, having first explained to the ghost the exact bounds which you wish him to keep. Of course no sooner is your back turned than the ghost starts for home too." Frazer was a master at constructing images like this with a few simple sentences.

But Frazer's influence was surely more than this. Marett gives an interesting account of Frazer's reception by official anthropology. According to Marett, the anthropologists were inclined to stand aloof upon the publication of the first edition of *The Golden Bough* (1890). Marett characterized them as asking: ". . . had he hobnobbed with cannibals, had he measured heads at the risk of his own, had he, in fact, spent a single working day outside the four walls of his study, so as to learn how to discriminate between the smell of his lamp and the genuine reek of uncultivated humanity?" By the time of the second edition, however, the pioneer field work in Australia of Sir Baldwin Spencer and F. J. Gillen had been received with universal acclamation, and their work supported many of Frazer's contentions, especially the irrationality of savage life. Thus, in acclaiming this field work, the anthropologists were largely committed to a favorable opinion of Frazer's work.

Frazer had a great influence among the anthropologists and workers in allied fields until classical evolutionism in anthropology fell into disrepute. As a representative of this school, his work suffered a severe criticism from which it has never recovered in official anthropology. One of the more generous opinions of Frazer among American anthropologists comes from R. H. Lowie who states that his "proper place is in the history of English literature and of the intellectual classes of Europe." Kroeber and Herskovits, in their recent surveys of Anthropology, hardly mention Frazer, although Herskovits refers to Frazer's work on totemism as a "monumental study."

Malinowski has, in comparatively recent years, been the foremost champion of Frazer as an anthropologist. According to Malinowski, "The vastness of the problems, the human interest and the dramatic beauty of anthropological facts were brought home to scholars and laymen alike by the monumental works of Sir James Frazer." Malinowski cites the "spiritual guidance of Frazer" in the field work of such pioneers as Fison and Howitt; Baldwin Spencer and F. J. Gillen; A. C. Haddon, W. H. R. Rivers, C. G. Seligman, C. S. Myers; Junod, Roscoe, Smith, Dale, Torday, and Rattray. He claims that the anthropological work of Freud and the French School of Durkheim, Hubert, Mauss, and Levy-Bruhl would have been unthinkable without the inspiration and achievements of Frazer. In Germany, Malinowski mentions Wundt and Thurnwald as benefiting from Frazer's work; and in England, he claims that Westermarck, Crawley, Gilbert Murray, Jane Harrison, Sidney Hartland, and Andrew Lang have taken "their cues and orientation from Frazer—whether they agree or disagree with him." He points to the importance of Frazer's work in history, psychology, philosophy, and ethics, and names Anatole France, Bergson, Toynbee, and Spengler as having been influenced by him.

Most of Frazer's specific theories, such as the development of magic and religion and the origin and development of totemism, are untenable today; but the mass of data he collected still stands as an imposing monument. Marett paid the highest compliment possible to Frazer's collection of data by stating in 1914, with reference to criticisms of Frazer's theories, that ". . . if he cannot be convicted out of his own mouth, the thing is not to be managed at all." He goes on to say that "To Dr. Frazer, who has laboured to such splendid purpose, our deepest gratitude is due; for by the magic of his pen he has made the myriad facts live, so that they tell their own tale, and we are left free to read their meaning as our several tastes and temperaments dictate."

Today, even Frazer's material is seldom used by anthropologists, partly on account of its unwieldy presentation which makes any systematic search for specific cultural data prohibitive, and partly because much of the field work from which it was taken has been discredited or super-

seded. Also, some claim, as does Goldenweiser, that "Frazer
displays a curious suggestibility towards the opinions of
those who furnish him with facts required by his theories."
But whether Frazer is guilty of this to a greater degree
than any other worker, past or present, seems a moot question. Those anthropologists who, paradoxically, seem to
have little sense or appreciation of the history of anthropology and dismiss or ignore Frazer as a contributor to
their field, might well consider Frazer's admonition to those
of his day who dismissed the efforts of previous workers:
"The amount of new knowledge which one age, certainly
which one man, can add to the common store is small, and
it argues stupidity or dishonesty, besides ingratitude, to
ignore the heap while vaunting the few grains which it may
have been our privilege to add to it."

In an address to Frazer in 1921, A. E. Housman said of
*The Golden Bough:* "There they find learning mated with
literature, labour disguised in ease, and a museum of dark
and uncouth superstitions invested with the charm of a
truly sympathetic magic. There you have gathered, for
the admonition of a proud and oblivious race, the scattered
and fading relics of its foolish childhood, whether with-
drawn from our view among savage folk and in distant
countries, or lying unnoticed at our doors. The forgotten
milestones of the road which man has travelled, the mazes
and blind alleys of his appointed progress through time,
are illuminated by your art and genius, and the strangest
of remote and ancient things are brought near to the minds
and hearts of your contemporaries."

# EMILE DURKHEIM

## *ONE MUST CHOOSE*

WHEN EMILE DURKHEIM's fellow students and professors at Ecole Normale Supérieure nicknamed him
The Metaphysician, they made a prophetic misjudgment,
for Durkheim became one of the great destroyers of all
metaphysical systems.

Although sensitive, intelligent, delicate, and aloof—the
essential traits of a metaphysician—Durkheim fought des-
perately against social alienation, for himself and for all
men. He was convinced that the social interdependence of
individuals was the reality and true glory of human life,
and he applied his own extraordinary independence to the
scientific foundation and application of that principle. The
true "Spirit" of human life for Durkheim was the "spirit
of collectivity." All metaphysical systems—religious and
scientific—are symbolic projections of man's everyday life
on earth, and that life is inherently a social one. The great
implication in Durkheim's work is that man alone or, more
precisely, men together direct their own fortunes. His work
and his life were inseparably dedicated to that belief.

Durkheim was born April 15, 1858, at Epinal (Vosges),
in Lorraine province, the descendant of a long line of rab-

bis. At an early age he began to prepare for the rabbinate and studied the Old Testament, the Talmud, and the Hebrew language and history. He abandoned these interests early in his life, but in the latter part of his career as a sociologist religion became the subject of one of his most daring studies. He would often remind people that he was, after all, the son of a rabbi.

Durkheim was always a brilliant student. At his first school, the Collège d'Epinal, he was put ahead of his class several times and won academic contests with ease. He was sensitive, delicate, and very keen, traits which persisted throughout his life. He decided to become a teacher and went to Paris to study at the Lycée Louis-le-Grand in order to prepare for admission to the Ecole Normale Supérieure. After three years of preparation he entered the Ecole Normale Supérieure in 1879. He was now twenty-one and quite mature in appearance and mind. He was extremely intense and serious, even solemn. These traits, along with a bushy beard and mustache, earned him the name of The Metaphysician.

Durkheim found the Ecole Normale Supérieure stimulating but uncongenial. The strong emphasis there on a rhetorical humanism conflicted with Durkheim's toughminded concern for what he considered to be serious, pressing problems for society. The solutions to these problems did not, Durkheim was convinced, lie in pretty words or mystical ecstasy. According to Durkheim, the methods of science and practical, co-operative endeavor in empirical enterprises must form the basis for any kind of diagnosis and treatment of society, and these remained unshakable tenets all his life. He never wavered from this position at the Ecole Normale Supérieure and was always outspoken about it. He finished next to the bottom in his class.

The stimulation and influence of the Ecole Normale Supérieure was due to Durkheim's close association with a few brilliant classmates and professors. The historian, Fustel de Coulanges, and the philosopher, Emile Boutroux, were especially influential in the shaping of his interests. From Boutroux he gained an interest in scientific methodology and a general taste for critical analysis. Three thinkers whose works especially influenced Durkheim at this time were Renouvier, Kant, and Comte.

Toward the end of his studies at the Ecole Normale Supérieure (around 1882), Durkheim decided to become a sociologist. His aim was to study social phenomena with all the rigorous objectivity of the scientific disciplines. Harry Alpert, Durkheim's biographer, attributes his decision to a dissatisfaction with the dilettantism of philosophy at the time and, on the positive side, to a determination to make a practical contribution to the moral consolidation of the struggling Third Republic. With the secularization of France there arose, according to many, the need for a new foundation for moral solidarity in place of religion and the church. Durkheim believed that a scientific analysis and evaluation of the phenomena of social life would be necessary for the establishment of a new moral order to reinforce the radical political changes that had taken place, and he set himself to that job. His philosophy was always guided by the practical consequences it would have on social and political life, and he insisted that any philosophy must always have practical application.

Durkheim was appointed Professor of Philosophy at Lycée of Sens in 1882 and served in that position until 1887. In 1885 he made a formal entry into the field as a collaborator on Ribot's *Revue Philosophique*. By 1886 he had made the first formulation of his theory of social solidarity and social evolution. By 1887 he was recognized in the field as an outstanding sociologist and began his thirty-year university career. At the University of Bordeaux a course in the social sciences was created for him—the first official recognition in France of the social sciences.

In 1897 Durkheim organized the *Année sociologique*. Many consider this immediately successful project as his greatest service to sociology. Its twelve volumes eventually covered the years from 1898 to 1914. It presented specialized monographs, many on the cultures of illiterate peoples, and made annual surveys of the work and literature of the social sciences. Durkheim gathered a group of brilliant men around him for this project, and they made a detailed and critical analysis of much of the sociological and anthropological literature. The *Année sociologique* became an important source for original, empirical investigation and also served as a lively forum for current theoretical discussions; its motto became "The Unity of the Social Sciences and Specificity of Research." It was always a collective enterprise, employing many of the best workers in the various specialized fields. The major headings of its great range of subjects were: General Sociology, Juridicial and Moral Sociology, Religious Sociology, and The Social Conditions of Thought.

Durkheim exerted great influence as a teacher. Alpert states that he was considered by his students as "one of the great heroes of human thought." He brought to his students a great wealth of subject matter and a profound, critical acumen in the treatment of the material. This, along with a persuasive eloquence and a devoted enthusiasm, made him an outstanding and popular teacher.

Durkheim, like Herbert Spencer, inherited genius, with its inevitable consequence, isolation. Spencer glorified isolation and made "individualism" the principle of life and all of nature—organic and inorganic. Durkheim, with the same inheritance, fought isolation and made "social solidarity" the principle of human life. He deplored the "cult of originality" that was so popular at his time. Although he did not have the physical constitution or the temperament for it, he drove himself to action in the practical world. He took many stands on the current problems in education, politics, and social reform.

Durkheim was intensely patriotic. At the outset of the First World War he devoted himself to education and propaganda related to the war effort. As a lecturer and writer he engaged in what he called "moral refreshment," both for the troops and the people at home. He accepted an official position with the government during this time and was known for his motto: "Patience, Effort, Confidence."

Tough and brave as he tried to be in the practical world,

his essential delicacy could not withstand personal tragedy. His son André, a promising student in sociology, was wounded twice in the war and died in 1915. Durkheim could not get over the sorrow of his son's death. He even forbade his friends to mention the boy in his presence. He became seriously ill in December, 1916 and knew he was dying. He made one last effort to complete a large work in the field of ethics, but died on November 15, 1917, with much of his contemplated work unfinished.

Durkheim is commonly called the heir of Comte and a positivist. Parsons, Benoit-Smullyan, Bristol, Bougle, and others take this as a commonplace; only Alpert is inclined to dispute it. Alpert states that Durkheim was probably not as indebted to Comte as is generally believed and that Durkheim objected to being called a positivist. If positivism be taken in the general sense as the doctrine which holds that the social sciences should adopt the spirit and, as far as possible, the methods of the physical sciences, then Durkheim was beyond any doubt a positivist. If taken in the strict sense as that school which will admit only the observations of the senses in the formulation of scientific explanation, then Durkheim was not, in practice, a positivist.

At the very least, Durkheim held that human and social phenomena must be included within the unity of nature, and as such, are in principle subject to statements of general law. Here, Durkheim believed that Comte and Spencer, among others, were on the right track. As examples of "necessary and legitimate sociological specialisms," Durkheim cites the works of Maine (Juristic history), Fustel de Coulanges (history), Schmoller and Buchon (economics), Prichard, Waitz, Morgan, McLennan, and others (anthropology), A. H. Post and Steinmetz (comparative ethics), Tylor, Robertson Smith, Frazer, Hartland (comparative religion and folklore), Lazaraus and Steinthal (comparative psychology), Quetelet (social status), Ratzel (social geography).

A conscious attempt to found a "social physics" can be found earlier than the eighteenth century in Hobbes (1588-

1679), but the idea was not seriously considered until the eighteenth century, when the implications of the Newtonian science were being discussed, along with the beginning of a radical reconstruction of the institutions of Western Society. This reconstruction, which was characterized by the emergence of the business spirit and the middle class, undoubtedly had much to do with the creation of the social sciences during that period.

France, of course, was conspicuous during this revolutionary period, and as a child of these revolutions, Durkheim was born into a period when the faith in reason and in the order of nature and social progress was still strong. One is reminded here of Herbert Spencer, who was especially influenced by the same historical developments. Durkheim, as will be seen, was much indebted to Spencer (although he criticized him strongly), and Spencer's ideas were very popular in France in the latter part of the nineteenth century.

Another important idea which Durkheim inherited was the French idea of progress. The history of this idea in France can be hastily drawn from Turgot (1727-1781) through Condorcet (1743-1794) and the French Revolution, and Comte.

The general idea of progress became a powerful force in France during the eighteenth century beginning with Turgot, who seems to have been the first to advance a "stage theory" of human development. In the economic development of man the three stages, according to Turgot, were the hunting, pastoral, and agricultural. In the development of human thought man had passed through the animistic, metaphysical, and scientific stages. Comte took over this idea later. Condorcet, who was much indebted to Turgot, was one of many who became enthused over Turgot's idea of historical development, and he developed a nine-stage theory of human development which is close to the classical evolutionary theories of the early anthropologists, and even makes use of the comparative method. Condorcet was able to translate his ideas into action during the French Revolution, which he saw as a necessary development in man's progress. Comte carried the French idea of progress into the nineteenth century and he had considerable influence on Durkheim. Durkheim became active at a time when the evolutionary theories of Darwin and Spencer had become the leading scientific ideas of the nineteenth century, and he became a loyal, if critical, adherent to the evolutionary hypothesis and the comparative method.

The basis of Durkheim's work in sociology was laid down during the five years (1882-1887) he served as professor of philosophy at the Lycée of Sens. It was during this time that he adopted what is called an "organistic" view of society. Here, he was indebted especially to the views of Spencer and Espinas, who conceived of society as some kind of "living whole." Espinas' portrayal of society as a super-individual with a collective conscious, analogous to the society of cells which comprise the human individual, may be taken as a prototype of the organistic idea. It has been seen what use Spencer made of the same general idea.

Durkheim's view of the "organic" nature of society differed, however, in important ways from those mentioned above. Suffice it here to say that Durkheim would often use such phrases as "social body," "social brain," "social protoplasm," and "cerebro-spinal system of the social organism," in describing social structure and function.

With Durkheim, as with Spencer, a necessary implication of the organic view of society was that, being a "reality" sui generis, society must be studied, described, and explained as a separate realm. Although obviously related to psychological phenomena, "social facts" cannot be explained by psychology; the whole, that is, is more than the sum of its parts and must be studied on a separate level. This "superorganic" doctrine, as it is now called, had, since Comte, important adherents. Also, there is a close parallel here to some of Wundt's ideas. Durkheim had visited Wundt in Germany and was very impressed by the scientific rigor of Wundt's work. Durkheim has often been criticized for this view as imputing a metaphysical reality to society, but, while his language often supports this change, it seems clear enough that he simply wanted to consider social facts as "things" so that social phenomena could be treated with the "scientific method."

Durkheim's contributions to methodology in the social sciences are of great importance. His general aim was to make sociology an empirical study, and he endeavored in his work to practice the "crucial experiment," used so successfully in the physical sciences. This was in sharp contrast to the philosophers, like Hobbes and Hegel, who attempted to construct systems which would embrace the entire field of human activity, and to the anthropologists, like Spencer, Tylor, and Frazer, who made great comparative surveys. Parsons calls Durkheim "one of the greatest empirical scientists of his day" and goes on to say that "Durkheim was a scientific theorist in the best sense of one who never theorized 'in the air,' never indulged in 'idle speculation' but was always seeking the solution of crucially important empirical problems."

According to Alpert, what impressed Durkheim the most during his visit with Wundt in Germany was the precise and restricting exactitude of Wundt's methods. In the preface to the *Division of Labor* (1893) Durkheim writes: "This book is above all an attempt to treat the facts of the *moral* life by the method of the positive sciences." Durkheim, according to Parsons, is faithful to the true positivist position.

Durkheim insisted that for an empirical treatment of social data it is necessary to treat social facts as "things." This important postulate, basic to all of his work, has caused much confusion; a condition which can, in some part, be traced to his use of language. Durkheim's insistence on considering social facts as "things" grew out of his determination to avoid the deductive, rationalistic approach which characterized so much of the work of Comte and Spencer, among others. As an empiricist, Durkheim had to work with data which could be observed, described, classified, and explained, not merely deduced from a few arbitrary postulates, such as the psychic unity of mankind, and unilinear evolution. For Durkheim, to say that a social fact is a "thing" is simply to identify social data: "All that is given, all that is subject to observation, has thereby the character of a thing. To treat phenomena as things is to treat them as data, and these constitute the departure of science."

In his zeal to emulate the methods of the "exact sciences," Durkheim probably over-dramatized the "reality" of the social realm and left himself open to the charge of attributing a metaphysical reality to social phenomena. But all he seems to be saying is that since social institutions are "exterior" to the individual and exert a power of constraint over him, they can be considered as a part of the individual's world and can be studied as such: "A social fact is to be recognized by the power of external coercion which it exercises or is capable of exercising over individuals, and the presence of this power may be recognized in its turn either by the existence of some specific sanction or by the resistance offered against every individual effort that tends to violate it."

Although they originate in a collection of individual minds, social facts come to any given individual from a realm outside himself (society) and must, therefore, be explained in terms of other social facts, not in terms of facts of a different order, such as the biological or psychological. Durkheim states: "Every time that a social phenomenon is directly explained by a psychic phenomenon, one may be sure that the explanation is false."

Social facts, although they come to each individual from an external "reality," do become internalized in the individual consciousness and represent what the individual has in common with the group; they are, so to speak, society within the individual and can be distinguished from the biological consciousness which defines a unique individual. In the social category Durkheim included such concepts as time, space, force, and causation, as well as legal and moral codes, and the like. The implications here for epistemology are very important, as will be seen, and have had an interesting history.

The implications of the methodology outlined above have

earned for Durkheim the title of Father of Functionalism in the social sciences. Radcliffe-Brown cites Durkheim's definition of social function: "The 'function' of a social institution is the correspondence between it and the needs of the social organism." The needs of a society are related to but are on a different level from the needs of the individuals who constitute that society. The individual is born into the social world as he is born into the physical world; it existed before him and will exist after him. The conditions of the existence of the social world are not necessarily the conditions of the existence of the individual and must be studied separately.

Radcliffe-Brown states that Durkheim was the first to make a systematic formulation of the analogy between society and organic life, and that his basic assumption was functionalism. As the *life* of an organism is considered to be the functioning of its organic structure, so is *social life* conceived by Durkheim to be the functioning of the social structure.

Durkheim made use, as mentioned above, of a general evolutionary hypothesis and the comparative method. Most students agree that he employed these ideas somewhat more critically than did Comte, Spencer, Tylor, and Frazer. In his use of the comparative method, for example, he insisted that comparisons be made only within the "interior of the same type" and he attempted to weight his comparative data. Where the classical evolutionists, like Spencer, Tylor, Frazer, and Lang, tended to regard all examples of a social phenomenon as of equal weight, Durkheim introduced a relativistic approach where normality was always viewed as relative to the stage of development of each given society.

Durkheim's concept of "normality" played an important part in all his work. There has been much dispute over what he meant by "normal" and "pathological," but a simple reading suggests that by "normal" Durkheim meant a kind of "average." He states: "We shall call normal those facts which present the most general forms and we shall

give to the others the name of morbid or pathological."
He insisted on applying this definition to only one society at a time, or, as he would put it (with his evolutionary approach), to a given stage of development of a
society.

Wholesale comparisons of social phenomena were thus
more or less excluded as reliable tools in the analysis of
social structure and function. Gehlke quotes Durkheim on
this subject: "One cannot explain a social fact of some
complexity, except on the condition of following its whole
integral development through all the social species . . ."
But one must "consider the societies, which one compares,
at the same periods of their development." It would probably be a mistake to attribute to Durkheim any significant
innovation in the use of the evolutionary hypothesis and
the comparative method. The most that can be said is that
he used them with more care and with a better awareness
of their limitations. As Gehlke says: ". . . our author Durkheim is certainly an adherent to the evolutionary hypothesis
school which he criticizes so vigorously for being, as we see,
a little more extreme than himself."

It was as an empiricist, then, that Durkheim earned his
reputation as a methodologist in the social sciences. As
Durkheim explains it, the goal of the sociological method
is to make the conceptions of Comte a reality instead of
a "philosophical aspiration." To this end Durkheim employed the "systematic specialization" that characterized
the great accomplishments of the *Année sociologique*.

Talcott Parsons lists four stages in the development of
Durkheim's general sociological theory.

*1)* Early Formative Period: *Division of Labor* (1893)

*2)* Early Synthesis: *Rules of Sociological Method*
(1895) and *Suicide* (1897)

*3)* Transition: *Individual Representation and Collective Representation* (1899), *Moral Education* (1902–3),
*The Determination of Moral Facts* (1907)

*4)* New General Position: *Elementary Forms of the
Religious Life* (1912)

The *Division of Labor* takes up as its central problem the nature of social solidarity and evolution. On the assumption that the hostile forces in man require some kind of enforced co-operation for survival, Durkheim undertakes an examination of social rules of conduct, both legal and moral, in order to discover the conditions of social solidarity and evolution. It must be possible, he thought, to find variations in a society which will serve as reliable clues to the internal structure and function of that society. He found these variations in legal and moral codes, social statistics (such as suicide rates), and religious practices. The *Division of Labor* concentrates on the legal and moral codes, which are seen as expressing the social needs of a society.

It was stated above that Durkheim, while an "evolutionist," did not subscribe to any simple, unilinear idea of evolution. In this work he states: "It is no longer possible to believe that moral evolution consists in the development of the same idea, confused and uncertain with primitive man, little by little growing clearer and more precise with the spontaneous progress of knowledge." Rather, he goes on, "The moral law . . . is formed, transformed and maintained in accordance with changing demands."

Durkheim agreed with Spencer that increased specialization among the individuals of a group led to the co-operative interdependence which has characterized the evolution from primitive to civilized societies. But where Spencer, a proponent of the utilitarian, individualist theory in economics, attributed this co-operation to "contractual relations" between individuals for their mutual advantage, Durkheim insisted that such regulations are "given" by society and are not created by individuals while pursuing their own immediate interests. The "happiness" or "self-interest" principle which, on the utilitarian view, was supposed to lead men to social co-operation, was entirely discounted by Durkheim. What may appear to be a "harmony of interests," says Durkheim, "conceals a latent or deferred conflict. For when interest is the only ruling force each individual finds himself in a state of war with every other since nothing comes to mollify the egos, and any truce in this eternal antagonism would not be of long duration. There is nothing less constant than interest."

Durkheim turned to a study of legal and moral codes as the place to look for the true sources of social cohesion, since, as he states, "the characteristic of moral rules is that they enunciate the fundamental conditions of social solidarity." He finds there a distinction between two types of law: "repressive" and "restitutive."

Repressive law is simply an expression of the traditional customs, beliefs, and sanctions of a society and is blindly adhered to under threats of punishment. Durkheim called the social solidarity based on repressive law, "mechanical solidarity." Mechanical solidarity, maintained largely by hereditary right, is found in primitive, "undifferentiated" societies which are organized on a "totality of beliefs and sentiments common to all members of the group." Durkheim calls this the "collective type."

Restitutive law stresses restitution instead of punishment and affects only certain segments of the group at any one time. Its function is to preserve the status quo, not to inflict punishment for crimes against the community. Restitutive law is an indication of "organic solidarity," that is, a solidarity based on the co-operation of specialized individuals.

Where restitutive law predominates, the society is organized on the basis of specialized difference, in which solidarity rests on "a system of different, special functions which definite relations unite." Since mechanical solidarity rests on the absorption of individuals into a totality of common beliefs and sentiments, it is achieved at the price of individual "personality." Organic solidarity, on the other hand, rests on the assertion of that which is personal and distinct in the individual. But it must not be supposed that in the case of organic solidarity the individual comes to depend less on society; the exact opposite is the case, for increased specialization (the assertion of individual differences) results in the need for greater interdependence, and society supplies rules for regulating the necessary relations between individuals. This type of social solidarity, like the unity of the organism, "is as great as the individualism of the parts is more marked," hence the phrase "organic solidarity."

In making the above distinction Durkheim sought to answer the question: "Why does the individual while becoming more autonomous, depend more upon society? How can he be at once more individual and more solidary?" There is evidence that Durkheim posed the problems in this way to support a polemic against the adherents of economic individualism, such as Spencer. Spencer, it will be recalled, denounced "social interference" as an evil force directed against man's natural tendency to improve. Durkheim is anxious to show that the regulative norms of society are presupposed by any concept of individual freedom. Parsons believes that Durkheim developed the idea of organic solidarity primarily as an answer to the economic individualists.

Durkheim appears vague and uncertain in this work about his major problem, the origins of a division of labor. Having found individual motives to be irrelevant he was forced to find an alternative explanation. He finally settles for an explanation based on the natural increase in population, where increased competition demands specialization and co-operation as the price of survival. In the "Conclusion" to the *Division of Labor* Durkheim reverts to the importance of the common values, attitudes, and sentiments which people in a society hold (translated by Parsons as the "conscience collective"), and attempts to place the two ideas of mechanical and organic solidarity in complementary perspective. He states, for example, "If there is one rule of conduct which is incontestable, it is that which orders us to realize in ourselves the essential traits of the collective type." Advanced societies do not require the close adherence to collective beliefs and sentiments that primitive societies do, but "the absence of some likenesses . . . is still a sign of moral failure. . . . There are common sentiments, common ideas, without which, as has been said, one is not a man." Thus, Durkheim concludes, the rule which requires us to specialize is limited by the contrary rule which orders us to be like each other.

In Durkheim's later work the idea of organic solidarity became less important and it is his elaboration of the "conscience collective" which became a permanent contribution. The *Division of Labor* clearly set the stage for the later work and some of its main features were never lost, especially the identification of social and moral life: "Society is not a simple juxtaposition of individuals who bring an intrinsic morality with them, but rather man is a moral being because he lives in society, since morality consists in being solidary with a group and varying with this solidarity. Let all social life disappear, and moral life will disappear with it, since it would no longer have an objective."

The *Division of Labor* was Durkheim's doctoral thesis and he was pressed hard to defend himself before a hostile Faculty of Letters of the University of Paris. According to witnesses, as reported by Alpert, Durkheim "constantly held the upper hand" and more than carried the day for his brilliant study.

Durkheim's famous study, *Suicide*, represents an extension of the basic idea found in the *Division of Labor* to another empirical field. There are important theoretical refinements and modifications in this study, however, which require special exposition.

In the *Division of Labor* Durkheim had cited the increased suicide rate in the nineteenth century as an argument against the "happiness" principle of the utilitarians. He now selects the phenomenon of suicide for intensive analysis. On the basis of statistical studies and theoretical constructs he isolates three factors operating in the suicide rate; he calls these the "altruistic," the "egoistic," and the "anomic."

The altruistic factor is associated with the idea of extreme mechanical solidarity where the collective attachments and pressures are so strong that the individual life becomes relatively unimportant. With so little value placed on the individual, both by himself and others, it takes little pressure to cause a person to take his own life. Also, there may actually occur a social command to commit suicide; Frazer's *Golden Bough* cites many examples of such cases.

The "egoistic" factor is at the other pole. With a progressive emphasis on the value of individuality (a characteristic of the social evolution and the growth of civilization) the individual tends to become exalted over all other objects and ideas, such as God, society, country, and all other repositories of collective sentiments. When, in the extreme, the individual becomes so detached from social institutions that he cannot recognize or feel the power of an authority beyond himself, he is faced with a desolation which can make life unbearable. In times of dislocation, stress, and anxiety he finds himself without group support and is likely to take his own life out of desperation.

Durkheim cites statistics from political, religious, and family life to support his analysis. He shows, for one thing, that the suicide rate has a significant relationship to family status: married persons have a lower rate than single persons and parents have a lower rate than childless couples—the parents of large families having the lowest rate of all. Durkheim interprets these statistics as showing the preservative power of strong group attachments.

In another field, religion, he finds that "free-thinkers" have the highest rate of suicide, followed by Protestants, Catholics, and Jews, in that order. The suicide rate is lower in the measure that the assertion of authority in the religious group is higher. But here Durkheim introduces a new idea: The distinction between the Protestant and the Catholic is not that the one is free of group pressure and the other not (in the sense employed in the *Division of Labor*)—the Protestant is under a social pressure too: the pressure to be *free*. He cannot choose to be free or not to be free, he must exercise his freedom. Individuality, then, is a product of the "conscience collective" and not, as claimed in the *Division of Labor*, the product of a weakened collectivity. Parsons considers this thinking a great advance over that in the *Division of Labor*. After *Suicide*, Durkheim's attempt to tie organic solidarity to differentiation and population pressure is abandoned and the "conscience collective" becomes the major concept.

The anomic ("normless") factor operates where the social norms are upset by rapid change in the interior of a society. In times of extreme prosperity or poverty, for example, the suicide rate goes up. In both cases the relationship between means and ends is upset: with sudden poverty the means for accustomed ends are gone; with sudden prosperity the ends are realized without the accustomed means. In the first case, there is direct and immediate frustration, in the second, there is an unbridling of appetite which must eventually result in frustration. The absence of a clear definition of ends is the common factor.

*Anomie* is simply the weakening or disruption of the "conscience collective"—that system of social norms which reflects a commonality of beliefs, sentiment, and feeling. It is a disastrous "freedom" from social constraint, where the individual can find no direction or meaning to life. Durkheim is eloquent on this subject, describing the freedom as that of "a being liberated from all external restraint, a despot more absolute than the ones history tells about, a despot whom no external power can control and rule." He goes on to say that "when our desires are freed from all moderating influence, when nothing limits them, they become themselves tyrannical and their first slave is the very subject who experiences them" (quoted in Alpert). *Anomie* is not to be confused with "egoistic" freedom which, as has been shown, is really a special kind of constraint and a positive expression of the "conscience collective." What is needed to counteract *anomie* is a new moral authority in step with the changes which have taken place in society. Durkheim recognizes this as a most difficult job at best.

In *Suicide* the main theoretical advance over the *Division of Labor* lies in the development of the idea of the "conscience collective" which, although foreshadowed in the earlier work, did not assume a central importance until his study of suicide. In the former work the concept was identified with an undifferentiated social group; in the latter it became a working concept applicable to all societies as a definition for the social element in every individual personality.

Characteristically, Durkheim formulated a practical program in accordance with the findings of his study, designed to combat the alarming increase in the suicide rate of his century. Suicide was not, for Durkheim, to be regarded as "abnormal" since, as far as we know, it is a phenomenon invariably associated with all societies. Indeed, Durkheim points out, "suicide is a close kin to genuine virtues, which it simply exaggerates"; he means here the virtues of social solidarity ("altruism"), individuality ("egoism"), and flexibility (*"anomie"*). But suicide can become abnormal when it passes beyond certain limits; the "limits" being relative to any given society. The great increase in suicide during the nineteenth century must, according to Durkheim, be classified as abnormal and pathological in origin. The question then is, What are the sources of the increased rate and how can it be reduced?

Durkheim finds that the "altruistic current" in suicide has not increased; in fact, it has diminished. The "egoistic" and "anomic" currents have shown a great increase and can alone be considered morbid. In both cases the underlying cause is a weakening of social solidarity due to the rapid expansion and differentiation of a revolutionized economic structure. The old institutions of solidarity—the political state, religion, and the family—no longer meet the needs of individuals. The modern State is too far removed from the individual and too complex to permit a day-to-day personal identification and assimilation. Religion had a positive adaptive value only at the expense of freedom of thought; when, in the course of human progress, the limits to reason and inquiry are set aside, religion must relinquish its arbitrary authority and therefore its power of socialization. The family, too, has lost its hold. Children do not remain for long within the sole orbit of a pervasive family influence; they are soon exposed to many different and conflicting influences. The importance of hereditary name and its binding associations has diminished with the emergence of the commercial class. The trend is toward the breaking down of barriers between local environments and a general leveling within the social milieu. These conditions favor the growth of egoistic and, to a large extent, anomic suicide.

What is needed, then, is an integrating institution which will be in accord with the changed institutions of modern society. Durkheim finds such an institution in the "occupational group" or "corporation." These groups are organized on the basis of common occupations and interests and have been observed to take on a "collective personality." Durkheim argues: "There is no reason for the corporative interest not acquiring in its workers' eye the respectable character and supremacy always possessed by social interests, as contrasted with private interests, in a well-organized society." The fact that it is "omnipresent, ubiquitous and that its control extends to the greatest part of life" suits it admirably as a means of social solidarity. A number of changes and recognitions would have to occur before the corporations could assume this role, but the framework is there.

Thus, Durkheim concludes his study with a practical recommendation for modern society. *Suicide* contains an excellent example of Durkheim's over-all program for sociology: To establish objective criteria of social health, to identify the sources of morbidity, and to prescribe remedies based on the general laws of sociology.

The *Elementary Forms of the Religious Life* (1912) is Durkheim's last major work. Unlike *Suicide*, which was based on original research, this work draws on secondary sources for its data, primarily on the anthropological material from Australia. It is important not only as a treatise on primitive religion but also as a major contribution to sociological theory and general epistemology.

Durkheim, in the early part of his career, recognized in the field of religion an important source of sociological material. It was the English anthropologists who had interested him in the origin and analysis of religion; Robertson Smith and Frazer were especially influential. He became acquainted with Smith's work as early as 1895 and called it a "revelation." He states that "all my researches had to be taken up again with renewed efforts in order to be placed in harmony with these new views."

When he finally applied himself to a full-scale study of religion, he decided against a comprehensive survey of the field (in the manner of Tylor, Frazer, and Smith), and instead selected a specific case for intensive study; namely, Australian totemism. He undertook this study with the familiar assumptions: that religion, like any social institution, must be regarded as a response to specific social needs and that, as a social phenomenon, it is a product of collective thought. (It was his earlier consideration of religion, in fact, which played an important part in the development of these assumptions.)

Durkheim defines religion as "a unified system of beliefs and practices relative to sacred things, that is to say, things set apart and forbidden—beliefs and practices which unite into one single moral community called a church, all those who adhere to them." He insists at the outset that religion must have its origin in some concrete reality. Such a persistent and universal phenomenon cannot be based on illusion, such as is required by Tylor's animism or Morgan's naturism.

Durkheim makes two distinctions which are basic to his entire study: the distinction between *beliefs* and *rites* as categories of religious phenomena, and the distinction between *sacred* and *profane*. The first distinction separates the elements of *thought* and *action* in religion, and the second separates religious attitudes from other human attitudes. It is the origin of *sacred* ideas that receives the most attention.

There is nothing inherent in an object, such as the totem, which evokes a sacred attitude; rather, it is the projection of belief upon an object that makes it sacred. In other words, a sacred object is a symbol; it "stands for" some reality, and our search should be not for the origin of sacred ideas and objects, but for the realities which are being symbolized. For Durkheim, the positivist, such "reality" must be observable, and that "reality" is society, for only society can be observed to exercise moral authority. Religion is society symbolized and elevated to a position of unassailable moral authority. Society, as the expression of the collective sentiments of a people, is, above all, moral reality; religion is the concrete representation of that reality. It is better to say, therefore (as Parsons does), that for Durkheim society is a religious phenomenon rather than that religion is a social phenomenon. Durkheim, in fact, states that "nearly all the great social institutions have been born in religion," and that "If religion has given birth to all that is essential in society, it is because the idea of society is the soul of religion."

A society cannot exist unless the conditions of solidarity and co-operation are kept intact. This takes continuous support and reaffirmation—a "moral remaking"—and can be achieved through religious practices and ideals where the required feelings, attitudes, and sentiments can be experienced and acted out, although on a symbolic level.

The function of religion, then, is to foster and perpetuate, largely on unconscious levels, the kind of human behavior necessary for social existence: restrictions on the indulgence of individual whims, sacrifice for a social cause, a disposition toward co-operation, and the recognition of a power superior to the individual. With this understanding of religion it is possible to make sense, for example, of certain religious rites which on any other view seem completely unreasonable. The separation of sacred and profane things, the "negative cult," prohibits freedom of action with respect to certain objects and events and promotes abstention, asceticism, and the toleration of suffering. On the positive side, certain practices, such as sacrificial rites, promote a sense of communion and dependence on powers above the individual.

In general, ritual permits an active exercise and expression of the social values and attitudes of a people which

Charles Darwin
(1809–1882)

Herbert Spencer
(1820–1903)

Edward Tylor
(1832–1917)

James Frazer
(1854–1941)

Emile Durkheim
(1858–1917)

Franz Boas
(1858–1942)

Bronislaw Malinowski
(1884–1942)

Alfred Kroeber
(1876–1960)

Ruth Benedict
(1887–1948)

Sigmund Freud
(1856–1939)

are not understood rationally and which need periodic reinforcement. For these common sentiments to become conscious they must be fixed to external objects and forces (sacred things) which can be experienced and manipulated. The error of most students of religion has been to mistake these projected human sentiments for forces exterior to man. They are, of course, "exterior" to any individual because they are collective, or social forces. Their human origin does not make them less noble. The ideals of all the great religions are the ideals of society, and although never perfectly realized by man, they keep him at least a little this side of destruction.[1]

The general conclusions reported above resulted from Durkheim's analysis of the totemism of Australia; or it might be better to say that the study of totemism confirmed his preconceptions concerning the relationships of the individual to society as they appeared in his earlier works. He has been shown to be factually mistaken on important points in totemism, and his detailed analysis has been weakened accordingly, but the insights emphasized above are still worthy of attention.

A major contribution of *Elementary Forms of Religious Life*, one that is generally neglected by anthropologists, is in epistemology. As a philosopher, Durkheim was acquainted with the subtle problems of the theory of knowledge. This was Kant's major problem, and Durkheim had read and studied Kant's work with great interest, although with considerable suspicion. Specifically, Durkheim was interested in the so-called categories of the understanding: the ideas of time, space, number, substance, cause, and so on. Are these categories, through which we experience and understand the world, prior to all experience and an inherent part of the human mind, or are they constructed by the mind after sense experience of the objects of the external world? This is the classic argument between the

---

[1] Durkheim might well have cited Socrates' last words as symbolic of his own insight here; for after discoursing about pure virtue and justice in that ideal world after this life, Socrates' last concern is for an obligation he has to the real world: "Crito," says Socrates, just before he expires, "I owe a cock to Asclepius; will you remember to pay the debt?"

rationalists and the empiricists. Durkheim can accept neither position. The universality and the external constraint of the categories argue against the empiricist position, for if these ideas are constructed by the individual, they can be changed at the whim of the individual. Empiricism here can result only in irrationalism. The rationalists, on the other hand, presume an objective reality for the logical life but can offer no explanation for the transcendent categories, except to say that they are "inborn" or that they emanate from a "divine reason"; explanations which cannot, in principle, be verified.

Only by admitting the social origins of the categories of the understanding can this unacceptable alternative be avoided, according to Durkheim. If the categories are collective representations, the objections to the classical positions can be overcome. As social ideas, they are imposed upon the individual and he is constrained to accept them without proof or persuasion. They are "necessary" in that a contact of minds would be impossible without them and human life would cease to exist. Logical conformity as well as moral conformity is a prerequisite of social existence. This explanation also does justice to the positive aspects of the empirical tradition because it relates the categories to observable phenomena: the realities of social life. In Australia, for example, some societies conceive of space as a great circle which is divided up just as the tribal circle is divided in their camp. Space, for them, is the image of the physical arrangement of the camp. The imitative rites of certain primitive peoples are based on the idea that like produces like; a definite conception of "cause." It may be assumed that the more sophisticated principle of causality is also a social product. Durkheim finds this true of all the rest of the categories of human thought.

This, in brief, is Durkheim's extension of assumptions, which were to all of human thought and experience formulated as early as the *Division of Labor*. Such a great and daring project necessarily involved him in contradictions and difficulties, but he was a stubborn man who could not be stopped from working out the most diverse and subtle implications of a central insight. He uncovered enough problems here to keep social scientists busy for a long time.

DURKHEIM has an important place in anthropology and sociology, and both fields must be considered in attempting to evaluate his importance. Anthropologists, for the most part, have emphasized his contributions to ethnological literature (especially as the editor of *Année*), his study of totemism, and his functional method. The sociologists have paid less attention to his specific contributions to the study of primitive peoples and have emphasized the importance of his general sociological theories, especially as they appear in the *Division of Labor* and *Suicide*. They have also hailed him as the founder of modern sociological method. It seems safe to say that the sociologists have given Durkheim a higher place in the social sciences than have the anthropologists, at least in the United States. In any case, he is without a doubt a great figure and is treated with considerable respect by the workers in both fields.

Durkheim has been called the First of the Moderns in sociology and the Father of Functionalism in anthropology. Both of these titles he has earned by his particular methodology. His idea of applying the methods of the physical sciences to sociological data, although not new, was insisted upon to a remarkable degree. Spencer, Tylor, and Frazer, among others, were committed to such a view, but they did not exercise the care and criticism that characterized Durkheim's work. His extreme confidence in the general application of the methods of science has not been justified; but this is a defect that is shared with others, including the physical scientists. The social scientists of today who claim that a "science of human behavior" is impossible usually overlook the difficulties and uncertainties that plague the physicists and chemists.

Durkheim's contributions to a scientific methodology for the social sciences were discussed above. His major substantive contribution lies in his understanding of symbolism and projection in society. Although often considered as hostile to psychology, he emerges in this area as a social psychologist of the first order. This is especially clear in his functional analysis of ritual and ceremony in primitive societies, where he insisted on relating these symbolic activities to what people actually do in their everyday social life.

On the negative side, Durkheim is routinely criticized for his neglect of psychology. In stressing the importance of studying society as a reality sui generis, Durkheim refused to acknowledge the relevance of individual psychology for sociology. A collection of human individuals create phenomena far beyond the capacities of any one individual, so how, Durkheim asked, can we explain these phenomena by making the individual the central problem? In fact, since man is primarily a social product, it is the study of society which must precede the study of individual behavior.

It has been pointed out (especially by Parsons) that contradictions in Durkheim's work lie in his commitment to the tenets of positivism on the one hand, and on the other, to his admission of goals, attitudes, sentiments, and values as phenomena of the greatest importance to a study of society. The cohesive forces in society are not accessible to sense observation (as required by the positivists) but are understood, if at all, only after considerable imaginative effort. But this criticism of Durkheim does not seem too important when we remember that the term "observation" is difficult to define, and what is more important, when we look to what a scientist *does* rather than to what he *says* he is doing. What Durkheim *did* was familiarize himself with a great and varied body of cultural data, look for general laws of relationship, and formulate hypotheses and theories which would explain and at the same time point the way toward the human improvement of society.

Durkheim has had a great influence in sociology and anthropology, especially in France and England. His followers there include Henri Hubert, Marcel Mauss, Georges Davy, Paul Fauconnet, Maurice Halbwachs and, in part, Levy-Bruhl. His general influence is difficult to ascertain. As the first systematic functionalist, his influence is inestimable. As an advocate of the "organic" view of society, he has contributed to the development of what are now called the "superorganic" ideas, as seen, for example, in Kroeber and, in the extreme, in Leslie White. Lowie states that Durkheim also illustrated the "pattern" idea which became so popular among American anthropologists, where the search is for a central idea, mood, or disposition which is expressed in all the practices of a society.

Durkheim today is of more than historical interest; his work, especially in the field of sociology, is seriously studied for what light it may shed on contemporary problems and theory. The full importance of his insights has yet to be fully recognized and appreciated.

# FRANZ BOAS

## ICY ENTHUSIASM

ACCORDING TO FRANZ BOAS, it was "in the sublime loneliness of the Arctic, and in contact with the active world" that he came alive. The amplification of this paradox—sublime loneliness and the active world—is found throughout Boas' life, and helps to explain the chain of contradictions that constitutes his work.

Mankind was a puzzle to Boas, and therefore a challenge. He could have easily become a great figure in the physical or the natural sciences. His natural bent was for the non-human phenomena of nature—from the billiard balls of the physicist to the ferns and flowers of the botanist. He chose instead to study man. Boas studied man—or more accurately, he studied men—with all the powers of his great mental and physical resources. He worked like a man fighting for his life. He reminds one of the athlete who compensates for a lack of natural talent by hard work, determination, and courage, and often succeeds where the natural athlete fails.

In his struggle to understand men he founded a disciplined anthropology—and never allowed himself one comfortable generalization about man. Although always forcing himself into the center of the active world, he still remained alone.

Boas was born July 9, 1858, in Minden, Westphalia (Germany). He was one of six children of Meier Boas and Sophie Meyer Boas, both of Jewish extraction. His father was a prosperous businessman, and his mother was an extremely active woman in civic and political affairs. The parents, especially the mother, were committed to the spirit and ideals of the German Revolution of 1848, and Boas speaks of that spirit of liberalism as a "living force" in his early home life. His mother was a close friend of many of the "forty-eighters"; her younger sister married Dr. Abraham Jacobi, one of the famous members of this revolutionary group.

Boas describes his mother as "idealistic, with a lively interest in public matters" and lists among her accomplishments the founding of the first Froebel Kindergarten in Minden. The father, while also "liberal," according to Boas, was not active in the causes which his mother served.

Of the six children only Boas and three sisters (one older and two younger) survived childhood. The relationship with his mother and sisters (especially the oldest one) was a strong and influential one throughout his life. Their intense, protective interest in him seemed at times to be too much for him, but he was steadfast in his allegiance to them.

Although quite a delicate child—a cause for much of the fuss made over him by his mother and sisters—Boas spent much time outdoors. He was a nature lover from early childhood, and was encouraged in botanical investigations by his mother. At the age of eighty, in one of his rare reminiscences, he recalls an early, "intense emotional interest in the phenomena of the world."

Boas valued very highly the liberal, freethinking background of his early family life. He states that his parents had "broken through the shackles of dogma," although the father "had retained an emotional affection for the ceremonial of his parental home." He was careful to say, however, that his father did not allow this affection to "influence his intellectual freedom." Boas was grateful for these parental attitudes, by which, as he says, "I was spared the struggle against religious dogma that besets the lives of so many young people."

He spent the first nineteen years of his life with his family in Minden, and attended school and the Gymnasium there. Very little is known about this part of his life, since he was not given to reminiscing about the past; a trait which Alfred Kroeber attributes to Boas' zealous concern for the present and the future. It is known, however, that he was quite an accomplished pianist. The piano remained a source of satisfaction and relaxation for him for many years. Of Boas' early life one gets the impression of a somewhat delicate boy, interested in nature, music, and school studies, whose life at home was dominated by maternal attention and concern.

At about the age of twenty Boas began his university career. He studied for four years at Heidelberg, Bonn, and Kiel and took his doctorate at Kiel in 1881, at the age of twenty-three. He first specialized in physics and mathematics, and then became interested in physical, and later, cultural geography.

His doctoral dissertation was in physics, and was entitled *Contributions to the Understanding of the Color of Water*. As was required at the time, he had to defend other theses along with the one in his major field. The title of the last one that he defended—*That Contemporary Operetta Was Equally To Be Condemned on Grounds of Art and Morality*—reveals a side of his personality that was to qualify much of his life and work.

Kroeber states that "Boas' university life may be presumed warm and rich," and cites in support of this presumption the facial scars Boas received from dueling during this period. Boas often attributed these scars to bear clawings in Baffinland; a characteristic way of playfully avoiding questions about his personal history. They were, however, received in duels which resulted from the hostile relations between the two university fraternities representing the aristocratic (*Korps*) and the ordinary (*Burschen-*

*schaft*) students. Boas belonged to the *Burschenschaft* and would not tolerate the insults—often anti-Semitic—of the *Korps* students.

He spent at least one year in the reserve officer-training program of the German army and another year in further study. Then, in 1883, he began his anthropological career with a trip to Baffinland; a crucial experience for him and for anthropology. He was financed for a year there by a German newspaper, the *Berliner Tageblatt*, which published his letters and articles.

His intimate experience with the Eskimos was a decisive one in turning his interests from the physical to the human phenomena of nature. He wrote of the Eskimos a few years later with sentiment unusual for Boas: "I had seen that they enjoyed life, and hard life, as we do; that nature is beautiful to them; that feelings of friendship also root in the Eskimo heart; that, although the character of their life is rude as compared to civilized life, the Eskimo is a man as we are; that his feelings, his virtues and his short-comings are based on human nature, like ours."

He spent the following year (1884-1885) in New York, and then returned to Germany as an assistant at the Museum for Volkerkunde, an institution founded by the famous anthropologist, Adolf Bastian. In 1886, as Docent in Geography at the University of Berlin, he studied a group of Bella Coola Indians who had been brought to Berlin, and became determined to make another field exploration, this time to British Columbia. He returned to New York from this trip in 1887 and took the position of Assistant Editor for the publication *Science*. In the same year he married Marie Krackowizer and decided to become an American citizen. His return to British Columbia in the summer of 1888 for a study of the Northwestern Indian tribes marked the beginning of a monumental anthropological study.

From 1888 until 1892 he served on the faculty of Clark University, where the first Ph.D. in Anthropology was taken (by A. F. Chamerlain) under his supervision. He resigned from Clark University in 1892 and took the position of Chief Assistant in the Department of Anthropology at the Chicago Exposition. In 1895 he became Curator of Anthropology at the Field Museum in Chicago, and worked there until a personal conflict resulted in his removal. In 1896 he worked for the American Museum as Curator of Ethnology and Somatology, and in 1899 he began his long career as Professor of Anthropology at Columbia University. He also served for several years (1901-1905) as Curator of the American Museum, and was responsible for much of the great study and exploration undertaken by that institution in the field of anthropology, shortly after the turn of the century. This was the period of Boas' greatest achievements in research, the most notable of which was the Jesup North Pacific Expedition, which sought to establish the relationships of the aborigines of North America to the mainland tribes of Asia.

His other major undertakings included an appointment, in 1901, as Honorary Philologist at the Bureau of American Ethnology, which resulted in his three-volume *Handbook of American Indians;* the founding of the International School of American Archaeology and Ethnology in Mexico, in 1910; the founding of the *Journal of American Linguistics,* in 1917; and the chairmanship of a committee on native American Languages for the American Council of Learned Societies.

Boas' later years were filled with personal sorrow. Two of his six children died suddenly, one by an automobile accident. His wife was also killed in an automobile accident in 1929. In 1931, at the age of seventy-three, he suffered a heart attack, but recovered sufficiently to return to steady work. He continued doggedly at his work for the next eleven years and died suddenly at a Columbia University Faculty Club luncheon on December 21, 1942.

Boas was a member of all the scientific honor societies in this country and a corresponding member of most of the foreign societies. He was President of the New York Academy of Sciences (1910) and President of the American Association for the Advancement of Science (1931), among many other honorary positions. He held an honorary doctorate from Oxford.

He wrote relatively few books, and of these, all but one were written in the later years of his life. He recorded most of his massive research and study in over six hundred articles in the professional journals. His great book, *The Mind of Primitive Man*, was published in 1911. Not until 1927 did he write another book, *Primitive Art*, which was followed in 1928 by *Anthropology and Modern Life*. His *General Anthropology* and a revised edition of *Primitive Man* were published in 1938. A valuable selection by Boas of his most important papers was published in 1940 under the title *Race, Language and Culture*.

Franz Boas hated authority. Authority, whether it was that of tradition or that of a university administrator, was to be resisted and defied. His students were exhorted to practice independence of thought and action, and woe to those who did not. He fought authority all his life, even his own authority; for when any of his ideas were threatened with systemization he went off on another tack, leaving his followers without a flag. He is the greatest hero in American anthropology, but there is no Boas "school."

One of the "unforgettable moments" of his life occurred when, as a student, a theologically-minded friend of his "declared his belief in the authority of tradition and his conviction that one had not the right to doubt what the past had transmitted to us." Boas was shocked, and years later he cited this conversation as having had a permanent influence on his life. In the same reminiscence he refers again to his abhorrence of authority: "The psychological origin of the implicit belief in the authority of religion, which was so foreign to my mind and which had shocked me at an earlier time, became a problem that engaged my thoughts for many years. In fact, my whole outlook upon social life is determined by the question: How can we recognize the shackles that tradition has laid upon us? For when we recognize them, we are also able to break them."

It has been suggested that a history of Boas' intellectual development is needed to explicate his doctrines, if, indeed, he can be said to have held doctrines. Such a history should begin with the freethinking background of his early family life, for which he expressed the warmest gratitude. The intensity with which he fought authority invites a careful scrutiny of this early freedom. It is known that his mother, a tireless worker for political freedom, was something of a matriarch in her own family, and that her constant attention often became a burden to him. When he was away she wrote to him three and four times a week. Although he always expressed the keenest interest in and affection for his mother, he found it necessary to declare to her that he had to live his own life.

It would also be interesting to ask to what extent his determination to "break the shackles of tradition" was tied up with his encounters with anti-Semitism—the Boas family was one of probably two Jewish families in Minden. His father was apparently the only one in the family who had not forsaken his religious ties. A freethinker from childhood, Boas received none of the strength and security that religion can provide, yet he was associated with the Jewish religion by others and persecuted for it. He paid the price for a tradition, the benefits of which he never received. Perhaps this played some part in his hostility to tradition and authority. In a paper, "Race and Progress" (1931), he juxtaposes the "garb of the medieval Jews" and the "stripes of a convict," as examples of symbols imposed on certain people by dominant groups "so that each individual no matter what his own character may be, is at once assigned to his group and treated accordingly."

Whatever his emotional investments in fighting regimentation, he used his independence in a dramatic, effective way. He is as much a hero for this as he is for the almost incredible amount of work he accomplished in anthropology. During the First World War, when loyalty was a major concern, Columbia University solicited reports by its students of any suspicious remarks made by the members of the faculty. Boas prepared a strong statement of his unpopular views, read it to his classes, and offered a copy to any student who would like to send it on to the trustees of the university. In 1918 he wrote an open letter to the *Nation* in which he castigated the behavior of four anthro-

pologists who had engaged in intelligence work for the
United States, while on a scientific expedition to Latin
America during the war. He referred to them as "men
whom I refuse to designate any longer as scientists" and
accused them of having "prostituted science by using it as
a cover for their activities as spies." He was formally rebuked for this letter by the American Anthropological
Association at a stormy meeting in Cambridge in 1919.
Although Boas was aware that his pro-German views—he
was never accused of disloyalty to the United States—
stemmed from a sentimental attachment to his native land,
he did not let that deter his outspoken criticism of his
adopted country's entry into the war.

With the rise of racism under the Nazis, prior to the
Second World War, he was one of the first to take a strong
public stand against Hitler. At a then advanced age he
fought Hitler's Germany with all the capacities of his great
knowledge, reputation and personality. His books were
burned in 1933 at Kiel, the university which had awarded
him his most valued degree.

Wherever important liberties were threatened Boas could
be counted on to fight for their preservation. This inevitably found him associated with unpopular groups and
causes, but he never shunned a fight for fear of any labels
that might become attached to him. As Lowie has put it,
"He stood by what he saw as right and let consequences go
hang." This attitude won him many loyal friends, even
worshipers, and, naturally, it evoked hostile feelings in
many quarters. But on the whole, he was the object of
overwhelming respect, largely because of his massive
achievements in anthropology; achievements which no one
could challenge.

A closer look at Boas, as teacher, colleague, friend and
family man, reveals a man of power and reserve, whose overt
affections were reserved for the most intimate—and for
total strangers. He was devoted to his wife, children, and
grandchildren, and to a small group of students and colleagues; and he was always ready to aid complete strangers
on the slightest evidence of their needing help. To the

large number between these extremes he often appeared removed, impersonal, and even hostile. Lowie was a student of his during the time Boas was feuding with the American Museum, and remembers "actually dreading meeting him on the way to classes." "Utter silence," says Lowie, "would follow a curt 'good morning' till I found the situation intolerable."

Although generally poised and undemonstrative, and accustomed to making cold, cutting analyses when engaged in polemics, he could give way, on occasion, to bursts of undisguised feeling. The driver of a sight-seeing bus almost threw him and his grandchildren off the bus after Boas threatened him with his cane because of the historical distortions in the driver's commentary on the trip. When he was a university student he became so annoyed at the failure of a neighboring girl pianist to get over a passage in a work by Mozart, that he would regularly pound it out for her on his own piano every time she came to the passage. These, however, were probably rare occasions. As a rule he was outwardly calm, poised, and determined. He once tried for three hours to get his son to say "thank you"; an example of emotional control that any parent can appreciate.

With his family and close friends he was not the austere figure familiar to the less intimate. He helped his children and grandchildren with their studies, took long hikes with them, and exercised a good sense of humor, being especially fond of jokes and riddles. He regularly reserved a part of his busy evenings for the family, and found most of his relaxation with them.

Boas' great influence as a teacher is closely related to his unwillingness, or inability, to ingratiate himself with other people. He won students solely on the merit of his work, never for the brilliance or facility of his presentation. Instead of a large number of uncritical, enthusiastic followers, he attracted a small number of devoted young scholars, whose future work would establish him as the greatest teacher in American anthropology. As a somewhat forbidding personality who refused to popularize his material, he discouraged the academic interest of all but the most highly gifted students. These students were drawn to him by the cold intensity of his work and personality, and only later felt the warmth he radiated in intimate associations. In time, he became known to them as "Papa Franz."

His main courses at Columbia for forty years were *Statistical Theory* and *American Indian Languages*. He imposed a heavy load on his students. Special skills essential to his courses, such as mathematics and linguistics, were assumed to be part of the equipment they brought to class, along with paper and pen. Most of the factual data which he used to illustrate and support the all-important principles and methods of anthropology had to be gathered, organized, and assimilated by the student without his help or interest. He was interested, primarily, in principles, theory, and methodology, and here, according to Kroeber, he demanded "an uncompromising adherence to his own values."

It is interesting that although he gratefully dropped an introductory course in anthropology at Columbia College (for men), he enjoyed a parallel course at Barnard College (for women) for many years. In fact, it was one of his favorite courses. Girls always seemed more attracted to him than boys, and he responded to their attention. Perhaps, with the intuition and devices of young females, they could more easily penetrate his austere armor.[1]

When his students matured and set out to do their own work, Boas continued to regard them primarily as "his students," with whom, according to Herskovits, he felt he was obliged to disagree. His attitude toward their work was always critical, and the fact that he was usually right in his criticism did not ease the discomfort that some of them experienced. His greatest talent lay in the critical analysis of theory and method, and no piece of work was safe from his patient, meticulous dissection. To many of his students he appeared unpredictable and impossible to

[1] In his letter-diary to his parents (Sept. 21, 1886), Boas revealed an early preference for women in an aside about the Bella Coola Indians he was studying: ". . . (it seems that the women are always more intelligent than the men). . . ."

please. But whatever personal disappointments and frustrations they received at his hands, they regarded him with the greatest esteem and respect, both for his almost omniscient position in anthropology and for the power and integrity of his personality.

Toward such a powerful and, as it may have seemed, capricious figure one would expect to find ambivalent and contradictory attitudes, especially on the part of those whose professional lives were at stake. And this is what one finds among many of Boas' students. A typical exaggeration of his place in the history of anthropology was written by Ruth Benedict in 1943: "He found anthropology a collection of wild guesses and a happy hunting ground for the romantic lover of primitive things; he left it a discipline in which theories could be tested and in which he had delimited possibilities from impossibilities." To this, another of Boas' students, R. H. Lowie, felt compelled to register his "vehement, uncompromising dissent," and to declare: "The notion that he was a culture hero of the type featured by aboriginal folklore, a bringer of light out of total darkness, was intensely distasteful to him; he explicitly repudiated it in a letter to me. . . ." But Lowie, on the other hand, went so far in his praise of Boas as to dismiss all of Malinowski's innovations in field methods as simply conforming to Boas' standards. Lowie concluded a memorial paper on Boas in 1944 with the sentiment, that ". . . through his gnarled discourse and personality I see shining a truer light than other men's."

"Icy enthusiasm," is the only motto Boas is known to have proclaimed. It supposedly originated with the great pathologist, Rudolf Virchow (with whom Boas has been compared), and it exposes Boas' personality as he would have it exposed. In response to an address at the celebration of the twenty-fifth anniversay of his doctorate from Kiel, he consciously presented himself in this light: "not less is my gratitude due to those of my colleagues and friends who have enthusiastically co-operated with me—a co-operation which I fear has not always been easy with one whose work rests essentially in an unfeeling criticism of his work and of that of others." This side of Boas' personality has generally been accepted as a complete portrait, but a closer look reveals "Papa Franz," whose icy exterior did not fool the Barnard girls.

The weakness the Barnard girls detected in Boas' armor was not enough to permit the flexibility that marks the natural student of man. The greatest credit that can be accorded Boas is that he refused to follow an emotional predilection for isolation, in fact did just the opposite and sought contact and knowledge in every field of human behavior.

His methods were from the laboratories of the physical sciences and his inspiration, according to his own account, came from the "spirit of liberalism," as interpreted by his mother. That calculated and militant spirit of liberalism just about closed out the old-fashioned father who maintained an "emotional affection" for the traditions of a great people. It is just possible, however, that it was the unrecognized influence of his father that turned Boas' retreat from the active world of people into an assault on the problems and mysteries of that world. Lacking a natural *feeling* for people, he sought to make up for that loss by *knowing* more about them than anyone else. Without the small but critical inheritance from his father he would not have felt his loss, and the determination—stronger for being blind—to make up for it would never have been born.

Kroeber has stated that Boas "initiated all his own new paths and only subsequently sought contacts with the like minded." Whether or not this is an exaggeration, one can at least point to some general influences.

During his university days he was attracted to the famous German geographer, Theobald Fischer, who directed his interests from physics and mathematics to physical and, later, cultural geography. After his return from Baffinland he became associated with Rudolf Virchow, who, according to Kroeber, influenced him more than any other scientist. Virchow was a rigorous scientist, whose greatest achievements were in pathology, but who also made some contributions to anthropology. His study of the distribution of blondes and brunettes among schoolchildren in Germany was the kind of patient, statistical study that characterized much of Boas' future work. Virchow, like Boas, was skeptical of speculative hypotheses in science; in 1877, eighteen years after Darwin's *Origin of Species*, he opposed the teaching of evolution in the schools on the grounds that it had not been "proved." Like Boas' parents, he was active in liberal politics, and joined the Revolutionists in 1848. He was well known for a pugnacious spirit in advancing and defending his views, both in science and in social and political matters. His attitude of "icy enthusiasm" made a great impression on Boas.

Boas' expedition to Baffinland in 1883 marked three important and not unrelated events in his life: it launched his career in anthropology, it established his independence from his family, and it came at a time when he had fallen in love. He reached maturity during this period, as the following quote testifies: "During these years in the sublime loneliness of the Arctic, and in contact with the active world, I have felt my strength ripen, and I became ready to learn how to teach." The conclusion of this reminiscence (in 1906) is a letdown, but the feeling of growing power and creativity is there.

He had gone to Baffinland primarily as a geographer, looking for the cultural effect on people of their physical environment, but as he lived and traveled with the Eskimos he became more concerned with the importance of social tradition as a determinant of culture and personality. His realization of the power of social tradition in shaping human lives turned his interests from geography to ethnology, and marked the beginning of his career as an anthropologist.

In 1888 he began his serious field work with the tribes of Northwestern Canada. He became especially interested in their folklore, noting its marked dissimilarity from European folklore, and started what was to become one of the greatest collections of folklore in anthropology. This trip to British Columbia was sponsored by the British Association Committee on the Northwestern tribes of Canada, whose chairman was E. B. Tylor. He became interested in Tylor's use of statistical methods on cultural data, and for a time believed that these methods could elicit answers to most of the problems in ethnology.

From 1888 to 1899 he gained much knowledge and experience as a fieldworker, museum curator, and teacher. By the turn of the century he was ready for one of the greatest teaching careers in American history.

Boas had a passion for collecting, classifying, and preserving vast amounts of raw data. With the help of a number of barbers in New York City he once had over a million single hairs examined with magnifying glasses as part of a study on the graying of hair. The most outstanding consistency in his work is his insistence on the importance of raw material from the field. He said of one of his former students that she had forgotten all the anthropology she knew, but her data were good; that saved her, in his eyes. There is much evidence to support Gladys Reichard's estimation that "The strongest rocks in Boas' self-built monument are his texts, his belief that what people record of themselves in their own words will in the last analysis reveal their motivations and ideas most accurately."

In the sharpest possible contrast to Malinowski's dramatic reports, Boas presents his material on a culture with a deliberate economy of literary and imaginative effort. After a very short preface, a work on the Kwakiutl Culture (his favorite people) begins with their Material Culture, then, under Houses, he gives the following description: "Houses are generally built on the ground. They are square. A large house measures ten by ten fathoms (c. 257)." He uses the same faithful economy under "Emotional Life and Ethics": "Pleasure is expressed by laughing . . . a woman because a man wants to marry her . . . people who have had fun . . . husband and wife laugh together . . . The people laugh at funny incidents." These descriptions go on without relief for 190 pages, marshaled under a careful categorical outline consisting of eleven major headings and about 160 sub-groups.

The restraint he used in describing a culture has been attributed to his zealous concern that only the strict methods of the sciences be employed in anthropology. His reports read much like a physicist's laboratory notebook. Much has been made of his early training as a physicist in accounting for these objective, unemotional descriptions. But, as in many other matters, this invites a comparison with Malinowski, who was also trained as a physical scientist—a fact which even Kroeber overlooked when he remarked that he thought Boas' training in physics was unique in anthropology.

According to Leslie Spier, who often differs with other Boas commentators, Boas probably did not wholly enjoy field work and had to discipline himself to it. Lowie, on the other hand, states that "Boas must be understood, first of all, as a field worker."

That Boas did not "wholly enjoy field work," as Spier contends, can be supported by excerpts from his letter-diary to his parents in 1886. In describing an interview with Bella Coola Indians he writes, in part:

> In the meantime, screaming dirty children run about, sometimes a meal is eaten. Dogs and children force their way between the people; fires smoke so that one can hardly see. . . . In short, the whole thing is a test of patience. (November 8)

He became unhappy and indignant when his work did not proceed on schedule, or when the quality of the data was not up to his expectations. He writes at about the same time:

> Today was my worst day since I have been here. I learned practically nothing as I had to spend the entire day running about in search of new people. . . . I was very tired at night from running about so much and went to bed in a bad humor. That was a profitless day. (September 25)

And a few days later he reports:

> Then I went to the Bella Coolas, who told me another idiotic story. . . . The fact that I obtain these stories is interesting, but the stories themselves are more horrible than some of the Eskimo stories. (October 3)

His celebrated respect and tolerance for cultural idiosyncrasy broke down when his work was affected by non-
conformity:

> I am very cross because my Tsimshian has deserted me. . . .
> From experience I should know that such things happen,
> but it is easier said than done not to be angry about it. I
> told the good man, who by the way is very religious, that he
> was the greatest liar I had ever known and that I would tell
> his pastor about him. (September 24)

From these personal and informal references to his experiences in the field, and from his formal ethnographical
reports, one can see the icy enthusiast at work. The weight
of his manuscript must increase every day: "My manuscript is becoming quite sizeable and I hope to have a valuable stock when I return to New York (October 3)." And he
is constantly worried about the size of the daily increase:
"I am unhappy for every moment lost (September 26).
. . . I wasted three hours without getting a thing (November 6). . . . I find that my notes are very scant these days
(November 8). . . . I did not get much today because I
missed seeing one man (November 21). . . . I did not get
much wiser today (November 30)." And always there was
the morbid fear of every great collector: "You cannot
imagine how I worry lest I lose my manuscript." (November 23)

Boas did not let sentiment creep into his observations
of people; any sentimentality was restricted to pastime observations of nature: "Magnificent tall firs as well as knotty
oaks and another tree, whose name I do not know, grow
there. It was a beautiful walk. The ground was covered with
lush ferns and naked grey rock showed here and there. Only
here can one find nature free and untamed, so close to the
turmoil of a city." One suspects here the emotional equipment for a botanist rather than an anthropologist. It can
be argued, however, that emotional distance is necessary
for scientific objectivity; that the botanist can be infatu-
ated with the turmoil of a city but must approach a fir tree
purged of feeling. By temperament or by choice Boas ap-

proached his field work with this kind of objectivity. He did not want the record distorted by his own emotional involvement. Whether or not this is a possible or desirable ideal in anthropological field work is a nice question. Malinowski's approach to field work will provide a useful comparison.

It is interesting, and confusing, that while Boas faithfully practiced the methods of the sciences in anthropology (especially the inductive steps), he was usually skeptical about arriving at useful generalizations in anthropology. "The danger is ever present," he states, "that the widest generalizations that may be obtained by the study of cultural integration are commonplaces." There is a difference of opinion among Boas' students and commentators as to whether or not he believed it possible to formulate laws of social development. One can find in his writing expressions on both sides of the question.

An early optimism regarding the formulation of laws of cultural development is found in his famous paper, "The Limitations of the Comparative Method of Anthropology" (1896): "We agreed that certain laws exist which govern the growth of human culture, and it is our endeavor to discover these laws." In a review of Malinowski's *Crime and Custom* in 1926 he comments on the "implied hope" in that study that general laws of social conditioning may be found, and observes that ". . . there remains a fundamental difference between a complex phenomenon that has grown up historically and generalized scientific laws. The complexity of historical events is such that the cultural life of any people and of any tribe can be understood only as an outgrowth of those unique conditions under which it has lived."

He believed it legitimate to ask "how far specific laws may be found that express analogous processes occurring in diverse societies," and this is probably a good general indication of how far he would go in drawing generalizations from comparative anthropological data. He refused to go beyond what he took to be direct evidence in describing a culture, and since considerable speculation is required for a more or less complete portrait of a community, he never attempted to give one.

It is easy to find in Boas' writings many contradictions in doctrines. The explanation is to be found in the fact that he formulated theories chiefly as a polemic against the fashionable doctrines of the day. He was, above all, a skeptic and an analyst. In 1896 he dealt a blow to the evolutionary theory and the comparative method from which American anthropology has never recovered. He proposed "historical reconstruction" in place of "evolutionary reconstruction," his aim being to replace a deductive approach with inductive methods. It was to be accomplished by carefully working many restricted cultural areas, and then comparing the processes of cultural growth in each area so as to arrive at sound inductive generalizations: "When we have cleared up the history of a single culture and understand the effects of environment and the psychological conditions that are reflective in it we have made a step forward, as we can then investigate in how far the same causes or other causes were at work in the development of other cultures. Thus by comparing histories of growth general laws may be found." His main point against the evolutionists and their "comparative method" is that they attribute cultural similarities to identical processes, on the unfounded assumption that the human mind obeys the same laws everywhere. It is never safe, he argues, to compare only the results of cultural growth, because similar customs, traits, and beliefs can develop from different causes. Only after intensively studying the processes of growth in small geographical areas and then comparing the histories of their individual development is it legitimate to look for general laws of cultural growth.

The period from 1895 to 1905 has been called Boas' "enthusiastic period." He checked the excesses of the evolutionists, and at the same time offered a positive program for limited historical reconstruction and the formulation of laws of cultural development. From 1900 to 1920, under his influence, culture history and reconstruction became the dominant concerns of American anthropologists. Boas, however, grew uneasy about the optimism which his ideas had generated and in the years which followed shifted his emphasis to acculturation studies, then to functionalism and, finally, to personality-culture problems. He became dissatisfied with any doctrine which threatened to explain too much, and would attack it as a dangerous oversimplification of the problems. That he happened to have been the author of the doctrine made no difference.

This attitude led to some interesting controversies with his students, the most famous of which is an exchange with Kroeber recorded in the *American Anthropologist*. As an early student of Boas, Kroeber was impressed with the possibility of useful reconstruction by means of comparative history, and he came to consider anthropology as a historical science. A number of years after Boas had turned against this view Kroeber protested. In his reply Boas chided Kroeber for being satisfied with less than a "high degree of probability for a conclusion," and called him an "Epicurean." He presented himself as a foe of all speculative theory, and concluded with the statement, that "Absolute systems of phenomena as complex as those of culture are impossible. They will always be reflections of our own culture." The implication here is that scientific generalizations about cultures other than our own are impossible; it has had a considerable influence in American anthropology.

This extreme skepticism, while useful at times, has had some unfortunate results. It is reported that when Kroeber offered to show Boas a list of comparative vocabularies purporting to show the relationships of some North American Indian languages, Boas refused to look at it, saying he was "not interested." The incident is supposed to have occurred during a controversy in the field of linguistics (started by Sapir's classification of North American Indian languages), in which Boas denied that the relationships proposed by Sapir existed. According to some experts, the opposition of Boas and his students to Sapir's work disrupted progress in this field for a generation.

Boas grew more skeptical of theory as the years went by and concentrated his great energies on the intensive working of restricted areas, with the use of the most precise and exhaustive statistical methods he could find. Being committed, as he was, to an almost exclusive inductive approach in science, he could never find sufficient evidence to support a generalization.

His insistence on "cultural relativism"—a consistent attitude throughout all his work—enabled him to study a culture with a minimum of ethnocentric preconceptions. In so far as this attitude guards against making value judgments about a culture founded upon the values of our own culture, it is undoubtedly a prerequisite for responsible field work and cultural analysis. Boas had great influence in making this attitude a commonplace in anthropology. It is when he carries this cultural relativism to the point where it seems to deny the possibility of making any comparative and general statements about cultures, that some students begin to wonder what anthropology can contribute to a knowledge of human behavior. This is a problem which continues to haunt anthropology. Kroeber, recently, seemed to be wistfully looking for a way to escape the relativity of modern anthropology and, as he put it, "to smuggle human nature back into the study of man."

It is possible, as suggested above, to link Boas with almost every major theoretical and methodological doctrine in modern anthropology. He worked always to keep anthropology free from "speculative theory," and held to any theory himself only so long as it served the purpose of destroying or weakening the current dogma. This impatience with theoretical speculation kept him always in the vanguard of anthropological theory, and opened important new areas of research and analysis. It is probably possible to say of every worker in anthropology since Boas that his methods stem from Boas' work, or that Boas practiced them first. This can be said, however, only if one disregards the importance of emphasis.

THE RANGE of Boas' interests and accomplishments in anthropology has not been approached by any other anthropologist, except, perhaps, by Kroeber. It included every major area in physical and cultural anthropology.

Boas was most comfortable with data that could be collected and classified so as to be susceptible of statistical analysis. In his famous studies of race and physical growth and development he made the fullest use of statistical techniques and analyses. He abandoned the conventional anatomic approach to the study of physical types and substituted the application of biometric techniques to great masses of data.

His main contribution to an understanding of race was his insistence on the plasticity of the human physical type. He conceived of man as a domesticated animal, possessing the instability of physical type characteristic of other domesticated animals. In a sensational paper published in 1912[2] he reported on the variations of head forms among the 17,821 subjects he and thirteen research assistants had measured. The results showed significant differences in head forms between American immigrants and their American-born descendants, the differences varying directly with the length of time the parents had been in the United States. The changes among those studied (Italians, Czechs, and Jews) were all in the direction of the Anglo-Saxon type dominant in the United States.

In selecting head form as a measurement of variability due to environmental influence, Boas selected the trait most commonly supposed to be stable. He did not offer any explanation to account for these changes; in fact, with disquieting modesty, he concluded that "all we have shown is that head forms may undergo certain changes in course of time, without change of descent." This work, however, along with other anthropometric studies, did much to establish the notion in human genetics that what are transmitted in the germ plasm are not fixed characters, but potentialities which are dependent upon the environment for the particular form they will assume. The "nature-nurture" controversy was largely obviated by this alternative.

[2] Boas, Franz, "Changes in the Bodily Form of Descendants of Immigrants," *American Anthropolgist*, N.S., Vol. 14, No. 3 (1912).

Among the most interesting of Boas' studies on the influence of environment on growth and development was his study of children in the Hebrew Orphan Asylum in New York City. The study demonstrated the value of a home environment over institutional environment in regard to general physical development, and further demonstrated the salutary effect on the development of children in the orphan asylum which resulted from a change in administration. The factors which affected the changes were not limited to diet and medical care, but included the degree of regimentation employed and the concern for meeting the individual needs of the children. Recent studies on the general health and development of children in foundling homes and similar institutions have corroborated and extended Boas' work in this field.

In his famous book, *The Mind of Primitive Man*, Boas probably contributed more than any other person to a general enlightenment on the question of race; it has been called the "Magna Carta of race equality." In it, he clearly demonstrated that races were mixed and unstable, and that physical type bore no inherent relationship to mentality, virtue, language, or other cultural traits. All his life he sought to further the practical humanitarian consequences of his work on race.

Throughout his entire career Boas was interested in folklore and was convinced of its primary importance for an understanding of foreign cultures. He made major contributions to the folklore literature of the Tsimshian, Kwakiutl, Kutenai, and Keres cultures. As editor of the *Journal of American Folklore* from 1908 to 1925 he was responsible for the interest which led to a great collection of North American Indian material.

In the study of Tsimshian mythology, his best known work in this field, he emphasized the direct relationship of myth to the daily lives of the people: ". . . those incidents of everyday life," he states, "that are of importance to them will appear either incidentally or as the basis of a plot. Most of the references to the mode of life of the people will be an accurate reflection of their habits. The development of the plot of the story, furthermore, will, on the whole, exhibit clearly what is considered right and what wrong. . . . They present in a way an autobiography of the tribe." The individual, for Boas, remained at the center of all social institutions, and he insisted that even the most esoteric philosophical and religious doctrines be seen as institutionalized manifestations of the everyday ideas, attitudes, and values of the mass of the people.

There are those who claim that Boas was a practicing "functionalist" long before workers like Malinowski and Radcliffe-Brown had written a line. To substantiate this claim they point to his efforts to correlate folklore, myth, philosophy, and religion with the daily lives of the people; they refer to his preoccupation with the relationship of physical and cultural development; and they cite his work with language in which he relates linguistic form to cultural experience. T. K. Penniman writes that in Boas' work on the Central Eskimo (1888), "We can see the relation of every feature to every other, and its true function in the whole culture."

Leslie Spier, a rather consistent dissenter among Boas commentators, does not share the view that Boas made significant contributions to an understanding of the relations of the individual to culture. He admits that Boas was aware of the problems and that his ethnographies contained the data for a functional analysis, but states that it remained for students such as Lowie, Mead, and Benedict to make specific contributions in that field. It is probably safe to say that when Boas finished collecting material on a culture there was data available for any kind of analysis, but there is an important question as to how valuable data can be which is not collected with definite theoretical, and necessarily speculative, preconceptions. Boas consciously avoided such a conscious foreshadowing of problems.

At the very end of his career he gave his blessing to culture-personality studies, but expressed unhappiness about the methods currently employed in that area. He was skeptical of the value of "life-histories," claiming that they were based on faulty memories and influenced by present concerns. He favored an eavesdropping approach, where the observer recorded the small events of daily life and listened in on informal discussions and gossip sessions.

He was suspicious of the work of psychologists and medical men in anthropology, and believed that their efforts had "led to much confused thinking." Psychiatrists in particular came in for criticism: "I believe particularly that the use of psychoanalysis for attacking the problems of primitive culture can not bear the light of careful critical examination. I accept as an important contribution the effect of experiences in early life upon the personality of the individual, but when the attempt is made to explain mythology, totemism, taboo on the basis of psychoanalytic theories I can not follow. There are so many hypotheses involved in each step that it seems to me that the results can no longer be called scientifically sound."

The inevitable absence of precise methods and techniques in cultural anthropology probably prevented Boas from pursuing the problems in this field with the consistency and enthusiasm that characterized his work in physical anthropology. Also, his extreme cultural relativism tended to inhibit any comfortable assertions about human behavior in foreign cultures. A tape measure is a safe guide in the measurement of head form and stature in any culture, but there are no such tools for measuring the happiness or evaluating the moral codes of a people. It is difficult to get "scientific results," such as Boas demanded, in many areas of cultural anthropology, and his achievements in this field reflect his uneasiness with intuitive and speculative procedures.

Murray B. Emereau has said that Boas "is the *guru*, the ancestor of learning, of all those in this country who work in descriptive linguistics." There is no doubt about the value of his *relativism* in this field. He refused to impose on primitive tongues the familiar forms and categories of the two great families of language (Indo-European and Semitic), insisting that every tongue must be studied according to its own structure. His free approach to linguistics and the work he accomplished with it resulted in the rapid emergence of comparative linguistics.

Boas considered an intimate knowledge of the language as indispensable to the ethnology of a culture. In his *Handbook of American Indian Languages*, a classic work, he emphasizes the importance of the observer's command of the language, which enables him to grasp the subtleties of daily life revealed through informal conversations and activities.

FOR HIS accomplishments in every major field of anthropology and for his unfailing integrity, Boas must be put down as one of the giants of modern anthropology. The problems that he discovered and the methods and attitudes that he developed to deal with them have, to an important extent, shaped the course that modern anthropology has taken, especially in this country.

First on the list of his achievements is the vast amount of ethnographic material he collected and preserved. His cultural, linguistic, and biometric data were taken from many tribes among the Eskimos and from the Indians of the Northwest Coast, the Southwest, the Plains, and California. Like Frazer, he believed that the collection of factual information was the safest and most permanent contribution the anthropologist could make. But while Frazer got his information from the libraries at Cambridge, Boas got his from original work in the field. He is the founder of modern field work in the United States.

As a methodologist in the social sciences, he is conspicuous for practicing, rather than merely advocating, certain scientific procedures, especially the application of statistical analysis to social data. He scrutinized his own work with critical caution and skepticism, and applied the same treatment to the work of others. He can be credited with curbing the excesses of almost every "school" of anthropology. His critique of the evolutionary theory and the comparative method in anthropology has been especially devastating.

It is difficult to estimate his positive contributions to ethnological theory. He can be associated with almost all theories, but can be identified with none. Always conscious of the bewildering complexity of man and society, he regarded all general theories as premature, if not, in principle, impossible. It was here, if anywhere, that his great virtues became a burden and a limitation.

Because of his massive reputation, the weaknesses in his work have had a far greater influence than they might have had. Extreme skepticism and a dread of making mistakes qualified most of his work from around 1910 on. The enormous complexities in the study of man and society and the problems of cultural relativism seemed to him to present overwhelming obstacles to any useful generalizations in ethnology. The rigid requirements of "scientific proof" were sacred to Boas, and he therefore imposed strict limitations on his work and on the work of others. What did not seem justified by inductive investigation should not be asserted; only the careful working of restricted areas by many workers over many years could lead to safe generalizations. It is no wonder that he remained pessimistic; the thought alone of the data from thousands of past cultures, lost forever, must have haunted him. And what if one did finally recognize the "emergence" of a generalization from all the material that had been collected and compared for many years? The data from the very next culture that came under investigation might refute it. This is the problem that all who invest everything in "pure induction" face, and it is the reason that modern science, popular opinion to the contrary, has never really practiced it.

To the day of his death, Boas was busy revising his material on the Kwakiutl, just as he had been doing sixty years earlier. This patient, indefatigable commitment to the establishment of precision and certainty in anthropology can be seen as his greatest contribution and his greatest weakness; for while it introduced a sorely needed discipline into the field, it also inhibited in him and in many of his students the speculative spirit and the accommodation to uncertainty that are indispensable to any science.

# BRONISLAW MALINOWSKI

## *THE MAN OF SONGS*

THE ABILITY TO UNDERSTAND very different kinds of people is often related to an innate lack of set values and standards. It is no accident that a great novelist like Balzac, who could penetrate and portray with impartial accuracy the character of bankers, prostitutes, and artists, was a moral relativist of psychopathic proportions. It is also no accident that the most successful field worker in the history of anthropology, Bronislaw Malinowski, was the most eccentric and controversial figure ever to enter the field of anthropology.

Malinowski recognized no boundaries. This trait infuriated professional anthropologists who wanted to establish an independent scientific discipline, but it won the confidence and trust of primitive peoples to a degree that has never been equaled. He ignored the academic partitioning of the field of human behavior into the cubicles of anthropology, sociology, and psychology, and moved freely from one medium to another according to the requirements of the problem. In the same spirit, he approached his primitive subjects free from intellectual or emotional preconception as to what constitutes the right way to live. His questions about individual behavior and cultural institutions were limited to: Does it work? How does it work? Why does it work? With these questions he founded the "functionalist" school of anthropology, and started the tradition of the "participant observer" in anthropological field work.

Malinowski was a natural "participant." He reveled in the unpredictable drama of human encounters. His home was usually crowded with students, friends, colleagues, and strangers. In fact, it was so crowded that his wife kept a house outside of London where she could escape the confusion periodically.

For Malinowski, however, a crowded house, like a large audience or a lively seminar, provided the ideal conditions for creative thought and work. The hand-to-hand combat and co-operation of the informal seminar was his favorite setting for teaching and research.

In contrast to his later life, Malinowski's childhood was a lonely one. He was an only child, and his father died when he was still a young boy. A lifelong attachment between mother and son began at that time. Until they were separated by the war, Malinowski's mother moved with him wherever he went and watched over him with affectionate care. His introduction to anthropology was from her lips, for she read to him for an entire year when an eye operation made it impossible for him to read at the very beginning of his career in anthropology. His mother's death in 1919, while a captive hostess to the Russian soldiers billeted in her house, was a tragedy from which he barely recovered.

Malinowski was born in Cracow, Poland, April 7, 1884. His father was a nobleman of the landed gentry, but followed an academic career as professor of Slavic philology at Jagiellon University, in Cracow. Malinowski's early education was at the King Jan Sobieski Public School. From there he entered the University at Cracow, where, in 1908, he received a Ph.D. degree in physics and mathematics. His degree was awarded with the highest honors in the Austrian Empire.[1]

---

[1] Cracow, a free city republic, was incorporated into the Austrian Empire in 1848.

A promising career in the physical sciences, which began with two years of study and research in Wilhelm Ostwald's laboratory of physical chemistry at Leipzig, was canceled by Malinowski's chance reading of Frazer's *Golden Bough*. Before he put down the last volume of that work, his career in the physical sciences had ended, and he had become dedicated to anthropology: "For no sooner had I begun to read this great work," wrote Malinowski, "than I became immersed in it and enslaved by it . . . and became bound to the service of Frazerian anthropology."

Unlike his idol and mentor, Sir James Frazer, Malinowski did not serve anthropology from the library. After four years of study, research, and writing at the London School of Economics, he set out on a field trip to Australia as secretary to a field expedition sponsored by the British Association for the Advancement of Science. He had been trained by the greatest field worker of the day, C. G. Seligman, who thought so highly of Malinowski's potential as an anthropologist that he had offered to have his own salary cut so that Malinowski could be hired for the faculty of the London School of Economics. Besides Seligman and Frazer, he had studied with Westermarck, Rivers, and Hobhouse in London. In 1913, he published his first book, *The Family Among the Australian Aborigines*. He was well qualified to make the field trip to Australia, and no anthropologist, before or since, made so much of his training and opportunities.

It was the accident of war, however, that determined the arrangement of Malinowski's life. "Accident" and "arrangement" are contradictory terms for most people; but there are others, like Malinowski, in whom flexibility and determination are so combined that chance takes a natural place in the causal chain of events.

Being an Austrian subject Malinowski had to be interned in Australia when war broke while he was on his way there. Instead of resigning himself to enforced idleness he persuaded the Australian government to let him explore their territories during his internment. He was so convincing that the government even supplied him with funds to carry out his work.

Malinowski stayed in Australia for six years, and made three extensive field trips, one to Mailu (1915) and two to the Trobriand Islands (1915-1916 and 1917-1918). The field work in Australia was the crucial experience for Malinowski's career. He lived like a native, and with the natives experienced directly the demands and comforts of their culture. His celebrated intolerance toward a relatively academic anthropology (based on historical reconstruction, distribution studies, and other impersonal investigations), was rooted in this experience.

Malinowski was married in Melbourne in 1919 to Elsie Rosaline Masson, the daughter of a well-known professor of chemistry, Sir David Masson. They left Australia shortly after their marriage and went to the Canary Islands for a year of relaxation and quiet work. Malinowski had become seriously ill in Australia, after he had received word of his mother's death.

In 1921 the Malinowskis, who now had a daughter, moved to Cassise where they lived for two years while Malinowski studied and prepared his work for publication. They then bought a house in the north of Italy from which Malinowski commuted regularly to London. He accepted the position of Reader in Social Anthropology at the University of London in 1924 and the chair of Anthropology there in 1927. The family, which had been enlarged by the birth of two more daughters, moved to London in 1929. Here, Malinowski could be closer to his students and colleagues and participate in the active social life which he always enjoyed.

Malinowski had visited the United States in 1926 and had worked during the summer of that year at the University of California. By the time of his second visit in 1933, as a lecturer at Cornell University, he was known as a famous teacher, anthropologist, and scientist whose works had been translated into a half-dozen languages and who had trained some of the best anthropologists in the field. He had also become a popular lecturer of wide appeal who had interested many laymen and scientists from other fields in anthropology.

In 1936 he was selected to represent the University of London and the Polish Academy at the Harvard Tercentenary. He was hailed there as "an anthropological explorer who initiated a new movement for the study of the gregarious habits of the human race." His popular lecture on "Culture" was attended by an overflow crowd, and hundreds of people had to be turned away despite the fact that other famous men, among them Sir Arthur Eddington, were lecturing at the same time.

Back in England in 1937, Malinowski became sick again and in 1938 left for the United States to spend his Sabbatical in Arizona. The Second World War started in 1939 as Malinowski was preparing to return to Europe. He decided to stay in the United States and took a position on the faculty at Yale. He made a study of the Zapotec of Mexico in 1940 and 1941. On May 15, 1942, Malinowski presided as President at the opening of the Polish Institute of Arts and Sciences. He died suddenly of a heart attack the next day at his home in New Haven, Connecticut.


WHILE it is a commonplace that a man's work is always some kind of expression of his personality, this is especially true of Malinowski, and the fact needs special emphasis. Malinowski was a man of great enthusiasm and directness who evoked strong and impassioned responses from other people; his personality and his work have always been the subject of heated controversy.

His success in dealing with the natives of the villages he studied and in reporting their most guarded thoughts and sentiments—talents which placed his ethnographical reports on a new level of descriptive excellence—must, in large part, be attributed to Malinowski's extremely sensitive nature. His curiosity and sympathy extended to all people and was spontaneous and intuitive as well as analytical. His likes and dislikes for other people were equally strong and freely indulged; one always knew where one stood with Malinowski. He had great talent for getting people to talk about themselves. His eldest daughter, Jozefa, recalls how, in a café in Italy, Malinowski soon had the large family of the proprietor around him pouring out information about themselves and their town. If he became bored with such a session, however, he would simply get up and walk away, the interview ending as abruptly as it had started. Malinowski was always free of the social niceties which at times interfere with the communication of thoughts and feelings between people, and although classed as eccentric in his own society, this freedom undoubtedly contributed to his great success in winning the confidence and loosening the tongues of those in whom he was interested. As an observer, he was especially alert to the nuances of human behavior which can elude the well-trained, conscientious, but less sensitive worker, and which are indispensable to an accurate report of a people.

From his own experience in life Malinowski was aware of the hidden motives which can influence human behavior and was conscious of the necessity of looking for them in studying other people. He practiced this motive hunting in all his personal, as well as professional, relationships. On one occasion, for example, he and his daughters were embroiled in a bitter quarrel five minutes after they met for the first time in a year and a half. At the height of the argument, which had to do with whether they should go to some fancy place to eat, as the girls wanted, or to a quiet place, where Malinowski could have all their attention, he withdrew himself and calmly analyzed the argument in terms of their respective, hidden motives.

According to Raymond Firth, an old and favorite student of his, Malinowski often behaved this way during a heated argument: "And if a crisis arose—because one could argue fiercely with him at times—he had a most disarming way of suddenly putting aside all emotion, and spreading the whole thing out on the table, as it were, for analysis of his own motives as well as those of the other person."

This capacity for objective, unemotional analysis was the fulcrum for two emotional extremes in Malinowski.

Although usually charming, witty, and optimistic, he was subject to moods of severe depression. He imagined himself besieged by illness and disease, and defended himself with ritualistic diets and exercises. His most feared and persistent fantasy was that he would end up in a workhouse.

Malinowski's revolt against orthodoxy began at an early age without apparent turmoil. His mother was a Catholic, and he was strictly reared in the Catholic tradition. One day, when he was a young man at Cracow, an elderly Jew in a railway carriage asked him why he "believed"; not having a satisfactory answer, Malinowski became an agnostic —and remained one. He was often a source of embarrassment to his daughters, whom he would not allow to be christened until they were old enough to make a mature decision for themselves. At the Church of England schools which they attended from time to time Malinowski would not dress "properly" on his visits nor attend the chapel services, which bored him. After a broadcast over the B.B.C. in which he proclaimed his agnosticism, the Salvation Army left religious tracts on the family doorstep.

Although Malinowski could not accept any kind of formal religion for himself, he argued eloquently for the importance of religion in society. He states, in one place: "A sound social life must be based upon a truly religious system of values, that is, one which reflects the revelation to us of the existence of spiritual and moral order." This kind of "inconsistency" was common with Malinowski. He was, for example, an enthusiastic advocate of "progressive education," but would not permit his daughters to be so educated, and said that he would not permit children reared in progressive schools above the first floor of his own house. What was good for society was not necessarily good for Malinowski. As a student of society, he seemed to consider himself free of the cultural imperatives which interfere with an objective analysis of one's own society.

Malinowski did not simply disdain the usual customs and proprieties, he took a positive pleasure in violating them, and there are many anecdotes concerning his unusual behavior. His daughter recalls that he would often dictate while lying in bed with his pajama tops on and the bottoms wrapped around his head. Firth remembers the time Malinowski was found lying on the floor of the gallery at the Covent Garden Opera House during a performance of *Das Rheingold.* When asked about his strange behavior Malinowski retorted: "One wants to *hear* Wagner, not to see fat Rhine Maidens."

From the fragmentary accounts of Malinowski's personality one gets the over-all impression of an unspoiled, or some might say, unsocial, child: he had great energy and used it recklessly; he was intensely curious; he could be tender or nasty, according to his true feelings; he could penetrate the disguised feelings of others; and he was always candid. These traits, together with a sympathy that, as Marett puts it, "could find its way to the heart of the shyest savage," played a large part in his legendary success as a field worker. Never securely tied to his own culture, Malinowski was better able to perceive the ideas, attitudes, and feelings of those in a foreign culture. He seemed a true cosmopolitan.

Although acutely sensitive, Malinowski was not a sentimentalist and he could not tolerate a naive, unrealistic attitude toward the world. He was scornful of any attempts to achieve success by intuition or faith and, although his own intuitions often suggested fruitful ideas and lines of inquiry, he scrutinized his own work and methods constantly for uncertainty, vagueness, and inconsistency. He seemed to combine the qualities of the poet and the scientist; the qualities, that is, that are commonly attributed to these not so different types.

Malinowski was a popular teacher and lecturer. His influence as a teacher and a popularizer was at least as great as that which emanated from his writings. His success as a teacher was, in many ways, due to the personality traits which made him such a successful field worker. He had an intense enthusiasm for anthropology and often appeared as a combative advocate for some definite and usually controversial point of view. His students often pictured him as a gladiator fighting heroically and brilliantly for a new or unpopular method, idea, or interpretation.

According to one of his favorite students, Audrey Richards, it was the intensity of his work that made the strongest impression on his students. Along with naïveté, Malinowski deplored above all an incapacity for, or an indifference toward, hard work and would not tolerate the signs of either in his students. He conceived of his students and himself as a unit, a team which would devote its entire energy to the solution of the most difficult problems. Those that could not, or would not, contribute their share were left behind.

It was easy for Malinowski to sustain a genuine enthusiasm in front of his students, because he ignored the University Curriculum and his classes worked only on the problems that interested him at the time. This practice may have resulted in the neglect of a comprehensive body of factual material, but it had the great advantage of introducing students to the methods and theories of anthropology at the frontiers of the field. Since there was always something important to Malinowski at stake in these classes and seminars, his zeal was great, if unpredictable. In any mood, he was always direct and provocative. Audrey Richards remarks that whether his pupils were "irritated by his intolerance, or inspired by his enthusiasm . . . They were never bored."

Malinowski preferred the informality of the seminar to the formality of the lecture room, although he was brilliant at both. He was always looking for the "general problem" which was at the bottom of any inquiry or study, and insisted on finding it in a "fundamental human situation." Malinowski considered this "coefficient of reality," as he jokingly called it (according to Firth), of the greatest importance to an understanding of our own society. It was, he said, the main justification for anthropology.

Malinowski's functional studies of culture, studies which always breathed life into their subjects, attracted students from all over the world and from many disciplines to his seminars. Colonial administrators, university lecturers, and beginning students would sit side by side and participate with Malinowski in four or five different languages. There were no barriers to communication, linguistic or personal. "There was nothing," says M. F. Ashley Montagu, one of his first students, "of the stuffed shirt about him; he put you at your ease at once, and made you feel that you and he were going to have a fascinating time exploring human nature together."

As a lecturer, Malinowski won a wide popular audience for anthropology. Kluckhohn, who holds serious reservations about Malinowski's over-all contributions, admits that "thousands of laymen in many countries came to entertain with fervor the attitude of an anthropology whose methods, purposes, and results had at last become intelligible." At meetings and conferences Malinowski was usually the center of a stormy interest. Richards quotes a missionary as saying: "Invite Malinowski to the opening session of a conference, half the audience will disagree with him violently, but the discussions will go with a swing from the start." And Braunholtz recalls that Malinowski "never failed to stimulate and enliven our discussions, occasionally prolonging them to a late hour. For he was a remarkably fluent and witty speaker, often provocative, never dull."

For some, however, especially among the professional anthropologists, Malinowski was not such a great or exciting figure. Kluckhohn states that to many anthropologists, including the majority of American professionals, "Malinowski appeared a little better than a pretentious Messiah of the credulous." He was accused of simply "capitalizing on the obvious" and advancing as new ideas those which other anthropologists, for example, Boas, had been quietly advocating for years. To these critics Malinowski's wit and light touch, which so delighted a popular audience, were in poor taste. A remark like, "The eating up of decrepit parents is a good method of old-age insurance, while expressing fully an appreciation of one's progenitors," was considered more flippant than entertaining or enlightening by certain anthropologists.

There is no doubt that, as a personality, Malinowski had

a great influence on the history of anthropology. All of his work—his field work, his theories, his teachings, and his popularizations—reflected the power of his personality.

THE EARLY background for Malinowski's work was broad and varied. His training as a chemist served as an introduction to the disciplines of physical science, and he never got over an uneasiness about the multiple assumptions and secondary inferences so common in the social sciences. His early anthropological readings (especially the works of Frazer), while they must have offended his sense of rigor, stimulated in him an enthusiasm for anthropology. At London he became acquainted with such men as Frazer, Westermarck, C. S. Seligman, W. H. R. Rivers, Haddon, Prince Kropotkin, Havelock Ellis, Hobhouse, and Marett. Of these, he was especially influenced and stimulated by Westermarck, Seligman, Frazer, Rivers, and Haddon.

Durkheim's functional approach to the study of society impressed Malinowski very much, although he criticized the French sociologist and his followers for exaggerating the social nature of man and neglecting individual variation and innovation. He attempted to modify Durkheim's social functionalism with the psychological theories of Pavlow, Wundt, and later, Freud. But Durkheim's main idea —that one must always look for the cultural realities behind the institutionalized symbols in society—became the hallmark of Malinowski's work.

An early enthusiasm for the psychoanalytic theories of Freud, Rivers, Jung, and Jones did not last very long. He found their claims "exorbitant," their arguments "chaotic," and their terminology "tangled." But he still expressed an indebtedness to them for a "dynamic theory of mind," and valued their concentration on child psychology and "life history." He also appreciated their candid treatment of sex. It was characteristic of Malinowski's receptivity of mind that, while he remained a behaviorist in his psychology, he made a useful synthesis of psychoanalytic doctrines in much of his field work. According to Kluckhohn, Malinowski "could translate from one intellectual idiom to another with matchless lucidity." Studies of the family and kinship, studies which required the integration of several theories and methods of inquiry, suited Malinowski's interests and talents very well.

Malinowski insisted on relegating the methods of evolutionary anthropology to a minor role in the analysis of culture. Cultural processes are subject to laws, but the laws are to be found "in the function of the real elements of culture," not in the "survivals" upon which the evolutionists reconstruct the stages and processes of culture.

This departure from evolutionary theory was not new with Malinowski. Functionalism had become popular in many fields by Malinowski's time and was influencing work in science, government, philosophy, and the arts. Malinowski himself traces the functional view of culture as far back as Bastian and cites many names and "schools" as having contributed to the view. Among those he mentions are Tylor, Robertson Smith, Wundt, Frazer, Westermarck, Marett, Boas, Wissler, Kroeber, Lowie, Radin, Sapir, Benedict, and the French sociologists. With himself, however, he names only the following as having applied the functional method systematically and exclusively in ethnological field work: W. Hoernle, Radcliffe-Brown, and R. Thurnwald. Lowie names Bachofen, Fustel de Coulanges, and Boas as having made significant contributions to the study of cultures in their "intertwined state" and goes on to state that "probably everywhere scholars have followed the practice intuitively." This, however, is a little like saying that in formulating the law of gravity, Newton only made explicit what everyone knew "intuitively." Somewhat more generous is Lowie's conclusion, that, while others had preached *or* practiced the "faith of functionalism," Malinowski did both.

However indebted he may have been to others for his functionalism, Malinowski was certainly the one who made the integrated study of culture a popular method in anthropology. The unusual length of time he spent in the Trobriand Islands, living as a Trobriand, convinced him that a culture can be understood only by an intimate knowledge of how the individual experiences his cultural environment.

Malinowski's methodology was based on the conviction that there exist "scientific laws of culture." It is essential in a scientific theory that its assumptions be made explicit and its refutation made easy by conceivable testing and analysis. Malinowski always attempted to state his theories so that they conformed to this rule.

Although he defined anthropology as the "comparative science of cultures," Malinowski was often critical of the use made of the comparative method by the evolutionary anthropologists. He was especially critical of the concept of survival, which played such a crucial part in evolutionary reconstruction. He could not accept the implication that an institution can outlive its function and pointed out that so-called survivals disappear as we learn more about a society and the specific cultural context of a given institution. In a typical polemic Malinowski suggests how "survivals" can be misleading: "Marriage in the past did not consist merely in the eating together of fish and hard-boiled eggs, nor in the tossing of rice, nor yet in the wagging of rods or green trees. There is no reason, therefore, to assume that because in some tribes the marriage act consists in a mimic capture, capture in dead earnest was the origin of marriage."

Malinowski shared Tylor's concern that anthropology not become preoccupied with "savage exoticisms" and urged that anthropology emerge from its "Herodotage" (coined from Herodotus) and "anecdotage." But, contrary to Tylor, it was the reliance on survivals that Malinowski feared would help perpetuate a distorted view of primitive societies. Society, for Malinowski, consisted of a body of institutions related to the current adaptive needs of man, and it is the study of these institutions—economic and political systems, education, law, religion, science, family organization—and the individual's relationship to them that must take precedence over historical reconstruction, whether in the hands of the evolutionists or the diffusionists.

While admitting that careful, sober, and limited evolutionary reconstructions and diffusionist hypotheses could be profitable, if secondary, enterprises, Malinowski made no such allowance for so-called "tribal-genius" studies. He criticized Boas and his students, such as Ruth Benedict, for fostering a concept of culture which was so general and vague as to defy any kind of scientific evaluation. Malinowski was uncompromising in his attack on this approach: "I have again and again indicated that it is illegitimate to cover our inability to deal with certain facts by such mystic labels as the 'genius of culture,' or to describe this 'genius' as Appollonian, Dionysiac, megalomaniac, or hysterical." And in another place: "We might feel that it would be best to paint the warlike Masai in exaggerated colors in order to bring out the martial, boisterous, licentious 'genius' of the culture."

Malinowski's criticism of the evolutionists, diffusionists, patternists, and others, must be seen against the background of his intense crusade for an individual functionalism in anthropology. Malinowski was an "advocate"; he exaggerated the weaknesses of opposing schools and overlooked or minimized their contributions. It would be better, therefore, to turn to his own affirmative views, rather than to dwell, as some have, upon his excessive and sometimes unfair criticism of competing schools of thought.

Malinowski has defined in many places the functional method in anthropology. One of the clearest general statements is the following: "The functional view of culture lays down the principle that in every type of civilisation, every custom, material object, idea and belief fulfills some vital function, has some task to accomplish, represents an indispensable part within a working whole." The functionalist, according to Malinowski, is concerned primarily with the present workings of human culture, not with "ambitious but questionable reconstructions of the past." Cultural laws—the relations that exist between individual needs and social institutions—can be discovered only through a comparative study of cultures where the individual is seen in his day-to-day adaptations, both physical and mental. Malinowski's creed and advice was, "never to forget the living, palpitating flesh and blood organism of man which remains somewhere at the heart of every institution." The history of an institution, its form and distribution, its evolution and diffusion—all these problems are of secondary importance. The important questions are, How does an institution function *now?* How does it satisfy individual and cultural needs in the given society, and How is it related to other institutions?

Malinowski defines functionalism more specifically as "the theory of transformation of organic—that is, individual—needs into derived cultural necessities and imperatives. Society, by the collective wielding of the conditioning apparatus, molds the individual into a cultural personality."

The human individual has certain basic, physiological needs which require organized, collective responses from the members of a society. These include the need for food, shelter, safety, relaxation, movement, growth, and reproduction. The organized responses to these "basic imperatives"—the commissariat for nutrition; shelter and dress for bodily comfort; protective devices and organizations for safety; marriage and the family for reproduction—represent another, derived order of conditions which must be dealt with by the members of society. The acquisition of food, for example, requires a more or less complicated economic system where the production, processing, exchange, and distribution of food is regulated by certain social rules; proper shelter requires co-operative endeavor and communal consent regarding production, maintenance, and style; mating and parenthood must be regulated by social rules which define the rights and obligations of the persons involved to each other and to the other members of the community, and so on. Thus the great institutions of society—economic, political, legal, educational, and social —are seen by Malinowski as responses to the problems of adaptation posed by the more or less direct collective responses to the basic, physiological needs of man.

Then there is a third order of imperatives, the "integrative" or "synthetic imperatives," which result in the creation of systems of science, magic, myth, religion, and art. These, too, can be traced, although less directly, to man's organic needs. Of all living creatures man alone can accumulate experiences, reflect on them, and use them to foretell the future. These capacities make man the tragic hero that he is; they reveal new possibilities and opportunities with each generation, but they also reveal man's relative impotence and leave him striving for more than he can rationally expect to receive. Systems of knowledge, such as *science*, serve to organize and integrate human activities, so that, by the wise use of past experience, the present and the future may be made to better serve the needs of man. The gaps in man's knowledge and power create anxiety and hesitation, and here *magic* can be employed as a substitute for rational systems and give man the courage to act, even without perfect knowledge. *Myth* enhances social tradition by endowing it with awesome and glorified beginnings and thus promotes, sustains, and integrates appropriate social behavior. *Religion* promotes individual security and social cohesion by sanctifying human life and making public (by dogma and ritual) the social contracts of co-operative existence. Malinowski sees *art* as satisfying the "craving of the human organism for combinations of blended sense impressions," whether in the rhythms of bodily movement or in the blending of tones, colors, and forms.

Malinowski regarded his functionalism as differing from other social theories in its emphasis on basic bodily needs. The intellectual, emotional, and aesthetic aspects of man's behavior—the "higher side" of man's activities and the primary concern of most students—must also be seen as rooted in man's physiological needs.

Social or cultural commands, whether in the form of legal or moral codes, religious rites, economic regulation, customs, or aesthetic taste, are the re-interpretations of organic drives and impulses. They must so shape individual motives that the individual unconsciously behaves in a manner which satisfies the conditions of cultural survival and harmony. Malinowski states here (contrary to Frazer), that "Sociological aims are never present in the minds of natives, and tribal legislation on a large scale could never have occurred."

It is the job of the anthropologist to discover the specific functions of the elements of a culture within the integrated scheme as outlined above. Malinowski's celebrated field work was devoted to that end.

For a caricature of earlier authorities on primitive peoples Malinowski cites the response of one of them to a question about the manners and customs of certain natives: "Customs none, manners beastly." Although Malinowski's work does not in any way represent the first advance beyond the approach ridiculed here, he was the first worker to explicate and publicize the methods for investigating a primitive community in the role of a participant, with one's own cultural values left behind, in so far as that is possible.

The goal of all field work, according to Malinowski, is "to grasp the native's point of view, his relation to life, to realize *his* vision of *his* world"; or, as he often put it, "to get inside the native's skin." While it is necessary to banish all preconceived ideas about how a culture must or should function, it is just as necessary that the worker have some positive theoretical framework with which to "foreshadow" the problems. For Malinowski, this was functionalism, as outlined above.

Malinowski breaks scientific field work down into three areas:

1) *The organization of the tribe, and the anatomy of its culture* must be recorded in firm, clear outline. The method of *concrete, statistical documentation* is the means through which such an outline has to be given.

2) *Within this frame, the imponderabilia of actual life*, and the *type of behavior* have to be filled in. They have to be

collected through minute, detailed observations, in the form of some sort of ethnographic diary, made possible by close contact with native life.

*3*) A collection of ethnographic statements, characteristic narratives, typical utterances, items of folklore and magical formulae has to be given as a *corpus inscriptionum*, as documents of native mentality.

These three categories correspond, in Malinowski's functional scheme, to (1) the routine prescribed by custom and tradition, (2) the manner in which it is carried out, and (3) the commentary to the routine, as contained in the native's mind. Malinowski insisted upon "statistic documentation by concrete evidence" as the method for acquiring this information about a people, but not through the procedure of the fixed interview and the native interpreter. To get an integrated picture a community worker must learn the language, live with the people, share their food and customs, and learn, as far as possible, to feel and think as they do.

This is the doctrine of the "participant observer." A field trip for Malinowski had to be a profound personal experience; from what we know of his personality it could not have been anything else. For Malinowski there was an intense personal satisfaction in studying a foreign culture which transcended the mere satisfaction of scientific curiosity. He states: "To study the institutions, customs, and codes or to study the behavior and mentality without the subjective desire of feeling by what these people live, of realising the substance of their happiness—is, in my opinion, to miss the greatest reward which can hope to obtain from the study of man."[2]

The justification of this method does not lie in its personal satisfaction to the observer, it lies in the fact that it is the only way to central insights about a people. Malinowski claims, for example, that he discovered the function

[2] Malinowski was known as The Man of Songs to the Trobriand Islanders, a simple but convincing testimony to his successful identification with the natives.

of magic when, as a frightened participant in a hurricane in Melanesia, he observed the work of a magician ordering the hurricane to stop and assuring the natives that no harm could come to the village: "I realized then and there what the real function of magic is. On the psychological side it leads to a mental integration, to that optimism and confidence in the face of danger which has won to man many a battle with nature or with his human foes. Socially, magic, by giving leadership to one man, establishes organization at a time when organized and effective action is of supreme importance."

More persuasive, however, than this personal testimonial, are Malinowski's examples of how, and how not, to get information. Do not, he urges, ask a native, "How do you treat and punish a criminal? . . . a real case indeed will start the natives on a wave of discussion, evoke expressions of indignation, show them taking sides—all of which will probably contain a wealth of definite views, of moral censures, as well as reveal the social mechanism set in motion by the crime committed." Malinowski gives some amusing descriptions of himself at work with this method: ". . . as they knew that I would thrust my nose into everything, even where a well mannered native would not dream of intruding, they finished by regarding me as part and parcel of their life, a necessary evil or nuisance, mitigated by donations of tobacco."

Although it is probably fair to describe Malinowski's method, as Kluckhohn has, as "the well-documented anecdote set firmly in a ramified context," it would be a mistake to attribute to him a lack of real scientific aims. He was convinced that cultural laws existed and that it was the primary job of the anthropologist to discover them. The job demanded more than a sensitive, intuitive participant; it demanded the patient and thorough collection and recording of vast amounts of ethnological detail, all according to a system dictated by theoretical considerations. Malinowski's reports and books, with all their maps, charts, photographs, illustrations, and case histories, still do not indicate the mass of material on which they were constructed. Much of this material has never been published.

Malinowski's serious field work was limited to the Trobriand Islands which he studied more or less intensively for six years. Although criticized as being an "ethnographic provincial" (by Lowie) and as having only a superficial knowledge of other ethnological data (by Kluckhohn), the field methods Malinowski practiced and publicized have a universal value and have been widely adopted, largely through his influence.

Before discussing Malinowski's specific ideas and theories regarding religion, magic, myth, and the family, reference should be made again to his general theory of culture.

To promote a functional analysis of society Malinowski found it necessary to define and distinguish the various elements in society. While it is true, as noted above, that other workers had, to one degree or another, employed a functional approach in their studies, Malinowski was the first anthropologist to formulate consciously and explicitly a theoretical basis for functional anthropology.

He defines *culture* as that "instrumental reality which has come into existence to satisfy the needs of man in a manner far surpassing any direct adaptation to the environment." A culture can be analyzed into *institutions*, which are defined as "a group of people united in a common task or tasks, bound to a determined portion of the environment, wielding together some technical apparatus, and obeying a body of rules." It is only by studying institutions that the worker gets a concrete picture of the social organization within a culture. Institutions are the structural units of culture. Institutions—not traits, forms, ideas, or adventitious complexes of these elements—are what diffuse and evolve, while maintaining a basic integrity. They exist to satisfy, directly or indirectly, the biological needs of man and must be studied with that central idea in mind.

Malinowski's functional approach to cultural studies marked a formal departure from the anatomical approach of many earlier anthropologists. By focusing attention on the actual behavior of the members of a community, Malinowski's institutional method resulted in a more integrated description and analysis of society. Instead, for example, of merely juxtaposing the data on dwelling construction and the data on family life, the two are considered together in the light of the functional relations which exist between them.

The key institution by which the instinctive drives of the individual are modified so as to satisfy the conditions of community survival is the family. The family, for Malinowski, is a kind of placenta through which the biological individual acquires the accumulated products of culture and is molded into a social individual. Malinowski was convinced that monogamous marriage provides the best foundation for the crucial functions of the family. It permits the most satisfactory form of sexual selection and fosters the kind of personal attachments by which the biological bonds of the family, especially between parent and child, are gradually transformed into social ties. "Love relations in the family," says Malinowski, "serve as prototypes and also as a nucleus for the loyalties of clanship, of neighborly feeling and of tribal citizenship." He cites authorities from anthropology and psychoanalysis in support of this view, including Lowie, Kroeber, Radcliffe-Brown, Freud, and Flügel. Recognition of this important function of the family was not, of course, new with these men; Darwin, in particular, had shown a very keen appreciation of the intermediary function of the family.

In focusing his attention on the family Malinowski was led to testing the psychoanalytic theories of Freud in the field. Although he found many of Freud's specific formulations inadequate and unsupported by comparative ethnological data, he considered Freud's general doctrine of repression as providing the first useful theory as to the functional relations between the instinctive life of the individual and social institutions.

When Malinowski showed (to his satisfaction) that in the matrilineal societies of Eastern New Guinea the Oedipus complex is absent, he claimed to have verified the main tenets of Freudian psychology; for when the relations between individuals within the family are basically changed there should, if Freud is right, be a change in the repressed desires, or so Malinowski argued. In these matrilineal societies it is the maternal uncle, instead of the father, who is the powerful male figure in the family and the agent of authority. It is the uncle, not the father, whom the boy is to succeed as a figure of power and authority. The father, on the other hand, represents no threat at all to the boy. He is not an instrument of authority and seldom interferes with the child's activities; he is more a friend and understanding helper. But what is even more significant, since it goes to the heart of the Oedipal theory, is Malinowski's assertion that these Melanesians are ignorant of the father's role in paternity. Malinowski argues that if Freud is right in his main idea then one would expect that in these societies the familiar constellation in the young male of awe, respect, fear, jealousy, hatred, and envy would be directed against the uncle, and that the incest taboo would center on the brother-sister relationship. And that, according to Malinowski, is precisely what occurs. The evidence for these attitudes is found not only in ordinary social life, but, what is perhaps more important, in the folklore of these people as reflected in myth, fairy tale, legend, and magic. It is also found in an examination of individual dreams and obsessions.

As a functionalist, Malinowski welcomed the offer of Freudian psychology to provide a way for understanding the functional relations between folklore and social organization. He had high hopes for applying Freud's main insights to anthropology and wrote, in 1923, that Freud's "doctrine of repression due to social influence allows us to explain certain typical latent wishes or 'complexes,' found in folklore by reference to the organisation of a given society. Inversely it allows us also to trace the pattern of instinctive and emotional tendencies in the texture of the social fabric." His subsequent disillusionment with psychoanalysis stemmed from what he observed as an inflexible attachment of psychoanalysts to the details of Freud's doctrines, often to the neglect of his basic insights. When Ernest Jones argued that the denial of the father's paternity, the hatred of the uncle, and the taboos on brother-sister relations all functioned to direct attention away from the father-son rivalry in matrilineal societies, Malinowski was amused and sarcastic. He takes Jones' analysis as a validation of his own conclusions; namely, "that in mother-right the family complex must be different from the Oedipus complex; that in the matrilineal conditions the hate is removed from the father and placed upon the maternal uncle; that any incestuous temptations are directed towards the sister rather than towards the mother." To ascribe this to the "repression of the Oedipus complex," as he interprets Jones to have done, is just double talk to Malinowski. He asks, "Is there a sub-unconscious and what does the concept of repressed repression mean?" Malinowski would not accept the Oedipus complex, or any other single condition, as the "unique source of culture, of organization and belief . . . prior to all things and not caused by anything." For Malinowski, the family complex was always a "functional formation dependent upon the structure and upon the culture of society."

Although magic and religion are less directly related to biological needs than other social institutions, they are the "very foundations of culture," says Malinowski. Religion, especially, was seen by him as a basic integrative force in society.

The urgency with which the individual denies his mortality and strives to perpetuate personal attachments beyond earthly life has its origin, according to Malinowski, in the culturally determined "human sentiments." These sentiments, or emotions, are the structural elements of social cohesion, and must be fostered and maintained by social institutions. Religion, by giving supernatural and public sanction to the beliefs, attitudes, and values which comprise a social morality and make social cohesion possible, affirms and reinforces the human sentiments which morality requires.

Religion, therefore, does not arise out of illusion, speculation, or misapprehension, but as a response to the needs of cultural survival. It is an integrative institution which conditions and compensates men for the individual sacrifices required by social existence.

Malinowski contradicted his idol, Sir James Frazer, on the function of magic in society. Magic does not represent primitive science, as Frazer believed, but, on the contrary, it represents the recognition by people that human art and knowledge have definite limits. Thus, as Malinowski says, "magic and practical art are entirely independent and never fuse." It is when crucial events appear completely beyond human control and influence that magic is called upon to provide illusory gratifications. The practice of magic is a substitute activity which, in the absence of any realistic solution to vital problems, gives at least psychological support to the individual and helps to prevent submission or disintegration. Its value and validity, then, is purely subjective, but it satisfies a real biological need. As mentioned earlier (p. 178), magic can also serve to organize a community in the face of a crisis by virtue of investing one or a few men with authority and leadership.

For Malinowski, magic and religion take their places alongside of rational knowledge as the foundations of culture: "Knowledge, magic and religion are the highest, the most derived imperatives of human culture. . . . Magic and to a much higher degree religion are the indispensable moral forces in every human culture. Grown, as they are, out of the necessity to remove internal conflict in the individual and to organize the community, they become the essential factors of spiritual and social integration. They deal with problems which affect all members of the community alike. They lead to actions on which depends the welfare of one and all. Religion and to a lesser degree magic thus became the very foundations of culture."

IT IS not easy to estimate Malinowski's importance in anthropology. He has been such a controversial figure as a personality that most commentators are inclined, or forced, to take a "for" or "against" position regarding his contributions. Generally speaking, his ethnological reports and his pioneer work in field methods and techniques have been acclaimed by almost all workers as belonging among the greatest contributions to cultural anthropology. But regarding his theoretical conceptions there is less agreement.

In this country Lowie and Kluckhohn have been Malinowski's chief detractors. Of these, Lowie is the more severe. He compares Malinowski with Boas on several counts and finds that Boas either anticipated Malinowski or surpassed him in insight. The only "positive achievement" that Lowie singles out is Malinowski's use of psychoanalytic concepts in his ethnographic work. Even in the area of field techniques, where few contest Malinowski's importance and priority, Lowie simply observes that his techniques "conformed to Boas' standards." Rising to a passion unmatched in the rest of his book (*History of Ethnological Theory,* 1937), Lowie writes: "In Messianic mood Malinowski is forever engaged in two favorite pastimes. Either he is battering down wide open doors or he is petulantly deriding work that does not personally attract him." And Lowie goes on: "Malinowski thumbs his nose at technology, flaunts distribution studies, sneers at reconstruction of the past. . . . In short, Malinowski's functionalism is avowedly antidistributional, antihistorical, and treats each culture as a closed system except insofar as its elements correspond to vital biological urges." Such an extreme condemnation by a responsible and conservative commentator must be partly attributed to Malinowski's provocative personality. Lowie himself softens his criticism by adding that "Malinowski's practice fortunately does not bear out the negative excrescences of his principle."

Kluckhohn credits Malinowski with great literary skill and the ability to dramatize field work. He also approves of Malinowski's contributions to our knowledge of the family, religion, economics, and law. Kluckhohn's chief criticism is of Malinowski's lack of "theoretical profundities." Malinowski is not subtle enough for Kluckhohn. He complains that Malinowski has "no flair for the intricate, tortuous [and precious] subtleties," and that he is only an integrator, "on a rather superficial level."

Such a general criticism is hard to evaluate. Physicists before Newton were too involved with the "subtleties" of moving objects on earth to look at the sky and bring all moving bodies under one general, unsubtle, law. One must look at Malinowski's work for himself and decide whether or not his "integrations" are superficial.

Herskovits agrees with Lowie that Malinowski's major contribution was the extension and modification of Freud's work in its application to cultural data. For his field work, Herskovits credits Malinowski with making explicit, if not inventing, field methods and procedures which facilitated a scientific treatment of anthropological data. And for his doctrine of the "participant observer," he credits Malinowski with "a real departure from the usage of many earlier students of culture. . . ." On the theoretical side, Herskovits singles out Malinowski's understanding of the family as "a link between instinctive endowment and the acquisition of cultural inheritance," as a major insight.

Peter Murdock, whose relations with Malinowski were sometimes stormy, ranks him with Morgan, Tylor and Boas in anthropology, and considers him to be one of the great innovators in the "behavioral sciences of man," standing with Adam Smith, Marx, Sumner, Freud, and Pavlov. He credits Malinowski with the establishment, in anthropology, of the concept of social institutions, which are the collective responses to basic human needs.

Perhaps one of the reasons that there is such a diversity of opinion among anthropologists regarding Malinowski's work is that he attempted to utilize ideas from other fields, particularly sociology and psychology. To many of the avowed specialists in the social sciences, "eclectic" is a bad word, and Malinowski respected no territorial limits in his study of man and society. If Malinowski's work is important, it is largely due to the use he made of sociological and psychological insights and techniques.

Malinowski's reputation and influence have been greater

in England than in the United States. In England he stands with Radcliffe-Brown as the standard bearer of functionalism in anthropology. His empirical approach and untidy theoretical formulations have caused students to look to his work for field techniques and inspiration, but more to Radcliffe-Brown's work for a defensible theory of functionalism.

Malinowski's position in the history of anthropology has not been decided. Ultimately, it will depend on what course anthropology will take as a scientific discipline in the field of human behavior. If anthropology persists in its preoccupation with "precious subtleties" and in its suspicion of the "integrator," then Malinowski will become a forgotten hero. If, however, there should be a rebirth of the conviction that anthropology can provide the framework and perspective for an integrated study of man in his fight for survival and self-realization, then Malinowski will be listed as a great anthropologist. His passionate interest and involvement in the workaday drama of human life kept him always in touch with the basic problems of man's co-operative endeavors to survive and to get some pleasure out of life.

Malinowski died with important work still to do, and his untimely death was a great loss to the social sciences and to society. He was intensely devoted to anthropology, and behind this devotion was a passionate sympathy for the human individual.

# ALFRED LOUIS KROEBER

*MAN, WHALES, AND BEES*

ALFRED LOUIS KROEBER, when he died in October, 1960, at the age of eighty-four, was the dean of American anthropologists and still one of the hardest workers in the social sciences. His career in anthropology covered sixty years. In these days of specialization he was probably the last anthropologist whose interests and contributions extended over the entire range of anthropological subjects. He was one of the most respected anthropologists and scientists in the world.

Kroeber was born in Hoboken, New Jersey, June 11, 1876. Order and strict discipline prevailed in the household of Florence and Johanna (Mueller) Kroeber. The father was a prosperous wholesale clock dealer and was able to send Kroeber to the best tutors and schools in New York.

He started his schooling with a German scholar, Dr. Gabriel Bamberger, who became the first principal of the Ethical Culture School, known then as Workingman's School, an institution devoted to a rational, humanistic approach to religion. He spent three years with Dr. Bamberger and then entered Sachs' School, at the time one of the best preparatory schools in New York. After Sachs' School he spent two years at a boarding school in Connecticut, and entered Columbia College in 1892. He graduated from Columbia in 1896, received his A.M. degree a year later, and took his Columbia Ph.D. degree in 1901.

He worked as Assistant in Rhetoric at Columbia from 1897 to 1899, and then, under the influence of Boas, began his life's career with a Columbia Fellowship in anthropology. The profound and complicated influence of Boas on Kroeber's life and work began at this time. Carl L. Alsberg gives as Kroeber's argument for going into anthropology that here he could do the most to free man intellectually, to liberate him from "hoary tribal taboos," especially the taboos of religion. These were the same motives Boas gave for entering anthropology.

After receiving his Ph.D. in 1901 Kroeber went to California as Curator of Anthropology for the California Academy of Sciences to organize an anthropological study of the state. He was affiliated with the University of California in this project and later became instructor, assistant professor, associate professor, and finally full professor and curator, and director of the Anthropological Museum at that institution. He retired from the University of California in 1946, and became active as a visiting professor at several leading universities, including Columbia, Chicago, Harvard, and Brandeis.

An impressionistic view of Kroeber's life and work reveals a person with an extraordinary sense of discipline and order, but one who was sometimes unhappy and restless within this confinement. As a young boy he formed with a friend a "scientific society" which was devoted to the collecting of biological specimens and the preparation and reading of "scientific papers." The "society," eventually composed of about fifteen boys, was active until the boys were college sophomores. Although this preoccupation with serious matters persisted in Kroeber's college career, it was occasionally relieved by daring and reckless exploits. His close friend and classmate, Carl L. Alsberg, recalls that on one escapade Kroeber led a group of students to Central Park, where they painted red walrus mustaches and blue stockings on the statues. Alsberg described Kroeber as the most unconventional and boldest of his friends, whose daring reached the point of recklessness.

In college Kroeber spent most of his energies on English literature, philosophy, psychology, history, and anthropology. He was always independent in his thinking and observations and enjoyed, according to Alsberg, the role of "doubting Thomas" and "pricker of the other fellow's bubble."

However independent and unorthodox Kroeber may have been in college or in later years, his name is most prominently associated with the view that individual acts are irrelevant in the sweep of cultural history, which he sees as an "inspiring inevitability which rises as far above the accidents of personality as the march of the heavens transcend the wavering contacts of random footprints on clouds of earth." A clue to the interesting juxtaposition of Kroeber's personal independence and his "cultural determinism," as it has been called, can be found in his obituary of the anthropologist, Elsie Clews Parsons, in 1943. He mentioned there "the struggle of what she felt as self-preservation against family and environment . . ." and goes on to say that her discovery "that culture could be viewed in itself, not merely as a reflex or aspect of society; in fact was largely determinative of both society and individual . . . helped her to shelve her old feud on behalf of the personality against society . . . society probably came to seem less of an oppressor, more of a smokescreen or perhaps blind instrument of an impersonal culture beyond." The "discovery" to which Kroeber referred is his own formulation of the relationship of culture, society, and the individual.

Kroeber, along with many others, always had difficulty trying to reconcile the acts of the individual personality and the "impersonal culture beyond." He studied psychology under Cattell before entering anthropology, and later on underwent a brief control psychoanalysis in San Francisco. Although he gained "insights into the human mind" from this experience, he gave it up because, as he said, "I did not feel that these insights helped me appreciably to understand culture any better; which was one of the reasons I quit psychoanalysis—fearing the split of trying permanently to carry two professions that seemed irreconcilable."[1]

Until the last days of his life Kroeber was fit and alert. He carried himself very erectly and walked with a quick step. He wore a well-groomed beard, which in no way disguised the quizzical, searching expression of his face. In a class he engaged in discussion and debate with the students as if he were one of them—just beginning to find the problems of anthropology fascinating. His careful, respectful scrutiny of students' questions and opinions and his enthusiastic comments convinced one that he was as anxious to learn as he was to teach.

A few years ago he was invited to give a talk on Culture for the weekly departmental meeting of the Philosophy department at Columbia University. The Philosophy faculty and graduate students—a formidable and critical audience—found him a good match for their dialectical skills. At one point, however, a young student asked a question and made a comment. Kroeber's expression changed suddenly, as if he had come upon a new and important idea, and he seemed preoccupied for the remaining few minutes of the talk. When the professors and more precocious graduate students crowded around him at the end of the talk—after giving him an ovation—he kept looking around for the young questioner, and was not satisfied until he was promised that the student would be found and told to get in touch with him in order to discuss the problem that had been raised.

---

[1] His friend, Alsberg, is less charitable to psychoanalysis, stating that he quit because ". . . he soon saw that he lacked utterly any trace of the charlatan's gift, without some measure of which only a limited success can be achieved in this sort of practice."

This anecdote points up Kroeber's persistent, insatiable curiosity, a trait that kept him young and enthusiastic. Busy all his life, he always found time to listen to new ideas. Although conservative and careful in his own work, he had an interesting penchant for the daring and eccentric in the thinking of other people. Ideas and facts, rather than individuals, interested him the most. His interests here seem to have had no bounds, running, on one level, from whales to the "language" of bees.

His life and his work reflected a general aloofness from the individuals who made up the cultural forms, patterns, and styles that fascinated him. Although often described as aloof in his personal relationships, he was always known for scrupulous fairness and thoughtfulness in dealing with people. When William Duncan Strong, now chairman of the Department of Anthropology at Columbia University, needed a job in his senior year at California, Kroeber gave him some work on an archaeological study he was working on. Strong, who was not especially interested in anthropology at the time, did the routine work usually asked of a student assistant. When the job was completed Strong found that in addition to the thirty-five cents an hour and carfare that he had been paid, he was, with Kroeber, co-author of the work.

Toward the end of his life Kroeber seemed to become more interested in individuals. While previously he used to insist on studying civilization as an "entity in itself, and of another order from life," he came to admit that he had probably gone too far in the past in tending "to assume or look for immanent causality independent of the human carriers of culture." He spoke of wanting to "smuggle human nature back into the study of civilizations."

A corresponding interest appeared in his attitude toward the people he contacted in his personal and professional life. His ability, for example, to find hidden, saving virtues in the least promising students became well known to his colleagues. At an oral examination of a doctoral candidate at Columbia a few years ago, Kroeber left the room for a few minutes; one of the professors on the examination committee leaned over to his colleagues and said: "Quick, let's flunk him before Kroeber gets back."

KROEBER's work falls into two main categories: his ethnographical field work, and his theories on cultural progress and the philosophy of history. In ethnography his work is of undisputed excellence. His theories on culture and cultural history are controversial.

As a great ethnologist, Kroeber expertly covered many fields. He was an expert on such subjects as pottery shards, basketry, secret cults, and forms of arrow release. On these subjects, and many more, he could discourse at length and in great detail at a moment's notice. He was fascinated by facts and collected and recorded them assiduously, in the best tradition of Boas. His was the "inductive method," and he invested everything in it.

His *Handbook of the Indians of California* (1925) is the basic reference work in the field and established him as the recognized authority on California. It is one of the great modern ethnographies. The bulk of the work is, as Kroeber states in the Preface, "a series of tribal descriptions." It "attempts to be a history . . ." he says, "in that it tries to reconstruct and present the scheme within which these people in ancient and more recent times lived their lives." The "tribal descriptions" cover "some fifty little nations," with (except for a few chapters of summary and comparison) the general conclusions "strewn at random through the course of several hundred pages. . . ." For the casual reader looking for some interesting personal information and neat generalization, this work is bound to be a disappointment. For a hard working, serious student it is a mine of material, gathered intermittently over seventeen years. It is a model of responsible, scholarly field work and research. Although California was his special field, Kroeber was active in other ethnological areas, including North America, India, Southeast Asia, China, Korea, Japan, and Indonesia.

From his ethnological experience has come an important

refinement and extension of the "culture-area" concept, a concept first systematically used by the Americanist, Clark Wissler. It is a method by which social groups are classified according to similar culture traits and marked out as "culture areas." The discovery and study of certain relationships—such as that between material culture and physical environment—are facilitated by the use of this classification. In his mapping of the culture areas of North and South America Kroeber went farther than anyone else in depicting specific correlations between culture and ecology.

Kroeber went beyond the descriptive use of the "culture-area" concept and used it for "historic understanding." He introduced the concepts of "intensity" and "climax" to describe and evaluate the achievements and influence of the social groups in different parts of a culture area, and to show the relationships between culture areas. By *intensity* he refers to the ways by which cultures arrive at and maintain their cultural level, the more "intense" cultures being ones which are rich in cultural traits and where institutions and relationships are more precisely defined. The *climax* of a culture area is the most highly specialized and integrated "center"—or "focus"—of the area, which radiates its influence, in decreasing intensity, out to the margins of the area.

The statistical methods used by Kroeber to measure "culture intensification" are the inductive methods made popular by Boas, and first practiced systematically by Tylor. The measure of culture intensification can be found by counting the number of discrete cultural elements in a social group—the higher the number of elements the higher the degree of specialization—or it can be measured more "subjectively" by evaluating the styles of the institutions that, according to Kroeber, should be heavily weighted as sensitive cultural indicators. These would include the religious cults of a group, the decorative arts, music, intellectual endeavors, and kinship systems; that is, the institutions of "higher grade." Kroeber points out in one study that the "discrete-element or point count" gave results which tallied closely with an evaluation of characterizable patterns and styles in the "sensitive indicators." Kroeber inferred from such agreements that "cult specialization—by itself is an excellent indicator of total degree of culture specialization or climax in native California—or perhaps elsewhere." Kroeber inclined to believe that the more subjective method—the selection of sensitive indicators by qualitative weighting—was the safer guide to the "intensive manifestations of a civilization," although the two methods often yielded the same results.[2]

It is possible, according to Kroeber, to use the culture-area classification to discover historical relationships. His use of the method in this way established him as the leading exponent of modern diffusionism. His book *Configurations of Culture Growth* (1944) can be seen as a far-reaching extension of his modified concept of culture-areas. Before discussing this work it is necessary to give a more detailed explanation of his superorganic theory.

ALTHOUGH he retreated to some extent in recent years on the superorganic theory, the idea, as it appeared in 1917, dominated Kroeber's thinking in the field of culture. In part, the 1917 essay was a polemic against the social evolutionists, who, in the wake of the evolutionary theory in biology, had gone to the extreme in viewing society as an organism subject to "evolutionary laws." In his criticism of these nineteenth-century views Kroeber was expressing a popular view, at least among social scientists. Boas' famous paper, "The Limitations of the Comparative Method in Anthropology," had been written twenty-one years earlier, and was accepted as the classic refutation of the evolutionary method in anthropology. Kroeber, however, felt it necessary to further proclaim the independence of anthropology from biology. Later, in 1952, he reflected that his chief purpose in writing the paper was not to pro-

---

[2] In spite of its inductive garb this method is admittedly subjective, intuitive, and arbitrary in its premises. If the question is how "intense" a social group is, the method of "sensitive indicators" begs the question; for it seems to say, If you want to measure the intensive manifestations of a group, measure its intensities.

test an annexation of anthropology by biology, but rather to correct public opinion at large in its acceptance of organismic views of society. "It was the intelligent man in the street," he said in 1952, "and those who wrote for him, social philosophers like Herbert Spencer, Lester Ward, Gustave Le Bon—it was against their influence that I was protesting." Specifically, he was criticizing "a diffused public opinion, a body of unaware assumptions, that left precarious the autonomous recognition of society, and still more that of culture."

The paper, however, went beyond this counter-propaganda and presented a concept of culture that excluded the individual entirely. In doing this he used, ironically, a term coined by Herbert Spencer, "superorganic."

According to Kroeber's formulation there are three distinct levels of phenomena: the inorganic, the organic, and the superorganic (civilization). The superorganic began with the introduction of "culture" by primitive man, and at that point began a development that has been independent of, and uninfluenced by organic life. The exclusion of the organic applied to the human constituents of the superorganic level; the "accidents of personality" amounting to practically nothing in ". . . the presence of majestic forces or sequences pervading civilization. . . ."

Kroeber made special use of the multiple discoveries in science to support his view. The many examples of two or more men, such as Darwin and Wallace, arriving independently at the same idea suggested to Kroeber that it is the transcendent forces or sequences in civilization that produce such ideas, and that it is accidental through which individual it is expressed. This is what people mean, for example, when they say that a certain idea was "in the air," just waiting for someone to discover it.

In the light of what Kroeber wrote about the superorganic idea since 1917 it would be fair to ignore his more extreme statements on the independence of culture from individuals and say that he used the concept as a heuristic device to facilitate an objective, scientific study of culture. He believed it was necessary to separate levels of phenomena, and in doing so he created a gulf between the social and the psychic which he believed to be analogous to that which exists between the organic and the inorganic. By using statistical and probability theories he attempted to show that civilizations proceed according to laws and sequences that cannot be related to individual acts. He never denied the obvious truth that civilization is carried by and exists through human individuals.

The difficulty with even this heuristic use of the idea is that any explanation, in the scientific sense, is either abandoned or couched in terms of "majestic forces" and other providential phrases. It is the function of science not only to describe but to explain; description may be facilitated by Kroeber's theory, but it excludes explanation. Along with Boas, Kroeber failed to grasp completely the methods of the physical sciences which he had, in many ways, tried to emulate. He stated, for example, that the champions of the Copernican doctrine had it in their favor that "they dealt with phenomena to which exactitude was readily applicable, about which verification or disprovable predictions could be made, which an explanation either fitted or did not fit." This was not so at the time Copernicus presented his hypothesis, nor is it so with most new theories in the sciences. There was little to recommend the Copernican hypothesis at first beyond the fact that it was a simpler explanation for the movement of the heavens than was the Ptolemaic theory. It was no more susceptible of verification, no more useful for predictions, than the system of Ptolemy. Not until eighty years after it was advanced, when Galileo discovered with his telescope a satellite system around Jupiter and observed the phases of Mercury, Venus, and Mars, did the Copernican hypothesis receive indirect verification. It is interesting and revealing that Kroeber viewed his superorganic doctrine as an analogue to the Copernican hypothesis.

In recent years Kroeber attempted to justify the "provisional freezing of cultural phenomena as such on the cultural level. . . ." by invoking Aristotle's "formal" and "efficient" causes to correspond to the cultural and individual levels, respectively. But for Aristotle science must tell us both *that* things are so and *why* they are so. A commitment to formal causes commits you to efficient causes, according to Aristotle, and you cannot, like Kroeber, simply say that you are not interested in efficient causes, that is, in individual acts. In Book II of the *Physics* Aristotle points out that it is permissible for the mathematician to separate form and matter, and to study form only, in terms of odd, even, straight, and curved; but the scientist who studies nature in terms of flesh, bone, and man, uses definitions like "snubnose," not like "curved." Nature has two "senses," the form and the matter, and "we must investigate its objects as we would the essence of snubness . . . That is, such things are neither independent of matter nor can be defined in terms of matter only."

That Kroeber chose to ignore "matter" (individuals) and concentrate on "form" can be illustrated by his comment in 1948 that "as for those who contend that cultures do not enamel their fingernails, we who are interested in culture phenomena can cheerfully concede this and keep on our way." And in 1952 he wrote: ". . . it is certainly justifiable, if one is so minded, to concentrate attention on the intrinsic significances and values, and to defer—or even renounce—causal explanations." In 1920, however, he felt differently. In a review of Lowie's *Primitive Society*, he complained of the absence of causal explanations in Lowie's work and observed: "In essence, then, modern ethnology says that so and so happens, and may tell why it happened thus in that particular case. It does not tell, and does not try to tell, why things happen in society as such." He insisted that "People do want to know why . . ." and went on to state: "That branch of science which renounces the hope of contributing at least something to the shaping of life is headed into a blind alley. Therefore, if we cannot present anything that the world can use, it is at least incumbent to let this failure burn into our consciousness." It would be difficult to write a more eloquent criticism of some of Kroeber's own views.

To the extent that the superorganic idea makes clear

the distinction between organic heredity and social tradition it serves a useful purpose. When it is used as a basic concept for scientific explanation in the study of man and society it is of questionable value, if not in serious error. In contemporary anthropology Leslie White has become the foremost champion of the superorganic concept and has pressed it with a vigor which matches, or surpasses, Kroeber's earlier and more extreme formulations. According to White, "cultural phenomena interact with each other on a 'superorganic' level and form new combinations and syntheses. The study and interpretation of these events can be carried on not only without reference to individuals, gifted or otherwise, but without reference to the human species." True, such studies can be carried out; the question is, What are they good for?

Kroeber's superorganic idea appears on the surface to be like Durkheim's "social facts" method, where social facts are viewed as "things" subject to empirical investigation. There are similarities, but the differences are more important. For Durkheim the individual was of supreme importance, and he dramatized the external reality of social institutions to emphasize their coercive power on the individual. What was important for Durkheim was the way society became internalized in the individual. Kroeber was never interested in this kind of functionalism, which attempts to show the interrelation of the individual and society.

IN TWO studies, separated by twenty-one years, Kroeber studied the changes in women's dress fashions over long periods of time. The first study in 1919 covered a period from 1844 to 1919; the second study, with Jane Richardson, covered a period of 300 years. These studies are good examples of the research conducted under the guiding concept of the *superorganic*. The first study was made, as Kroeber stated, in "the era of thinking that produced 'The Superorganic.'"

Kroeber finds in the notoriously capricious field of

fashion "rhythms" of change in which the wave length of periodicity was around one hundred years. He concludes that in dress fashion changes, as in economic changes, there is a "stateliness" in their march, or trend, and "in their superimposed cycles or oscillations. Here we have a concrete example, "inductively" arrived at, of the "majestic forces" and "great pulsations" which operate on the socio-cultural level. The individual is excluded from these studies, not because Kroeber denies that psychological motives may be operating, but because such data are, according to him, unmeasurable and undefinable. "Functional correlations," according to Kroeber, can be established without including the individual. The trouble is that they are the pure mathematician's correlations and, as Kroeber used them, have little relevance for the world of "flesh," "bone," and "man."

In a review of Kroeber's "Superorganic" paper in 1917, Edward Sapir noted that Kroeber had taken his examples from the fields of science and invention, where the accumulation of knowledge leads to a general inevitability in discoveries, and observed that had Kroeber "occupied himself more with the religious, philosophic, aesthetic, and crudely volitional activities and tendencies of man, his . . . case for the non-cultural significance of the individual would have been a far more difficult one to make." In 1944 Kroeber published *Configurations of Culture Growth,* which he had been working on for thirteen years. It can be viewed as an acceptance of Sapir's challenge, for it attempted to find wave-forms of cultural growth in the fields of philosophy, philology, sculpture, painting, drama, literature, and music, as well as in science. His procedure in this study was to determine "value curves" in terms of time and geographical location of recognized intellectual and aesthetic activities. "Quality-time configurations" were determined for philosophy, and the other fields, in six major cultures of the world, and these separate configurations were then compared with one another.

On the ground that "universals are to be found in abstracted properties or processes, not in specific phe-

nomena," Kroeber viewed the individual geniuses throughout history as "inevitable mechanisms or measures of
cultural expression," and used them as "symptoms" for the
reconstruction of the wave-forms of cultural growth. He had
noted that it was a "frequent habit of societies to develop
their cultures to their highest levels spasmodically . . ."
and it was this general cultural recurrence that he wanted
to investigate. His chief conclusion is that the highest
aesthetic and intellectual achievements in history have
occurred in temporary bursts of growth, as indicated by
the clustering of recognized geniuses in time and space.

He defines the higher values of a society—the aesthetic,
intellectual, and scientific—as "those qualities of human
productions which normally appear in historical configurations thus limited and shaped." The individual components
of cultural patterns or plans are not the agents, but rather
the vehicles or instruments of culture. The works of individual geniuses indicate the culmination of a certain cultural pattern or plan. The culmination comes "at the
moment when the full range of possibilities within the pattern is sensed; the decline, when there remain only minor
areas of terrain to be occupied." Thus there are "pulses"
and "lulls" in the growth of high-value cultural patterns.
Lower-grade cultural patterns, however, do not show such
transience; they "can apparently go on with much less
change and much longer. . . ." Why this is so is, according
to Kroeber, far from clear. He can only say that "it may
be something in the constitution of the human mind."

Kroeber's aim in this work was to investigate cultural
phenomena "empirically," instead of "intuitively or *a
priori*." It was to be "behavioristically factual rather than
explanatory." For the all-important ratings of genius and
values in the study, Kroeber states: "I have followed the
books . . ." by which he means, primarily, textbooks ("on
account of their timidity about departing from the accepted
norm") and encyclopedias. His treatment of St. Augustine reveals how arbitrary the *inductive* method can be in
this field. The appearance of a man like Augustine during a
cultural lull presented a problem. Kroeber solved it by

denying Augustine was a genius, arguing that only the subsequent success of Christianity as an institution made him important as a philosopher. To this, one can simply say that if science had not developed as an important institution, we would probably not have heard of Aristotle.

*Configurations of Culture Growth* is a culmination of Kroeber's persistent advocacy of the *superorganic* doctrine. At the beginning of the book he states that "there seem to lie certain forms of happenings which are more or less recurrent or generic, perhaps necessary and universal." At the end of the book, under "Review and Conclusions," he states: ". . . I wish to say at the outset that I see no evidence of any true law in the phenomena dealt with; nothing cyclical, regularly repetitive, or necessary." In 1951 he wrote that he would have entitled the book *Profiles of Cultural Growths*, presumably to emphasize the purely descriptive, non-explanatory nature of the work. It is clear, however, despite his disavowal of explanations, that he believes that somehow cultural patterns act as efficient causes. Although he calls them formal causes, he refers to cultural patterns as forces and pulsations, and speaks of their march or trend, their growth, realization, exhaustion, death. He anticipates this criticism by saying that the limited technical vocabulary in the historical and social sciences forced him to employ figurative, metaphorical language. One suspects, however, that the difficulty lies with the paradox of separating individuals from their cultural creations, and not with a limited vocabulary.

Although it fails, admittedly, to account in any way for cultural behavior, this work is a great tour de force, and a testimony to the magnificent scholarship and range of interest of Alfred Kroeber. It is a valuable descriptive work in comparative culture history, and raises important problems. If Kroeber did not provide the answer to the problems raised, he was at least aware of the difficulties and did not, like others, rush in with easy, deceptive solutions in an area which continues to present the greatest challenge to social scientists.

Periodically in recent years Kroeber sought a rapprochement with theories which include the individual in an attempt to provide causal, dynamic explanations in history and the social sciences. In a second review of Freud's *Totem and Taboo*, entitled "Totem and Taboo in Retrospect" (1939), he modified considerably the negative criticism in his first review in 1920. He was prompted to write the second review after hearing a seminar student demolish Freud's work. "An iridescent fantasy," said Kroeber, "deserves a more delicate touch even in the act of destroying its unreality."

His earlier criticism of *Totem and Taboo* stemmed from a solid conviction that a psychologist had no business entering the historical field. He criticized the historical material Freud used for his theories as conjectural and disputed. He pointed out, for example, that we do not have reason to believe that man's earliest social organization was like that of the gorillas, nor that blood sacrifice was universal, nor that incest and exogamy are the oldest taboos; nor do we have proof that sons killed their fathers. In 1939 he was willing to say that Freud's historical claims were beside the point and he would now "consider whether Freud's theory contains any possibility of being a generic, timeless explanation of the psychology that underlies certain recurrent historic phenomena or institutions like totemism and taboo." He went on to say that in a different form Freud's hypothesis might have helped anthropologists and sociologists in their search for explanations of "both the repetitions and variations in culture." Freud might, he said, have helped them to find "that underlying something" which would have served as a basis for cultural understanding.

Kroeber repeated much of his earlier criticism of Freud's *Totem and Taboo* but added that Freud made a large and permanent contribution with his concepts of repression, regression, and infantile persistences, dream symbolism and overdetermination, guilt sense, and the affects toward members of the family. He did not, however, believe that other Freudian concepts, such as the superego and the castration complex, have anything to contribute to anthropology. He concluded by writing: "As a construct, neither science nor history can use it; but it would seem that they can both accept and utilize some of the process concepts that are involved in the construct."

In a wistful, classroom statement in 1950 Kroeber spoke of a desire to "smuggle human nature back into the study of man" and warned of ignoring psychological explanations, as Leslie White wants to do. Cultural forms are the important ones, he insisted, but for causal and dynamic explanations one must go to the individual; for explanation of culture, he admitted, we need more than historic sequence.

In 1952, with Kluckhohn, he attempted a formal and detailed clarification of his theoretical position on culture and the individual. He admitted the legitimacy of the joint cultural-psychological approach, but expressed the fear that there is implicit in these efforts an attempt "to get rid of culture by resolving or explaining it away." At the same time he believed that eventually it would become the approach that could penetrate further into causality in culture; but for the "foreseeable future," he said, the best hope "for parsimonious description and 'explanation' of cultural phenomena seems to rest in the study of cultural forms and processes as such, largely—for these purposes —abstracted from individuals and from personalities."

There is no doubt that Kroeber ranks with the great anthropologists. His work on the California Indians is not likely to be surpassed. He made major contributions in anthropometry, linguistics, archaeology, and ethnography. It remains to be seen whether or not his theoretical formulations in the fields of culture and culture history will stand up. They are contingent on so many disputed views in the philosophy of history and the philosophy of science that it is difficult to evaluate their ultimate value. At the very least, his frank and provocative views have consistently challenged other workers to stay with the fundamental problems in anthropological theory. With a man like Kroeber, whose curiosity never rests, one may expect contradictions, and be glad for them.

# RUTH BENEDICT

## *SCIENCE AND POETRY*

A SENSE OF ESTRANGEMENT moved with Ruth Benedict all her life. Although intensely sympathetic and kindly she always gave the impression of standing apart from the world she lived in. Even her physical appearance had an unearthly quality. Victor Barnouw described her as "a tall and slender Platonic ideal of a poetess." She had large, penetrating, gray eyes set under heavy, dark eyebrows, and a fine head with short, prematurely white hair. Erik Erikson sketched her portrait toward the end of her life and described her as one "who looked as much like a young girl, as she looked like a man, without being in the least juvenile or mannish." Late in her life, G. E. Hutchinson sat next to her at dinner and was struck by her "unearthly beauty." She impressed him as "a sybil, a mythical wise woman, at once from the remote past and the distant future. . . ."

Students and colleagues held her in reverent esteem. She was especially helpful and sympathetic to those who were confused and struggling to find their place in life. On many occasions she gave financial aid to students whom she hardly knew, and whose interests were often far from her own.

Although these relationships brought her veneration and gratitude, they did not result in familiarity. The core of her personality was out of reach; an easy but unassailable dignity kept people from getting too close.

One of her early fascinations—before she studied anthropology—was the deviant personality; the person who stood at odds with his cultural environment. She was especially interested in the lives of the poets, many of whom she found to be out of step with society. Under the name of Anne Singleton, she herself wrote poetry in which she struggled for freedom of feeling and expression. A persistent theme in her work as an anthropologist has to do with the reconciliation of individual freedom and cultural integration. With the poet's sense of the essential she asked important questions and resisted pedantry. As an inspired student of Boas she was severely indoctrinated with the codes of scientific integrity. She remained enough of a poet, however, to keep from being enslaved by the rituals of scientific procedure, a fate that her teacher, Boas, did not completely escape.

Ruth Fulton Benedict was born in New York City on June 5, 1887 to Frederick Samuel and Beatrice (Shattuck) Fulton. A sister, Margery, was born a year and a half later. The father, a promising young man in surgery and medical research, died before Ruth Benedict was two years old, leaving his wife to support their two daughters.

When Ruth Benedict was seven years old the mother and her two daughters left the family farm, near Norwich, N. Y., and moved to the Middle West where the mother had accepted a teaching position. Four years later they returned to New York and settled in Buffalo, the mother taking a position as librarian at the Buffalo Public Library.

Despite the years of financial struggle and hardship, Benedict was able to take a college degree at Vassar, her mother's alma mater. She graduated in 1909 with honors but, according to her close friend Margaret Mead, with no "sense that her period offered her any intellectual or broad social role which had any meaning." A brief career as an English teacher at a girls' school in California was

followed by her marriage, in 1914, to Stanley Rossiter
Benedict, a professor of chemistry at the Cornell University
Medical School in New York City. She hoped to
have children right away. Fourteen years later, and childless,
she expressed desperate disappointment in this failure:

> *Be desperate in that hour. Lift up your heart*
> *As any cup and drink it desolate—*
> *A drained and ruinous vessel that no fate*
> *Shall fill again in pity, and no art*
> *Make brim quick-passionate.*
>
> *Leave not one drop for heart-broke artifice*
> *Against the stricken years. You shall know now*
> *The quiet breathing of the apple bough*
> *Past blossoming, peace of the Chrysalis,*
> *The rain upon your brow.*

This pathetic resignation to a life barren of children
came at the exact time when her career as an anthropologist
had its first blossoming. The verses above from her poem
"Lift Up Your Heart" were published in 1928, the same
year that her paper "Psychological Types in the Cultures
of the Southwest" was published. This paper followed ten
years of academic study and fieldwork in anthropology,
first under the supervision of Elsie Clews Parsons and
Alexander Goldenweiser, and then as a student under Franz
Boas and A. L. Kroeber. From that time on much of her
work in anthropology was an elaboration of the basic idea
and methodology contained in that paper. The end of one
life marked the beginning of another for Ruth Benedict,
as she herself realized in 1930:

> *. . . Death and birth*
> *Are whimsies of the wind—nothing avails;*
> *Yet till its term is spent no star beam fails.*

Robbed by the whimsies of death and birth she lived the
remainder of her term with a steady, detached passion.

In 1922, at the age of thirty-five, Benedict conducted
her first field study among the Serrano Indians in Cali-

fornia under the supervision of A. L. Kroeber. She received her doctorate from Columbia in 1923 and was appointed Lecturer in Anthropology at Columbia the same year. Field studies followed of the Zuni (1924, 1925), the Cochiti (1925), and the Pima (1926).

Benedict's field experience with the Pima was crucial, because here she tried out the idea of studying and understanding people through an analysis of their characteristic "culture patterns." This was the concept first formulated in her paper, "Psychological Types in the Cultures of the Southwest" (1928), and later made familiar to a wide reading public in her famous book, *Patterns of Culture* (1934).

In addition to her field work with Indians of the Southwest in the twenties, she studied, in the forties, Asiatic and European culture patterns by using acculturated informants in the urban areas of this country. Her book on Japanese culture, *The Chrysanthemum and the Sword* (1946), is her best known work in this field.

Her field work was done in the summers when she was not teaching at Columbia. At Columbia she carried heavy teaching and administrative responsibilities. During the war she made valuable contributions to the government as Social Science Analyst with the Office of War Information.

In the summer of 1948 Ruth Benedict attended a UNESCO seminar in Czechoslovakia. She died in the fall of that year on her return to New York, at the age of sixty-one.

Benedict's instinct for integration and generalization prompted her from the first to take a comprehensive view of culture. A listing and analysis of discrete culture traits seemed to her to offer little help in the attempt to explain culture. With the functionalists, such as Malinowski, she insisted on studying cultures as more or less integrated wholes. But where Malinowski started with the individual and saw cultural phenomena as derivative of individual needs, Benedict started with "cultural configurations" and saw individual behavior as largely a conformance to given cultural imperatives.

Most societies have, according to Benedict, a "dominant drive" which tends to elaborate recurring human situations —birth, death, and the quest for food and shelter—according to its own bent. Death, for example, among the Indians of the Western Plains is an occasion for violent, uninhibited, and extended grief among the mourners, whereas among the Pueblo of the Southwest the cultural injunction is to forget the departed ones as quickly and quietly as possible. These two cultures have opposing "drives" which Benedict summarized under Nietzsche's terms as Dionysian (Plains) and Apollonian (Southwest); the first is characterized by frenzy and excess, the second by measure and order. The exercise of religion, warfare, and sex in both cultures is fashioned so as to serve as occasions for the indulgence of the respective cultural drives. Thus the meaning and function of these and other institutions will be different in the two cultures; the variability in any cultural trait is, according to Benedict, "almost infinite."

For Benedict, therefore, there can be a functional interpretation of *cultures* but never of *culture*. In fact, there can never be a science of culture for Benedict, although she does not admit this. For if there is "almost infinite" variation there can be no scientific explanation. That is the outstanding implication of Benedict's radical cultural relativity, and it can be traced directly to her teacher Boas.

Benedict's earlier work can be seen as one great effort in behalf of the idea of cultural relativity. She insists there may be very little individual freedom, but there is unlimited cultural freedom. In arguing for a relative definition of normality Benedict writes: "It seems to me that cultures may be built solidly and harmoniously upon fantasies, fear constructs, or inferiority complexes and indulge to the limit in hypocrisy and pretensions." For Benedict it was always possible to point to an existing or possible cultural situation where the deviant in any given culture would be at home. Although this implication has no practical value for any human individual at odds with his society, it seemed a comfort to Benedict to know that his behavior would be appreciated in the appropriate cultural situation.

In her best known work, *Patterns of Culture*, Benedict cleverly put together several articles and field studies that she had produced over the preceding twelve years. She also made extensive use of the field studies of Franz Boas (Kwakiutl), Ruth Bunzel (Zuni), and Reo F. Fortune (Dobu). The studies of Zuni, Dobu, and Kwakiutl were presented as documentation for her central idea: the almost limitless variation of cultural patterns.

In her field experience with Indians of the Southwest in the twenties Benedict was struck by the observation that the Pueblo culture differed in a radical way from that of the Indians of North America at large in spite of the fact that there were no natural barriers to isolate them from neighboring peoples. The Pueblos seemed, incredibly, to be invisibly insulated from the cultural influence of their neighbors. Whereas the behavior of North American Indians at large was characterized, according to Benedict, by ecstasy and orgy, the Pueblos were committed to measure and sobriety. The Pueblos and their neighbors illustrated for Benedict Nietzsche's famous formulation of the Dionysian-Apollonian antithesis in the ancient Greek world.

For a specific contrast with the Pueblo, Benedict chose the Kwakiutl from the tribes of the Northwest coast, who had been described in great detail by Boas. All their activities, from the religious dances of the Cannibal Society to the practical affairs of their economic systems, revealed the basic drives of violence and self-glorification. In any kind of relationship or activity only two consequences were possible: total triumph or abject shame. In clinical terms they were, for Benedict, "megalo-maniac paranoid." The ecstasy and the depression that qualified their lives are Dionysian traits and were shared by most of the American Indians, with the remarkable exception of the Southwest Pueblos.

Benedict apparently picked the Dobu of New Guinea as a case history to support her thesis that a culture can function well enough even when possessing what Western civilization labels the most perverse human traits. "The Do-buan," says Benedict, "lives out without repression man's worst nightmares of the ill will of the universe, and according to his view of life virtue consists in selecting a victim upon whom he can vent the malignancy he attributes alike to human society and to the powers of nature." Ill will and treachery are institutionalized virtues in this society and are practiced within the prescribed cultural forms. The "good man" is the man who has survived his daily conflicts and has achieved a measure of prosperity—"It is taken for granted that he has thieved, killed children and his close associates by sorcery, cheated wherever he dared."

The cultures described in *Patterns of Culture* illustrated Benedict's idea that a culture can be viewed as consisting of cultural configurations integrated under the domination of one general, master pattern. A culture, therefore, is analogous to an individual being in that it is "a more or less consistent pattern of thought and action." Psychological terms could be used to analyze and summarize cultural characteristics. Cultures, she states, "are individual psychology thrown large upon the screen, given gigantic proportions and a long time span." It is this use of psychology that places Benedict among the modern anthropologists who have attempted an inter-disciplinary approach to the study of man and society. It must be noticed, however, that in her earlier work especially no use is made of the functional and adaptational aspects of psychological theory in an attempt to explain why one culture is different from another. The characteristic group ethos of a people appears simply as "given" in Benedict's study, in much the same way as does Kroeber's "style" in his studies of dress fashions. Benedict in fact used the term *style*, with its overtones of fortuity, to suggest the nature of a "psychological set" in culture.

The background for Benedict's "tribal-genius" concept is not psychology but the *Volksgeist* tradition in German historical scholarship. The works of Wilhelm Dilthey and Oswald Spengler were especially influential on Benedict. Behind them stood the great systems of thought of Kant and Hegel. Kant speaks of a "plan of nature" in history analogous to the "laws of nature" in science. Man is conceived as fulfilling this plan without being aware of it. For Hegel there was no plan of nature or of God behind historical events, but the reason and passions—the rational and irrational—of men. Although historical events, as seen from the outside, do not necessarily exhibit logical connections, the "thoughts" of men behind them do. The historian, therefore, must work both from the outside and the inside. He must penetrate the events to find the logically connected "thoughts" behind them—to the "spirit of the time" (*Zeitgeist*). Dilthey is close to Hegel when he speaks of the necessity for reliving the particular "spiritual activity" of a given culture in order to understand it. Philosophical systems are seen by Dilthey as expressions of various cultural moods; moods which cannot be resolved into one another. Spengler emphasizes the special character of each culture. The culture expresses its character in all the details of its existence. As with Dilthey there is an insistence on the independence of cultures from each other.

With an assist from Gestalt psychology on the importance of subjective frameworks, Benedict applied the *Volksgeist* idea from the German historical tradition to the data of cultural anthropology. Even in her later work, such as *The Chrysanthemum and the Sword* where she used adaptational psychology to account for the continuities in culture, her approach is still based on the tribal-genius idea. This method is understandably congenial to a poet, who strives to distill for us the essence of an experience or a complex of events. Exaggeration and omission dictated by a central preconception are necessary to this art. When poetry is practiced by the scientist, however, there are obvious dangers.

The most persistent criticism of Benedict's work is that she selected and exaggerated the cultural traits in a society which supported her conception about their particular "genius" and overlooked the ones that seemed to reflect a conflicting drive. The Dionysian and the Apollonian spirits often exist side by side in a culture and in the individual, although one may predominate. It was the coexistence of these drives in the ancient Greek world that attracted the interest of Nietzsche in *The Birth of Tragedy*.

The labeling of a culture as Apollonian or Dionysian can be useful to suggest the general bent of a culture, but it can be misleading when used as a scientific premise to order and interpret the entire range of cultural and individual behavior in a society. Benedict herself had warned against the dangers in this approach: "It would be absurd," she says in *Patterns of Culture*, "to cut every culture down to the Procrustean bed of some catchword characterization. The danger of lopping off important facts that do not illustrate the main proposition is grave enough even at best." This stricture, coming where it does, suggests a picture of the tough, scowling face of Boas looking over the shoulder of his favorite pupil as her attention strays from science to poetry.

Margaret Mead has inadvertently summed up very nicely the strength and the weakness of Benedict's scientific anthropology: "Two of her characteristics which all those who worked closely with her will remember vividly were the smile which accepted the general proposition the details of which she had only half caught, and the rephrasing of a question which made the questioner out to be so much more intelligent than had the original question; both were connected with her deafness, combined with her willingness to trust to what she felt were the essential elements in other people and in problems." The deafness (a result of childhood measles) that Mead refers to does not adequately account for Benedict's tendency to create simplicity out of complexity by poetic paraphrase.

Benedict's contribution lies in her attempt to make some sense out of the cultural phenomena that confront the student of culture. She was not satisfied, as was Boas, to go on recording information and postponing explanation until that time in the distant future when the patient bookkeeping of generations of anthropologists would reveal sound inductive generalizations about man and society. She was impatient with this attitude and seized upon the concept of cultural integration as a means for understanding and explaining cultural studies. If, in her enthusiasm, she pressed too hard, it was a mistake in the right direction.

It has been pointed out many times that Benedict's insistence on cultural relativity is inconsistent with her concern for improving the lot of mankind; a concern which is apparent in her theoretical work and in her practical efforts in behalf of freedom and tolerance. She hoped that eventually there would be a rational order to the now blind, unconscious patterns in culture. Social engineering, however, requires standards and judgments. If the many different, coexisting patterns of life are "equally valid," as she seems to want to say, then one must go all the way with Spengler and accept man's foolishness as inevitable. She does not accept this implication, however, and has spoken eloquently of the disaster inherent in certain kinds of social organizations: "It is possible to scrutinize different institutions and cast up their cost in terms of social capital, in terms of the less desirable behaviour traits they stimulate, and in terms of human suffering and frustration. If any society wishes to pay that cost for its chosen and congenial traits, certain values will develop within this pattern, however 'bad' it may be. But the risk is great, and the social order may not be able to pay the price. It may break down beneath them with all the consequent wanton waste of revolution and economic and emotional disaster."

More than any of her contemporaries, perhaps, Benedict exposed the weakness of the functionalist orientation as originally stated by Durkheim: that institutions are things, are related to each other, and can only be explained in terms of other institutions. She stepped out of this circle by invoking the analogy of institutional clusters with human character types. This had a certain illustrative value; but it failed as a dynamic. Such a system of evaluation could never mix with the psychodynamic approach she attempted in *The Chrysanthemum and the Sword*.

Benedict was a severe and perceptive critic of our own culture and used, paradoxically, a strict cultural relativism as the chief argument in her criticism. Only a fascination for formal contradiction, however, will mislead one about Benedict's contributions. Her insights reflected the great virtues and minor faults of the poetic nature. The faults can be corrected by more rigorous, if less poetic, social scientists.

PART 2

*THE NEW DIMENSION:* **Man**

## INTRODUCTION

CERTAIN social conditions and necessities lead to the generation of a new interest. The first attempt to implement this interest may not be successful or creative, but it establishes a precedent, a style, and a frame of reference. It is customary to say that this style or frame of reference has a momentum. But this metaphor obscures the facts. There are specific, identifiable factors responsible for the perpetuation of a style of thinking, the most important being the academic apprenticeship served by every new generation of students. Idealization of the teacher is common, and teaching often takes the form of indoctrination. A critical, creative approach to the problems of an academic discipline takes place, if at all, long after the apprenticeship. In the meantime the prevailing mode of thinking is strengthened.

A new approach to the problems in a field of work may reflect a personal need for rebellion by a student, but if the new approach has any value it is because it also reflects the needs of society. It is this correspondence which distinguishes the creative from the quixotic.

As social changes occur the solutions to new problems become imperative, and sooner or later the inertia of a sanctified mode of thought encounters forces which alter its course. Consequently, the history of a field, such as anthropology, is not so much a history of "falsehoods" and "truths," as it is a record of man's attempt to solve the problems that a constantly changing world presents.

From a study of the lives, the works, and the times of some of the major contributors to our knowledge of man and culture, we are encouraged in the belief that man has the capacity to invent new methods and ideas when the old ones fail him. A brief summary and interpretation of the vogues of thought surveyed in the preceding chapters reveals a slow but progressive adjustment in anthropological thought to the needs of modern man.

The theory of evolution gave the great impetus to the study of "primitive man." Darwin had many more enduring ideas on social evolution than did Spencer, Tylor, and Frazer. It was his idea that social evolution was a hit-and-miss, trial-and-error affair and that successful forms of social patterning survived while others less successful either vanished or changed. However much the evolutionary anthropologists might have endorsed this view, they did not have the data to establish it. The Spencerian idea concerning the unilinear evolution of mankind gave to Tylor and Frazer the license to borrow freely from a large variety of cultures the data of folklore or custom to back their views. In adopting this assumption Tylor and Frazer were more Aristotelian and Lamarckian than Darwinian. They failed to make the effective transition from organic to social evolution. Perhaps the specific reason for this was in their failure to establish a frame of reference for the study of social adaptation. Once this shortcoming existed, there was not much left for these investigators to do but to be topical in their approach. The study of isolated culture traits like sex customs (with particular reference to incest taboos), totemism, religion, and magic, could only be studied in accordance with a master plan. These early workers did not have any idea of the adaptation of individual cultures. The vogue of the evolutionary anthropologist declined as soon as fact finding became the undertaking of certain anthropologists like Boas, or when a new frame of reference was used, as in the case of Durkheim.

The decline of evolutionism was probably due to the fact that it was not an investigative technique but a series of discrete *ad hoc* explanations based on questionable assumptions. Instead of explaining social evolution, it really by-passed the whole issue. Social evolution was assumed to have involved all of humanity even in widely scattered areas. Adjustment to particular local conditions and insulation from other groups were ignored. It was this assumption that gave Frazer the license to draw his conclusions from the folklore of different groups as it suited his convenience. The evolutionists failed because their assumptions defined their problems, and prevented them from engaging in the most pressing need; namely, to gather data.

Emile Durkheim introduced a new idea into the technique of anthropology. He wanted to avoid the extremes of Spencer and Comte. He did not want to be deductive and rationalistic, drawing conclusions from arbitrary postulates like unilinear evolution, or the psychic unity of mankind. According to Durkheim, social facts must be treated as "things," and social facts can only be explained in terms of other social facts and not in terms of some other discipline like biology or psychology. This is the basic position of functionalism. The only available unit for study therefore is the *institution*. Institutions, in Durkheim's scheme, were related to each other as are the meshes in a gear system. This became, therefore, a technique for working within a closed system, where the individual entities—institutions—were related to each other. There is an attempt at a dynamic formulation. But precisely how the needs of the social organism related to the institution is not clear. We are told that social facts came from external reality and then became internalized. It is difficult today to make sense out of this, but in 1910 this kind of statement seemed adequate. Durkheim could not tolerate the idea of explaining a *social* fact with a *psychological* fact. He was quite certain the result was "false." In a way, Durkheim could not be blamed. In his day there was no psychology that had any relevancy to the problems he was working on.

Durkheim's technique led him to conclusions that today seem to be in error. When institutions relate to each other and not to the creatures who conceive and implement them, then one has to see society as an organism. In this case the needs of society are different from the needs of the individuals who comprise it.

Notwithstanding the limitations of his frame of reference, Durkheim's work was an essential building block in the structure of modern anthropology. He fell just short of the modern conception of social homeostasis and how it is achieved. He realized that in primitive religion the sacred object was a symbol and that the search must be for the realities that stand behind the symbol. This reality, he insisted, must be observable within society itself. He recognized that society cannot exist unless the conditions for co-operation exist, and he also recognized that religion was a way of maintaining co-operation in society.

Although Durkheim was inimical to psychology as a way of explaining sociological facts, he had a homemade and implied psychology to which he owed many of his brilliant insights. Considering that Durkheim was not really an anthropologist, his influence was profound. His *Elementary Forms of the Religious Life*, with all its errors, is still an enjoyable and instructive work.

The man who appreciated the poverty of anthropological data was Franz Boas. Being himself the severest critic of the evolutionary anthropologists, he set a new example in the methods of gathering field data. He was one of the two workers who, by plan or accident, began to study cultures as *entities*. His studies of Northwest Indian cultures set a new pattern for field studies, and he defined the necessity for exhaustive studies of individual cultures. Boas was not a great innovator of interpretive ideas; his emphasis was on what data to gather and how to gather it.

Among the functionalists it was Malinowski who may be credited with new styles of interpretation. It was an accident that he was interned in the Trobriand Islands during World War I. This gave him four years in which to live with the Trobriands and to gather the data that would take him the rest of his life to organize and assess. Malinowski never really described the total Trobriand culture. Instead, he divided it up topically, and no doubt there is much that he never got around to documenting.

His study of the Trobriands is a landmark in anthropological literature. Being a culture whose basic social organization is very different from our own, it furnished an opportunity for studying the sources, functions, and interrelations of adaptive patterns other than our own. Furthermore, Malinowski had a true conception of social adaptation. Institutions were not *things* to him; "they exist to satisfy, directly or indirectly, the biological needs of man." He recognized that toward this end the family was a prime necessity; he also recognized that the monogamous family satisfied these needs more effectively than other family structures. Notwithstanding this, he insisted that the structural units (institutions) evolved and were diffused.

In the midst of these activities Malinowski got the opportunity to lock horns with the psychoanalysts, notably Ernest Jones. The issue is a particularly instructive one. The question concerned the Oedipus complex in the Trobriand Islands. Jones claimed that in this community—a matrilineal society in which the mother's brother stood *in loco patris*—the Oedipus complex was repressed. Malinowski quite rightly pointed to the differences in social organization between the peoples of the Trobriand Islands and Western countries. This argument was lost on the psychoanalysts because the concession that social organization could have something to do with the family constellations would destroy the Lamarckian position of the Freudians and put them under the obligation to revise a major part of the libido theory. At all events, the kind of double talk that constituted Jones' defense is not much in vogue nowadays.

Malinowski remained a controversial figure. He incurred great animosities and some of his colleagues admitted his accomplishments grudgingly, if at all. If, as some claim, Boas said everything for which Malinowski took credit, the general student cannot find it in Boas' work and cannot therefore be so partisan as to deny Malinowski credit for high achievement. He is the most articulate of the functionalists, and it is his work rather than that of Boas that made possible some approach to the use of psychology by anthropologists.

When we look back at Durkheim and Malinowski we can locate the central problem in technique. Once doctrinaire evolutionism had died the technical problem began to shift from institutions as "survivals" to institutions as useful instruments of adaptation. They were the units in which social adaptation could be described. It was finally conceded that they existed for man. Durkheim however insisted that institutions could be defined only in terms of other institutions. Psychology was ruled out as a method for investigating and explaining institutions.

Psychology, on the other hand, was taking its turn at anthropomorphism. Under Freud "instincts" were given a life and direction of their own, and the individual was viewed as going a predetermined way, irrespective of the impact of social institutions. The anthropologists had no place for the individual in their frame of reference, and the psychologists had no place for society in theirs. This impasse exists to some extent even today.

Both Kroeber and Benedict must, in spite of many contrary indications, be classed with the functionalists. In keeping with the functionalist approach, both consider institutions to be the working units of the anthropologists. They both agree that institutions interact with one another. Kroeber proposed a superorganic theory which in effect anthropomorphizes institutions; reference to human agencies is purely incidental. In the case of Benedict, the arrangement of institutions forms a "culture pattern," a total *Gestalt*, which has a certain resemblance to human character types. This idea, originally an inspiration of Friedrich Nietzsche, was promoted and popularized by his faithful annotator, Oswald Spengler. Because of the unmistakable analogy to character types, Benedict's work is often credited with a psychological orientation which it does not possess.

A more psychological approach was effected by Ralph Linton in his book, *The Study of Man*. It was grounded, however, upon ineffectual psychological assumptions, so that no systematic technique emerged. It is a certainty that he did not agree with the functionalists in their view of the interaction of institutions.

Leslie White states a position similar to Kroeber's when he declares that "cultural phenomena interact with each other on a superorganic level and form new combinations and syntheses. The study and interpretation of these events can be carried on not only without reference to individuals, gifted or otherwise, but without reference to the human species." This is similar to Freud's position that man's fate depends on the outcome of a capricious battle between Life and Death instincts. It is a *reductio ad absurdum* of the whole functionalist position. We must seriously question the heuristic value of any view that lands us, as this one does, in such a hopeless predicament. In addition, we must point out that any doctrine which denies to man responsibility for his own fate tends, if taken seriously, to greatly augment his social anxiety and to make such anxiety the pretext for hopelessness, hedonism, or social ruthlessness.

Margaret Mead has made an effective effort to reconcile culture pattern with adaptive psychologies. The transition in her work came with her studies of Balinese character. It is quite apparent in this work that, although the data was gathered with the intention of documenting a culture pattern, what was actually recorded served to establish the "basic personality" of the Balinese. Despite her prodigious efforts and ceaseless productivity Mead could not buck the tide of conservatism in her own discipline. When the vast storehouse of knowledge that is encompassed by cultural anthropology is opened up again—as it surely will be—then the efforts of Mead will emerge as a real contribution.

The invasion, as it was regarded in some quarters, of anthropology by psychodynamics in the early nineteen thirties resulted in an emphasis on a neglected dimension of the "study of man," namely, man. The next section will trace the development of an effort to include the human individual in a comprehensive study of man. It will begin with an account of the work of the founder of psychodynamics, Sigmund Freud, and will then proceed to a consideration of the different uses that have been made of psychodynamics in cultural anthropology.

# SIGMUND FREUD

## *CHIMNEY SWEEPING*

A<small>N</small> <small>INTELLIGENT</small>, imaginative, and very stubborn young woman, known in history as Fräulein Anna O., imposed her will on a well-known Viennese physician in 1881 and invented a technique for exploring the human mind. She called the technique the "talking cure," and "chimney-sweeping." As developed and modified by Sigmund Freud it became known as psychoanalysis.

When Fräulein Anna O. became a patient of Josef Breuer, the Viennese physician, Freud was a young man of twenty-five, just completing his medical studies. He and Breuer had been friends for some years. Breuer reported to Freud that the girl had, with very little assistance from him, cured herself—by *talking*. By talking she had cured herself of paralytic contracture and anesthesia, disorders of vision, speech, and hearing, neuralgia, coughing, tremors, and miscellaneous phobias. While in a self-induced hypnotic state the girl insisted on reporting to Breuer in detail the experiences—real and hallucinatory—that she had accumulated since his last visit. By the greatest good fortune Breuer was a patient, sympathetic man who was content to listen to her ramblings, although he had no preconceptions as to the possible consequences of such a novel doctor-patient relationship. It developed that this "talking" had the salutary effect of relieving the girl's many anxieties and tensions, at least temporarily. A calm, cheerful, agreeable state of mind lasted for about a day, then the procedure had to be repeated.

The next stage in the treatment of Fräulein Anna O. occurred when, by chance, her hypnotic ramblings hit upon a series of events that were directly related to one of her current phobias. Upon relating the events the phobia disappeared and never returned. After that she and Breuer attacked one ailment after another by dredging up—while she was in a hypnotic state—her recollection of the occasion when the symptom first appeared. Once she had given free verbal expression to the events associated with the appearance of a given symptom, it disappeared. In this way she was cured of some of her symptoms.

The case of Anna O. impressed Freud very much. However, no one with whom he discussed the case shared his enthusiasm, including Charcot, the great French psychiatrist, and Breuer himself.

During the next ten years Freud treated mental patients with the generally accepted methods of the time, such as hydrotherapy and electrotherapy, and occasionally experimented with hypnosis. With hypnosis, he used from the start Anna O.'s talking cure, which Breuer had later named the "cathartic method." Encouraged by his success with the cathartic method in the treatment of hysteric cases he persuaded Breuer to join him in a study of hysteria. The collaboration began with the "Preliminary Communication" in 1893 and was completed by the publication, in 1895, of *Studies on Hysteria*. This volume marks the beginning of psychoanalysis.

Freud soon abandoned hypnosis and the cathartic method in favor of the method of "free association," and it was this decision that set the true course of psychoanalytic theory and practice. It was Anna O., however, who first revealed the causal connections between the mental limbo of phantasm, absurdity, and hallucination, and the mundane realm of rational life. In tracking down these connections Freud created an instrument for the examination and treatment of the human mind.

The step that led to the beginning of psychoanalysis proper was Freud's recognition of the patient's resistance to the recollection and divulgence of certain events and feelings in his past life. He learned to interpret this resistance not as obstinacy to be overcome by the patient's will, but rather as a clue to the discovery of past experiences and emotions in the patient's life which had been driven from conscious recall for some good reason. Only a man with an extreme confidence in the efficacy of human knowledge, coupled with a tolerance and sympathy for human failure—a rare combination—could have seen in this obstacle an opportunity for cure.

In making the patient's area of resistance the center of his inquiry Freud abandoned hypnosis, since under hypnosis resistance is not evident except at induction; there is no opportunity for discriminating focus. He substituted for hypnosis the method of free association, in which the patient is encouraged to "think out loud," reporting everything that comes to his mind no matter how absurd, trivial, or embarrassing the thoughts might be.

It is not a simple matter, as Freud learned, for a person to speak freely of all the thoughts that enter his mind. One's very sense of identity and existence is determined in large part by what Durkheim called the "common sentiments" of a society—the social conventions of thought and behavior that are integrated in the individual beginning in infancy. A censorship develops in the individual which protects him from giving vent to whimsies that would endanger his culturally determined integrity. It was this censorship that Freud had to break in introducing his patients to the free association method. In the account of his first successful case with this method he revealed how this was to be done: "Finally I declared that I knew very well that something *had* occurred to her and that she was concealing it from me; but she would never be free of her pains so long as she concealed anything." For what seemed to be damaging, humiliating, or just nonsensical revelations, Freud offered in exchange relief from pain. With this relief as a motive Freud's patients revealed to him an undiscovered dimension of the human mind.

Having accommodated himself to the frequently irrational products of free association in his patients, Freud was quick to recognize the significance of dreams as a source of information about the hidden motives and conflicts within the individual. The familiar reality distortions in dream sequences were interpreted by him as an attempt on the part of the dreamer to solve an inward conflict— "a kind of inward dishonesty," as he put it later. In this sense, a dream is like a neurotic symptom—a compromise solution to some conflict that the patient cannot deal with directly. Freud's success in making dreams intelligible through analysis and interpretation helped sustain his conviction that the entire neurotic structure of a patient would yield to rational analysis and eventual cure. But the interpretation of dreams served as more than a hopeful analogy; it became a powerful instrument in operating directly on the neurotic structure. It offered the patient another opportunity to discover the hidden conflicts that caused his pain.

Most important of all, Freud's discovery of the significance of dreams made possible his own psychoanalysis. By subjecting his own dreams to interpretation he achieved an understanding that has seldom been equaled in the history of men's efforts at self-examination. Fortunately, Freud had a grandiose nature. He believed that what went on in his mind must, at least in general outline, go on in all other minds. Once he understood himself he felt qualified to understand man. Although this conviction inevitably led to error and miscalculation in certain instances, it undoubtedly prompted the great insights that revolutionized psychology.

From his own analysis and from analyses of his patients Freud soon arrived at a central insight: neurotic symptoms derive from outmoded or misguided programs of adaptation. They are not whimsies of nature, but attempts, based on experience, to deal with the problems of daily life. The experiences that require adaptive maneuvers begin at birth. In infancy and childhood the choice of modes of adaptation is dictated by the simple requirements of survival. If abject submission to parental demands is, under the circumstances, the obvious way to gain the love and protection that a child needs in order to survive, that is the course he will follow. He cannot have the forethought to consider what damaging effects the adoption of this behavior pattern might have in his adult life. Carried into adulthood this behavior, which at an earlier age kept him alive, can become the basis of a neurotic disorder.

Freud discovered, in other words, that neurotic symptoms have a history. He was not led to this discovery solely by induction; he was aided by an a priori conviction that mental events, like physical events, have a strict determination. But the human individual is not a ball rolling down an inclined plane. There are many more variables, and the conditions responsible for his behavior are not open to direct inspection and measurement. Inference and reconstruction from a potpourri of fantasies, distant recollections, dreams, mistakes, and rational productions are required. By regarding these various manifestations as allusions, and rejecting very often their face value, Freud was able to locate central themes of which the patient was often unaware; themes which were related to events and feelings that the patient had concealed from himself. Freud called this process of self-concealment *repression*. In the example given above, the individual who is forced to submit to every demand made of him as a child might reasonably be expected to covet murderous wishes toward his parents. A conscious desire is bound to be exposed sooner or later, so the greatest safety lies in rejecting the dangerous desire. It becomes, according to Freud, *repressed*. A repressed thought, memory, feeling, or desire is not obliterated. Freud applied to the human mind the principle of the conservation of energy, which states that no quantity of energy in an isolated system can be destroyed; the fate of an unacceptable impulse is change, not destruction. Under Freud psychology became a study of dynamics.

Starting with a symptom or character trait, Freud traced its mode of development back through the patient's history until he arrived at the conflict that called the mechanism of repression into action. Between conflict and symptom lay a history of change and accommodation made possible by certain identifiable psychic maneuvers. These adaptive maneuvers—unsuccessful in the case of a mental patient—can be classified as defensive, substitutive, and compensatory. They are protective in function, and when successful, effect tolerable and even happy compromises. Using the above example again, the man with a justified but unacceptable hostility may direct his energies into rewarding avenues of aggressive behavior: he may become a politician, an army leader, a business tycoon, a surgeon, or a football player. Or he may take another tack and capitalize on an avoidance of aggressive behavior: he may become a priest, a teacher, a diplomat, or a bookkeeper. This is not to say that repressed hostility is a necessary or sufficient condition for the attainment of any of the above goals. These are illustrations, in the broadest terms, of the possible pathways of successful adaptation. It is not necessary, although it can be helpful, for the normal individual to have insight into his hidden conflicts and resulting modes of adaptation. For the disturbed and ineffective person, such insight will, in some cases, enable him to modify and redirect his adaptive efforts. This was the medical value of Freud's treatment.

Up to this point Freud's discoveries involved a low level of abstraction. They were derived very directly from the data—observations of himself and his patients. But science moves in the direction of ever more abstract and comprehensive levels of explanation, and Freud inevitably aspired to gain these levels. It is this climb that holds the greatest rewards—and the greatest risks.

Freud's ascent to the regions of universality began with the observation that the crucial conflicts in the lives of his patients were of a sexual nature. The expression of sexual drives encountered forbidding obstacles from infancy on through adulthood. It was in this area that the individual's adaptive capacities were put to the severest tests. Freud saw here an opportunity to provide a theoretical structure for his dynamic psychology. The result was the *libido* theory.

By postulating the sexual drive as the fundamental biological instinct in man, Freud was able to construct a theoretical framework in which the observable dynamics of adaptation were viewed as alterations in instinct gratification. The phases in the development of the libido (the energy associated with the sexual instinct) follow, according to Freud, a "prescribed course," that is, they are historically determined. The influence of the evolutionists, particularly Haeckel, is evident here; "ontogeny recapitulates phylogeny" was a popular dictum at the time. As Freud generalized it, instincts can be characterized "as tendencies inherent in living substance towards restoring an earlier state of things. . . ." The dynamics of adaptation consist in an adjustment to this preordained development, compatible with the demands of contemporary life. A compromise is sought between the demands of the past (phylogenetic history) and the needs of the present. Pathology results from an unsatisfactory compromise.

The resolution of the Oedipus complex illustrates how such a compromise can be made. The Oedipal phase in the genetic course of libidinal development occupied the central role in Freud's scheme. The famous Oedipus complex resulted, according to Freud, from an inevitable sexual attachment of the child to the parent of the opposite sex. Repression of the libido at the time of attachment saves the child from overwhelming fear and guilt over the attachment. Later on, at puberty, the libido is released and directed to a nonincestuous object of the opposite sex. Failure to resolve the Oedipus complex in this way results in neurotic disorder.

The libido theory proved to be very useful to the psychoanalyst as a frame of reference for the neurotic disorders peculiar to a society in which sexual development is greatly inhibited. It accounted very well for the observed phenomena and suggested a course of treatment. It was of no practical concern whether or not the precise stages of libido development were dictated by phylogenetic history; in Freud's patients the succession of stages did occur in ontogenesis in a predictable way.

The validity of a theory, however, is not settled by how successfully it accounts for phenomena at a particular place and time. The Ptolemaic theory of the solar system was founded on erroneous assumptions, but it accounted for the movements of the sun, moon, and planets for almost fourteen centuries, and provided reliable methods for prediction. When new problems appeared, *ad hoc* alterations were made in the machinery of the theory, while the basic assumptions were left undisturbed. The result was an increasingly complex and cumbersome system that eventually gave way to a theory based on radically different assumptions, assumptions which were later shown to be justified.

In the case of the libido theory the questionable assumption of a phylogenetically determined series of events in the ontogenesis of the sex drive was retained by Freud, and new problems were solved by gratuitous modifications of derivative concepts. Freudian psychodynamics became rooted in an instinct theory, and the concept of adaptation —so important in Freud's early clinical work—became one of many appendages. This development had important consequences for Freud's work in the social sciences.

KNOWN chiefly for his innovations in psychology and as the founder of a system of psychopathology and of psychotherapy, Freud is an anomalous figure in the social sciences. In this area he has written five major books: *Totem and Taboo* (1913), *Group Psychology and the Analysis of the Ego* (1921), *The Future of an Illusion* (1928), *Civilization and Its Discontents* (1930), and *Moses and Monotheism* (1939).

These five works, which would have been in themselves

a remarkable achievement for any individual, form only a fraction of his great output. As the matter stands today, one would be loath to say that these works represent the best that can be done with his ideas in the social sciences. But Freud is a force to be reckoned with in the social sciences because he provided access to a dimension long known to social science, but ignored for want of an adequate approach. This new dimension was man—the effective unit of society, and its creator.

No discussion of Freud's sociological works is of any value without a knowledge of his sources. In 1910 there appeared a work bound to stimulate a great many new ideas in Freud. That was Sir James Frazer's *Totemism and Exogamy*. In addition, he read all the evolutionary anthropologists, especially Marett, and Robertson Smith's *Religion of the Semites*. Smith's conclusions represented just the kind of "confirmation" Freud was looking for. With these works, together with what he had absorbed from Herbert Spencer and his "stages of development," and Haeckel's law of biogenesis that ontogeny repeats phylogeny, Freud had an armory of assumptions with which he could operate.

Freud referred to anthropological material to find evidence in primitive culture for his contention that what was once conscious in primitive man would be "unconscious" in modern man. He had originally given this assignment to Jung. But instead of following the trail of the evolutionary anthropologists, Jung was off on the track of mysticism. The break between the two men came when, in place of what had been agreed upon, Jung set to work on a book, *Symbols and Transformations of the Libido*. This was in 1911. Freud, therefore, had to do the job himself. The result was *Totem and Taboo*.

By the time *Totem and Taboo* was published much of the work of the evolutionary anthropologists had been questioned and many of their assumptions repudiated. Still, they lived on in Freud's libido theory. The theory that man's Oedipus complex derived from a primal parricide, or that animal phobias in children represent the "infantile return of Totemism," or that the latency period represents a recapitulation of the "ice age," are all derived from repudiated theories of cultural evolution. Robertson Smith "confirmed" Freud in his conviction that totemic feasts were repetitions of the original parricide and the ensuing mourning and euphoria. In true evolutionary manner Freud set to work to find in Christian ritual (largely of Greek origin) a repetition of the totemic feast. The added feature in Christianity is that the parricide is expiated in the death of Christ. Thus Freud unwittingly gave endorsement to the concept of "original sin," which he saw as parricide. According to Freud, this idea was perpetuated through the ages "by the inheritance of psychic dispositions."

*Totem and Taboo* has not stood the test of time because it ultimately shared in the fate of the evolutionary anthropologists. The assumptions were wrong; the technique was wrong. It really espoused an Aristotelian conception of social evolution. This does not mean that the whole concept of social evolution has been discredited. There has been evolution. But it could not be studied according to the assumptions of the cultural anthropologists—which Freud all too hastily endorsed. Unfortunately Freud could never free himself from his early convictions. He reaffirmed these early views in 1939 in *Moses and Monotheism*.

From 1911 to 1914 Freud was torn by the defections of Carl Jung and Alfred Adler. The first he dismissed more easily, although Jung's thinking had a profound influence in shaping Freud's ideas. Adler was particularly irritating because he accused Freud of omitting the influence of social directives, in fact, of omitting the effect of society altogether in human adaptation. It therefore became incumbent on Freud to prove that his frame of reference could account for social relationships. This undertaking was necessary because in *Totem and Taboo* he completely ignored the problem of what held societies together. He saw each individual as a monad in the company of other monads who lived "among" but not "with" each other. In *Group Psychology and the Analysis of the Ego*, the relations of human beings to each other were described in terms of the libido, the grossest manifestation of which is sexual love. By way of illustrating how this libido worked, Freud studied two artificial groups, both non-familial hierarchies: the army and the church. This was an unfortunate choice because these two artificial groups are not prototypes of the social life of man. Although Freud's thesis was that they operated through love (libido), they really operate on the principles of dominance and submission, obedience and reward, and mutual protection. Freud, however, subsumed all these relationships under the concept of libido. But since these relationships were in the main utilitarian and not amatory, Freud invented the concept of "desexualized libido." Friendship between men is aim inhibited, that is, sublimated love. When these love ties are severed, as in cases of panic, the group disintegrates. Love bonds however do not exist in one single modality; they are mixed with hatred, hence the phenomenon of ambivalence. In addition to aim inhibited love and ambivalence, there is another important mode of social relationship, effected through the agency of a mental mechanism called "identification." In this concept Freud recognizes four modes: (1) the wish to take someone's place, (2) to incorporate the object, (3) to have the same claim as someone else, (4) to replace a lost object by identifying oneself with the lost object.

In addition, there is the role of conscience, ego-ideal, and later, super ego. Thus Freud is able to define a primary group as one composed of a number of individuals who have substituted one and the same object for their ego-ideal and have subsequently identified themselves with one another in their ego.

Here at last we begin to have something of a social psychology. It establishes certain dynamics that are concerned with social cohesion. It attempts to answer the question of what holds human beings together in society. This question was never asked before, or if it was, the answer was usually in terms of some instinct or other, for example, the herd instinct. *Group Psychology and the Analysis of the Ego* is a much sounder sociological work than *Totem and Taboo.* It was original and not an imitation of the evolutionary anthropologists. However Freud was still tied to the limitations imposed on him by the instinct theory. Concepts like "desexualized libido" do not make semantic sense. Libido cannot be the energy of the sexual drive on the one hand and then suddenly alter its character and become desexualized. We do not know of any agency that performs such transformations. We must conclude that the vernacular, poor as it is in psychological concepts, nevertheless makes better distinctions between love, interest, and exploitation as modes of human relations than does the concept of desexualized libido, neutral energy, and the like. Terms like these lack descriptive power because they represent a translation of the vernacular into the lingo of an artificial construct without any empirical basis. It really is a verbal trick. The real damage that it does is to prevent further investigation and create the illusion of knowledge.

*The Future of an Illusion* is a mature and sober work. Here Freud sees culture as serving to render nature subservient to man and to govern the relations of the constituents of society to each other. Culture is a protection to the individual. In return for this protection he is obliged to make certain renunciations. Society has to compensate him for his renunciations and at the same time control the hostility unleashed by the demands for renunciation. This entire process is facilitated by the tendency to incorporate external pressures. Through the agency of conscience and ego-ideal the individual is rewarded for fulfilling the group ideal.

Among those social forces that tend to hold a society together is religion. Religion, according to Freud, is a social illusion used to overcome the individual's feeling of helplessness against the forces of nature. By personifying the forces of nature into specific entities like deities, man acquired a technique for dealing with them, thus putting them to some degree under human control. Freud showed that the techniques advocated by religion to placate or move the deity are the very ones that the child learns in order to placate his parents and to guarantee for himself their continued solicitude and protection.

Here Freud reached one of his great insights. While considering the methods man used to control, govern, or placate the deity, Freud recognized that they were based on a prototype of real experience—that of the child with his parents. Religion thus can be seen as having a remarkable governing function: it tended to regulate relations between individuals in society, and served as a protection against dangers in the outer world. For the first time, Freud describes here the origin of what may be called a *projective system*, that is to say, a system for structuring the outer world and one's relations to it in accordance with a pattern laid down in an earlier experience during ontogenesis. This is a powerful idea and one with many uses.

In *The Future of an Illusion* Freud was on the brink of a new technique for studying the adaptation of man. He did not follow through. A new influence shifted him from this approach to another one founded upon a revised theory of instincts. This shift was occasioned by the fact that serious incompatibilities were arising in the operational value of some of his assumptions in the libido theory. He sought to resolve the difficulty by defining new types of instinct: *life instincts* and *death instincts*. In addition to this, Freud had worked out a topological personality scheme consisting of the *id*, the *ego*, and the *superego*.

His new reflections on culture were embodied in *Civilization and Its Discontents*. In this work Freud tries to answer the question of how culture influences the instinctual endowment of man. Obviously, instincts must be controlled in order for society to exist. According to Freud, they are absorbed into what are called character traits. As an illustration he cites thrift, cleanliness, and orderliness. "How this happens, we do not know," he says, but he does note that orderliness and cleanliness are cultural demands. Here we note the paradox in Freud's theoretical position. The transformation of instincts into character traits was one of the assumptions of the libido theory, but now he notes that cleanliness and orderliness are cultural directives, the origin or evolution of which we do not know. Cleanliness, in the second view, is seen as an acquiescence to a cultural demand. This is the point of view of common sense. But Freud insists at the same time that character traits are "sublimations" of instinctual energy. In the end, cultural directives remain outside the theory. This was one of the consequences of the libido theory.

Unfortunately Freud sought explanations of the origins and course of culture by making the control of instinct the central point in his investigation. He was looking for some formula for the curbing of instinct in order to permit the society to function effectively. The first method of control that he identifies (but never defines) is "desexualization." Secondly, he notes that culture sets restrictions on sex life in the form of incest taboos and monogamy. Freud assumed, incorrectly, that these restrictions are universal. The whole formula on which culture operates is one in which the quantitative disposition of instinctual energy is the chief factor. Then the formula must work out in such a way that society or culture is antagonistic to, or opposes, or restricts the individual.

This restriction operates chiefly on the sexual and aggressive instincts. Aggression is considered an instinct on a par with the sexual drive in the sense that it seeks satisfaction. Society erects barriers against this satisfaction in the form of identifications, desexualized love relationships, restrictions on sex life, and the command to love one's neighbor. In exchange for the renunciation of aggression the individual secures some measure of social protection. This formulation of Freud's concerning the eternal struggle between life and death instincts has had great vogue, particularly among those who think of society in terms of ideologies, slogans, and formulas, but who tend to avoid all empiricism.

*Moses and Monotheism* was Freud's last sociological endeavor. For the greater part it is a reaffirmation of the position taken in *Totem and Taboo*. For all practical purposes, the works discussed above contain Freud's major literary contributions to the social sciences.

Freud's work in the social sciences suffered from the incorporation of two false assumptions, both of which have been discussed: the assumption that ontogeny recapitulates phylogeny in cultural evolution, and the assumption that instinct is the guide to all psychological processes. By concentrating on the problem of instincts Freud exposed himself to the dangers that go with identifying instincts by qualitative criteria, thus ignoring the systems of action by which instincts are carried out. Moreover, as time went on the instincts became anthropomorphized and took over properties of the entire personality. This was due largely to the use of instinct not as a structural concept but as an energic concept. The instinct drew its energy from phylogenetic sources, was capable of being transformed (according to the principle of the conservation of energy), of being moved around from one object to another (displaceability), and was capable of desexualization. In the use of instinct as an energic concept Freud unwittingly ignored the central co-ordinating apparatus that he had posited in his early works and in the *Interpretation of Dreams*. The so-called ego was squeezed out of the frame of reference and all adaptive contact of ego with the external world was thus ruptured.

What were the practical consequences of the anthropomorphism of instincts? Mainly, that cultural conditions, although recognized, had an extraterritorial position with respect to theory. One example may be taken from Freud's analysis. Anal character traits, according to Freud, are arrived at by a process of sublimation of libido. These traits are: thrift, cleanliness, and orderliness. But Freud also recognized that these traits are cultural demands. Either cleanliness is a form of compliance or it is a sublimation of energy—it cannot be both. One has to be sacrificed. Freud sacrificed the contact of the ego with cultural demands and thus could arrive at the meaning of culture only through the concept of instinct.

This is precisely what happened. He accounted for culture on the basis of the vicissitudes of two instincts, life and death, and their eternal struggle against each other, like God and the devil for the soul of Faust. Social evolution, the trial and error of improvised patterns of human relations, and the survival of the most expedient because they enhance the adaptability of man—these were all jettisoned. The ego lost all contact with the social environment, leaving the responsibility for man's survival to the barriers erected against the satisfaction of the death instinct.

These later ideas of Freud have proved to be of little use. Being for the most part tautologies, they have no explanatory value, and as guides to action they have no pragmatic value. How can man deal with the "death instinct" or the Eros? Man would be powerless in the face of a capricious struggle between so-called life and death forces. It is safe to say that no idea will ever be of use to man that takes the responsibility for his fate completely out of his own hands. He stands a much better chance with religion. At least he can pray.

Human suffering must be seen as resulting from failures in individual and cultural adaptation. To blame human suffering on an inborn death instinct, or to explain it as a satisfaction of the need for punishment and pain, is to further human helplessness and to encourage every form of social opportunism and oppression.

# THE INFLUENCE OF PSYCHODYNAMICS

## ON THE STUDY OF CULTURE

PARADOXICALLY, it is Freud's early work in the field of individual psychology, and not his later sociological studies, that contains something of value for the social scientist. He described a psychodynamic system in which the reactions of the individual to the problems of adaptation can be recorded. It became possible, therefore, to relate the conditions under which ontogenesis takes place to the end product—that is, to the character of the individual, or his neurosis.

Instead of making use of this verifiable procedure, most sociologically minded followers of Freud have attempted to use some part or combination of Freud's instinct theories.

It may come as a surprise to some to learn that there are several major "schools" in modern psychodynamics, with widely divergent points of view. Even the social scientists often overlook these differences and group the different approaches under the single headings of "Freudian" or "psychoanalytic." Psychodynamics is not a unified theory and method, any more than is "cultural anthropology," or "social psychology." Since there is no uniformity of theory and method in psychodynamics, there can be no uniformity of results in its application to the study of culture. It is necessary, therefore, to distinguish several psychodynamic procedures that have been employed in this field.

First, there is the Freudian concept that employs the Lamarckian idea that acquired characteristics of the individual can be genetically transmitted to offspring. The general assumption that what is unconscious in contemporary man was conscious in primitive man is derived from this concept. It led to the theory that the Oedipus complex originated with primal parricide, that the "latency period" in the individual is a recapitulation of the ice age, that the Eucharist is a repetition of the primitive totemic feast, and that infantile phobias are repetitions of totemism.

These ideas of Freud have been given publicity by Geza Roheim and Theodor Reik, and more recently, by Warner Muensterberger and George Devereaux. They are extrapolations of a questionable assumption and are of no empirical value. As explanations, they are more suited to the Jungian system of archetypes than to Freud's over-all system.

Another line of psychodynamic thought has Freud's libido theory as a central idea. Attempts have been made to employ this theory as a schema of social evolution. Freud himself never made serious use of this application, but later writers, notably Geza Roheim, have made ambitious efforts to do so.

Roheim has used at least two versions of the libido theory in attempts to explain cultural phenomena. In his early work he tried to follow Freud directly by uncovering Oedipus and castration complexes in all cultures. The concept of adaptation—of a culture to the external environment, or of the individual to cultural demands—did not enter the picture. In 1950 (in *Psychoanalysis and Anthropology*) Roheim made some concessions to the adaptational point of view and discussed cultures as separate entities, with different problems of adaptation. He disavowed the theory of primal parricide and rejected certain applications of the libido theory. He took instead Melanie Klein's revisions of the libido theory as his guide, and in his revised scheme included her idea that some of the fantasies of schizophrenic children represent normal stages of ontogenetic development. In this revised approach culture was considered to be a projection of the stages of ontogenetic development, with all its reality distortion.

To illustrate the confusions and inconsistencies that Roheim's theories accommodate, his analysis of the Central Australians can be cited. Roheim finds that these people are "genital" in their behavior because they had no oral frustrations in early life. On the other hand he finds that they have body-destruction fantasies, which he finds in folk tales in which parents devour their children. Here, says Roheim, is confirmation of Melanie Klein's body-destruction fantasies as a normal stage of development. Roheim refuses to relate these myths to the fact that when famine strikes this culture, the people kill and devour their children. The children know that in the event of famine the youngest child is sacrificed first, the third youngest next, then the fifth youngest, and so on. For Roheim, this reality apparently has nothing to do with the folklore. He posits, instead, a body-destruction fantasy which has never been demonstrated to exist except in schizophrenic and extremely deprived children.

This example, one of many that could be taken from Roheim's work, reveals how dangerous it is to extrapolate from assumptions that are faulty.

The energic aspect of the libido theory has also been applied to an explanation of social phenomena. As clinical phenomena were seen as transformations of sexual energies, so were social phenomena, such as friendship and co-operation. In this scheme friendship was seen as a manifestation of desexualized libido. Since it is impossible to conceive of an apparatus that can accomplish such transformations, this idea has no explanatory value. It fails to take into consideration the conditions under which human beings do or do not co-operate in a society, and it cannot account for what happens when co-operation fails. These are the crucial issues.

Erik Erikson pays lip service to the concept of "libidinous energies," but actually takes the energic concepts out of the libido theory. He proposes that the body orifices or organs are the sources of experiences which form the cognitive basis for certain concepts and attitudes in the individual's life. In Freudian theory these organs are considered to be the foci for the distribution of libidinous energies. In Erikson's conception, we no longer hear of character being formed through the transformations of anal and oral erotism. Instead, the experiences of eating and evacuating become in themselves the primary sources of certain attitudes, such as incorporation, retention, and expulsion. It should be noted that this idea was first proposed by Franz Alexander in 1924 and restated with modifications by Sandor Rado and Abram Kardiner in 1938. Erikson's work represents an escape from the severe restriction placed on empirical investigation by the libido theory, but it is limited as a method for tracing the impact of social institutions on human behavior. It does not offer a technique for the study of culture and history. Except for the modification of the libido theory as an ontogenetic scheme, Erikson's work is a continuation of Roheim's. In his practical applications he makes a feeble case for the Sioux, and none at all for the Yurok.

Freud's second version of instinct theory, which posited an autonomy of life and death instincts, has been hailed by some writers as a liberating insight for the social sciences. Herbert Marcuse, in particular, has been impressed by this view of cultural dynamics.[1] We cannot share his enthusiasm.

The so-called culturalist schools of psychodynamics represented by such writers as Harry Stack Sullivan, Karen Horney, and Erich Fromm, have not produced any enduring contributions to the social sciences. Although Fromm has devoted almost exclusive attention to this field, he has not presented a statement of principles nor has he suggested any techniques for the systematic investigation of cultural data. The supposed "mechanisms" of Fromm's "Escape from Freedom" thesis are not based on any recognized system of psychodynamics. The conception of masochism as an effort to lose oneself in something bigger than oneself is a belletristic conception introduced by Horney. In the end, Fromm's ideas can be extracted from a mixture of Martin Buber and Zen Buddhism, and as such, are in prin-

[1] Marcuse, Herbert, *Eros and Civilization.*

ciple incapable of scientific validation. As an essayist, however, Fromm is provocative and has acquired a large and faithful following.

In addition to these different efforts of the psychoanalysts mentioned above, workers from other fields have attempted to apply a knowledge of Freudian psychology to the study of culture. The result, as with some sociologists, is usually a translation of clear and simple propositions into a confused and complicated psychoanalytic jargon. The translation of known relationships into abstract constructs serves only to please the obscurantists and penalizes the student who is making a genuine effort to learn something.

The Freudian psychology was eventually subjected to a new synthesis by members of the faculty of the Columbia University Psychoanalytic Clinic, notably Sandor Rado, Abram Kardiner, and David M. Levy. This new synthesis emphasized the *adaptational* rather than the *instinctual* aspect of Freudian theory. Rado concentrated on the general theory of neuroses, Levy on childhood disorders and experimental psychology, and Kardiner on the uses of adaptational psychodynamics in the social sciences.

Kardiner's use of psychodynamics in anthropology can be distinguished from other psychodynamic procedures by the following tenets:

1. Social evolution has not followed a unilinear course. Hence each society must be studied as an entity in itself. In this, he agrees with Malinowski and the functionalists.

2. In order to understand the institutions of a society an attempt must be made to reconstruct the problems of adaptation the society has faced. It is recognized that there are many ways of solving the same social problem; in some communities where there is starvation and the population must be limited, the problem is solved by female infanticide, in others, by eating children.

3. Social institutions are the patterned relationships which accommodate the individual to the human and natural environment.

4. The success or failure of social patterning is a matter

of consequence. The extreme relativists, who hold that in social patterning anything goes, are in error. There is a penalty for bad social patterning: the effects on the human unit are disastrous, and the entire culture is put in jeopardy sooner or later.

5. Freud's methods of investigation can be used to relate social institutions to the individual and his genetic inheritance. The result of this interaction is not stereotyped, but falls within a fixed ambit of variations, known as personal character. The individuals of a society in their interaction create new institutions, some which promote co-operation and others which stimulate anxiety and rage. The success or failure of a society depends on a balance in favor of the former.

The techniques that were developed in this new application of psychodynamics to anthropological data resulted in the acquisition of three related bodies of knowledge: (1) a description of the homeostatic processes that operate in society, (2) a description of the "basic personality" that results from the particular homeostatic patterns of society, (3) a description of the dynamics of culture change. Material from studies in the Marquesan, Alorese, and European cultures will serve to illustrate the kind of information that can be derived from these three areas of investigation.

In Marquesas, a Polynesian island culture in the central Pacific, periodic starvation because of severe droughts constituted the chief problem in social adaptation. The Marquesans dealt with the problem of a limited food supply by the expedient of female infanticide. They did not kill female infants themselves; the children were simply exposed to marauding tribes who did the job for them. The destruction of these potential child-bearers served as an effective control over population growth, keeping the population within the limits of the available food supply. In this simple solution to a basic survival problem we have a gross illustration of social homeostasis, or adaptation.

In any homeostatic process the solution of one problem poses derivative problems. In Marquesas the control of population by female infanticide created an excess of men over women in the ratio of about five to two, and this discrepancy created an inequitable distribution of sexual opportunity. The obvious solution to this problem was polyandry, a marriage institution which permits a woman to have two or more husbands. This was not an ideal situation, but under the circumstances it was probably the best compromise.

This necessary compromise had important effects on the attitudes and behavior of the Marquesans, beginning in infancy. Even in a monogamous family set-up the woman has the problem of equitably dividing her time and attention between her husband and her children. With several husbands to satisfy, the problem is greatly magnified. The children, especially, suffer directly from this deprivation, since their needs are more pressing and unalterable. Frustration, fear, and anxiety among children were inevitable consequences in Marquesas where the mother spent most of her time with her several husbands, and, when not with them, at the local version of the beauty shop maintaining the conditions of her status and prestige. This maternal neglect was partially offset in Marquesas by the attention shown the children by the chief husband, secondary husbands, and aunts and uncles. This attention was enough to give the child minimum protection against physical dangers and to indoctrinate him in the simple social conventions and taboos. It could not, however, provide the emotional security and affection that is associated with a devoted mother-child relationship.

The husbands, too, suffer from female neglect in Marquesas. However, for them this was a condition to which they had been forced to adapt since childhood; the destructive manifestations of this neglect were better disguised. Jealousy among the men, for example, was suppressed in the interest of socially productive co-operation. It emerged only when the men were drunk. Also, the men turned to each other for a sense of social solidarity and identification, and joined at times in a united front against the women in the form of certain ceremonial taboos. Beneath the formality of these taboos lay a commonly shared hatred of women.

The most convincing evidence of the animosity toward women in this society is to be found in Marquesan legends and folk tales. In these tales women are commonly represented as wicked, heartless exploiters; they are portrayed as cannibals, seductresses of innocent young men, and robbers of children's food. In the fantasies of their folklore the Marquesans expressed a fear and hatred of women that to a large extent had to be suppressed in real life.

Viewed as isolated traits, some of the by-products of parental indifference in Marquesas have a positive connotation. Lack of care implies lack of restriction, and in the area of sexual behavior the absence of childhood restrictions contributed to an enviable degree of sexual potency; the Marquesan men can be said to have made the most of their limited opportunities. Marquesan culture also fostered a high degree of independence and precocity, due to the absence of dependency ties and restrictive injunctions. The early cultural relativists might have cited such evidence as an argument for introducing parental neglect in modern Western culture as an antidote to sexual impotency and crippling dependency, but they would have been guilty of ignoring the unique homeostatic pattern in which these cultural traits had a specific significance.

In Marquesas the food scarcity, the institution of polyandry, and the relative absence of basic disciplines in childhood constituted the main primary influences in the development of the individual members of that society. The effects of these social influences could be observed in the general personality make-up of the Marquesans, as described by the ethnographer. In addition, the entire institutionalized fabric of this society could be seen as reflecting, complementing, and expressing the basic personality of the Marquesans. In this frame of reference the social institutions of Marquesas did not appear as fortuitous, or evolved, or borrowed patterns of cultural behavior, but rather as specific implements of human adaptation within a unique homeostatic pattern.

The Marquesan study suggested a method and a frame of reference with which to study the effects of specific social institutions on the individual members of a society. It opened up the possibility of creating a useful critique of the structure and dynamics of human social organization. Thus from the start, the application of adaptational psychodynamics to cultural data was devoted to a practical end—social survival and human happiness.

A thorough and systematic attempt to use psychodynamic techniques in anthropology began in 1936, with the participation of Cora DuBois. After a preliminary attempt to work with existing ethnographies (Trobriand Islands, Chuchchee, Zuni) it became clear that the data would not yield the information necessary for a systematic psychodynamic analysis. It was decided, therefore, to initiate a field expedition designed to meet the methodological specifications of an approach that would furnish information about social adaptation, as effected through the lives of the individual members of society.

In 1937 DuBois departed for the island of Alor in the Netherlands East Indies with these general aims in mind: (1) To determine and describe the institutional constellations of the Alor culture, (2) To participate actively in the life of the culture, (3) To document the biographies of individual members of the culture, using such psychoanalytic criteria as dreams and fantasies, (4) To administer Rorschach and intelligence tests to selected individuals.

The study of Alor that resulted from this expedition illustrates, above all, the importance of "indirect evidence" in cultural studies—evidence that can be found and evaluated only with the help of experts trained in psychodynamics. The social scientist needs the psychologist for the simple reason that human adaptation involves the operation of processes which cannot be identified in the conscious life of man. Ethnographical data cannot be taken solely at its face value, any more than can the conscious productions of the individual mind. The observer must be trained to look beneath the surface of social institutions, and attempt to discern the relationships that exist between social pressures and the integration of the individual. Some highlights from the Alor study illustrate the nature of these relationships.

In Alor the vegetable food supply is controlled by the woman, while the meat supply is controlled by the man. On the face of it, this may not appear to be a critical or even particularly significant feature of this culture. But then a question occurs. What happens to the mother's infant children while she is in the fields tending the vegetable crop? The answer is that they are left back in the village, usually in the care of a reluctant older sibling, or a grandparent. Maternal neglect, because of the particular division of labor in this culture, is a persistent influence during the critical and formative years of Alorese children. Further observations reveal some of the corollaries of this condition: feeding frustrations continue throughout childhood. The direct training of children is unsystematic and sporadic, even in such basic activities as walking, talking, and sphincter control. Conformity to parental demands does not guarantee rewards. Punishment for misbehavior is inconsistent and capricious—behavior which brings approval on one occasion may just as well bring punishment on another.

The over-all treatment of children in Alor can be characterized as one of neglect and inconsistency. From studies in our own society one would suspect that these conditions would produce serious integrative disorders in the individual. The biographies and psychological tests of individual Alorese confirm this suspicion. The Alorese are suspicious, mistrustful, and anxious. They lack confidence and self-esteem. They are fearful and unaggressive, but prey on their neighbors by means of lies, deceptions, and chicanery. They are unable to sustain a love relationship or a friendship based on voluntary interest. They have a limited capacity to master or enjoy the outer world. The appearance of these traits as the common inheritance of the Alorese does not surprise us, knowing what we do about the early experiences of these people with their parents and the environment. What is more interesting, however, and what constitutes a real addition to our knowledge of cultural processes, is the observation that these traits are reflected throughout the entire social structure of the culture.

In the folklore and religion of Alor we note themes and motifs directly related to the life experiences and character traits of the Alorese. In their folklore the most common motif is parental frustration and hatred. In one tale, for example, a child is told by his mother to fetch some water with a water tube which she has deliberately punctured at the bottom. While the child is vainly attempting to fill the tube the parents abandon him. Years later, at his marriage feast, the parents reappear and are presented with food tubes filled with feces.

In their religion there is no idealization of the deity. The deity has no great power for beneficence and is therefore not placated in the expectation of rewards and benefits. Sacrifices to the deity are offered reluctantly and grudgingly, and then only in emergencies. There is no concept of forgiveness and no storing up of virtue as a form of insurance. The only comforting theme that appears in Alorese religion, myth, and folklore concerns supernatural Good Beings who bestow favors capriciously and without solicitation. They are, significantly enough, always total strangers to those whom they help.

The underlying tone in Alor religion and folklore is one of severely constricted affectivity. Considerations concerning the formal structure of these institutions, their origin, evolution, and diffusion, are of secondary importance in our efforts to find out how this culture functions. The correlation between the early strangulation of affectivity in the individual and the impoverished nature of institutionalized religion and folklore should lay to rest once and for all the idea that institutions interact with each other on a superorganic level, and without reference to human individuals.

Once we have reached these central insights about Alor, many seemingly idiosyncratic features in this culture take on meaningful and significant relationships. This applies to individual traits, such as the tendency to collapse and wait for death in the event of any kind of illness, and it applies to social institutions, such as the socioeconomic system which greatly exaggerates the importance of status and wealth. In the first example we recognize the Alorese conviction that one can expect only the worst from life, and in the second we recognize a frantic and desperate effort to bolster self-esteem.

When all the individual traits which the Alorese share in common are put together we have a record of the specific imprint of a given set of social institutions. It must be noted, however, that there are no two Alorese who will show exactly the same traits. Each individual has a specific and unique combination of traits which we call *individual character*. But all these individual traits are selections from the general ambit of potentialities offered by Alorese culture. This wider ambit of traits can be called "basic personality structure," "national character," or "modal personality."

The study of personality, as illustrated by the Alor study, is important because the personality structure of the individual is a critical factor in social homeostasis. Society is not an organism, so the term homeostasis is used metaphorically here only to suggest the balance that is maintained in society by the capacities of individuals to co-operate and share common interests. Social homeostasis is vested in the kinds of human beings it creates, hence the study of personality in culture is the only guide available to indicate how effectively a society is functioning.

Anthropology offers the source material for the demonstration of the effectiveness of one type of social patterning as compared with another. When the data and analysis of Alor were compared with similar studies of Marquesas, Comanche, Plainville, U.S.A., and Tanala, a useful method for the study of contrasts in social patterning emerged.

The study of Alor represented an important verification of the hypothesis first stated in *The Individual and His Society* (1939). It remains to this day the most complete collection of data gathered for this purpose. It was conducted as an interdisciplinary experiment in which three collaborators—Cora DuBois, an anthropologist, Emil Oberholzer, a psychologist, and Abram Kardiner, a psychiatrist—contributed to the collection and analysis of the data.

The first step of the experiment was a study of the institutions, mores, and folklore of Alor, on the basis of which a hypothesis was formulated concerning the impact of the institutions on ontogenetic development. The second step was a test of this hypothesis by the study and analysis of the eight native biographies that had been secured by the ethnographer through extensive life history interviews. The third step was a comparison of the results of the psychodynamic analyses of the eight biographical subjects with the results of the psychologist's study of thirty-eight Rorschach protocols and a collection of children's drawings. Kardiner and Oberholzer conducted their studies of DuBois' data independently and did not know of each other's conclusions until each study was completed. The correspondence of the results of these two methods of analysis was remarkably high, and quite beyond the range of chance.

The institutional setup in Alor indicated that it would create a serious interference with normal integrative processes within the individual. This was due to a lack of parental (chiefly maternal) care during the formative years of infancy and childhood. The effects of this deprivation were traceable both in the individual characters and in the character traits common to all Alorese. In addition, the effects of this deprivation were observable in the "secondary institutions" of Alor, such as religion, art, and folklore.

The traits of the Alorese—individual and cultural—reflected, above all, the emotional constriction in the individual, with the resulting secondary impairment of congnitive functions. In some instances the combination of character traits was beyond the emphatic understanding of a Westerner.[2] It seemed incredible that a society could survive

[2] See, for example, the biography of Lomani, *The Psychological Frontiers of Society,* p. 206.

whose institutions created such a severe degree of wide-spread emotional constriction.

The technique for cultural investigation that was developed in the study of Alor did not provide all the information we would like to have about a society, but it did reveal the limitations of the functional methods in anthropology. There is no way of relating institutions to each other, whether by the conceptual agency of the "super-organic," or by analogies with characterological types (culture patterns), or by any other arbitrary system. The functioning of a society depends on the social arrangement necessary to insure co-operation in dealing with the environment, on the impact of this arrangement on the integrative processes of the human unit, and on the institutions created by the members of society in response to the adaptive problems associated with a particular process of individual integration. The human unit is the variable that makes a functional analysis of cultural institutions possible.

Any investigative technique in the social sciences that is based on psychodynamics has the human unit at the center of the inquiry. The different approaches, however, yield very different results. Erikson's work begins with the identification of *Gestalten* associated with the alimentary experiences of the mouth and anus—ingestive, retentive, evacuative. These primary *Gestalten* are seen as the prototypes for emotionally charged thought processes which appear later in the individual's life. This concept is quite different from Freud's conception of the derivation of character traits by the transformations of libido. Erikson is on much sounder ground by deriving these *Gestalten* on the basis of congnition, rather than on the basis of instinctual energies and their transformations. He is limited in his analysis, however, to the identification and extrapolation of such *Gestalten* as bear some superficial resemblance to one of the institutions found in a given society. With the Sioux, for example, Erikson featured in his analysis the prolonged nursing period and the hostility of the child toward the mother which began with the long-delayed weaning period. The guilt that resulted over this hostility was the motivation behind those institutions associated with self-inflicted injury to the breast. When this kind of extrapolative procedure was applied to the Yurok it yielded even less information than with the Sioux.

Except for the translation of the bodily orifices into cognitive instead of energic terms, Erikson's procedure is the same as that used by Roheim, who speaks of the "projection on the outer world of an arrest of a stage of development." Roheim never made clear what the arrest of development consisted of, nor how it affected the subsequent development of the individual and the culture.

The analysis of Alor, by contrast, started with the institutional patterns, the origins of which we do not know. This pattern involved an unusual division of labor which deprived the child of maternal care. Here was a life condition which seriously affected the entire integrative process of the individual. There is an arrest of development, but this arrest is not a function of any particular bodily zone or the instinctual energies clustered around it. It is a disrupted configuration of integrative processes, both with respect to the self and the outer world, which resulted from the condition of parental neglect. The end products of distorted integrative patterns are apparent to one trained and experienced in psychodynamics. The adaptive value of the resulting integrative end products are the same whether they take place in New York or in Alor. Their adaptive value is low and so is the gratification they can yield. Hence the pleasure function also becomes disordered and loses its homeostatic value. The world becomes a disordered place and the social emotions fail to develop. The only emotions left to mediate between the organism and its environment are fear and rage—the inevitable consequences of defective or collapsing adaptive patterns.

The common error made by those without psychodynamic training who employ psychological concepts in cultural studies is that they fail to identify the kind of influences which interfere with the creation of effective integrative patterns of adaptation. Thus Gorer and Mead identified infant swaddling as being responsible for the Russian character, without any evidence that swaddling does anything to interfere permanently with the development of effective integrative patterns. The decision that a given factor operates in a damaging way must be based on many sources of information, because it is the nature of a malformed integrative pattern to operate in every aspect of adaptation. In Alor, for example, the evidence that maternal neglect was the damaging factor came from: (1) direct observation, (2) folklore, (3) religion, (4) biographies. The origins of some character traits in Alor were understood only with great difficulty; for example, the tendency to give up easily and surrender, the absence of depression, and the low order of artistic capacity. The lack of art seemed to be the result of preoccupation with inner tensions and an effort to exclude the external environment, hence the failure to idealize anything outside the self. The absence of depression appeared to be related to the failure to develop aggression and conscience patterns; the collapse in the face of adversity occurred in place of depression.

The importance of the technique employed in the Alor study lies in the fact that it can identify the effects of social patterning on the human unit. Such information cannot be secured by any of the extrapolative procedures derived from the libido theory, the dual instinct theory, or Erikson's modifications of the libido theory.

Unfortunately, this particular approach to culture-personality investigation in anthropology has ground to a halt. One of the main reasons is that this approach requires an expert knowledge of psychodynamics. This imposes a severe restriction on the recruitment of workers and collaborators. Another reason is that this work constitutes an invasion by psychodynamics of another discipline (anthropology). Academic resistance can be a powerful deterrent. Sooner or later, however, we are confident that these obstacles will be overcome, for the simple reason that if man is to survive in the modern world he must learn how society works. Man has probably reached the stage where organic evolution is no longer a factor in adaptation. Man is now in a position where he can practically remake the natural environment according to his bodily needs. It is now social evolution which will determine man's fate. Unfortunately, patterns of social co-operation carry no guarantees of success. One pattern will be successful under one set of conditions and fail under another. No society has a permanent tenure, especially those that are subject to constant change. Man must be given every opportunity to exploit the limited power he has to direct social evolution.

Existing primitive cultures present the only opportunity for the study of widely differing social patterns and the extent to which they meet the adaptive needs of man with varying degrees of success. The most instructive for us are those whose social patterns differ in marked degree from our own. However, the acculturation of these groups to modern culture is proceeding so rapidly that before long we will be deprived of the opportunity to do comparative cultural studies. There is no time to lose.

# HISTORY, PSYCHOLOGY, CULTURE

As an illustration of the usefulness of psycho-dynamics in identifying the dynamics of culture change, we want to attempt an explanation of how the scientific interest in man and culture happened to develop in the nineteenth century. This explanation is an exercise in the study of history and culture with the aid of some knowledge of human motivations. It is a good example of the effects a change of social institutions can have on emotional patterns.

When one speaks of political or social changes in a society one must bear in mind that men instituted these changes in the expectation of certain benefits, and that these changes did in fact have an effect on man, although perhaps not the same as those anticipated. Change can also be foisted upon man as a result of changes in the natural environment, or it can be forced on him by other men. In any case, man will react to change in a definite way. He is conditioned to respond by at least two identifiable factors: (1) his inherent nature, and (2) the immediate basis of his present expectations.

It is one of the features of so-called primitive societies that when the environment is stable, and contacts with other cultures limited, they tend not to change, at least not with any appreciable speed. But from its very inception Western culture has been given to continuous and rapid change —at times with explosive speed. It is therefore very difficult to take one period like the nineteenth century and insulate it from its past, particularly when some of the factors active at this period can be identified as having a continuity from the twelfth century on. We cannot therefore talk of things in the nineteenth century apart from the time that preceded it and that which followed it.

The transition from the feudal to the modern ethos has been described by many scholars. A description that has recently attracted some attention is the one by Erich Fromm. His thesis is that there was no *freedom* in the Middle Ages; that when freedom was finally achieved the burdens of man ultimately became too great to maintain it and so man decided to *escape* from freedom.

This is an interesting thesis. But we do not quite know what *freedom* is. Fromm tries to define it in terms of freedom to something and freedom from something but there is no absolute definition of freedom—to or from—except in terms of existing values, choices, opportunities, and available forms of security. If we consider these strictures, then we cannot complain of the fact that there was no freedom in the Middle Ages any more than we can complain that there was no electricity or express trains. The concept freedom acquired meaning only after a new order of social machinery came into existence—an order that created new goals, new values, and new types of security. Nothing can be considered a restriction of freedom that does not interfere with the access to opportunities that exist. One cannot talk of freedom in relation to nonexisting opportunities or with reference to those created centuries later.

From this illustration we can conclude that we are much safer talking about social machinery—to use a metaphoric expression—and evaluating its effects on man, than in talking about freedom, which is a derivative of these effects.

What is social machinery? It consists of the patterns of human relationships for the purposes of co-operation, and the instrumentalities used to effect them. For example, the social machinery for manufacturing articles for human use requires a definite kind of social organization, which is quite different from that required by the feudal organization. The goal of feudalism was not to create anything, but to defend status and property. One's status in the feudal system was—to a large extent—defined by birth; in the social organization for manufacture it was decided by enterprise and inventiveness.

When we attempt in our study of society to take the human unit into our frame of reference we are merely recognizing the fact that man reacts to his different external environments so that he feels differently about them and about himself in relation to them. Some give him a sense of pride; others depress his self-esteem. Each patterning provides different goals, directives, and values. When we study culture we are studying all of these things, and when we study history we are studying culture in motion over a span of time.

When we try to answer a topical question like, Why were the people of the nineteenth century interested in the study of man? we can only attempt an answer in very general terms and in probabilities. Everyone is in general agreement that such interest "caught on" because it had a bearing on the life of the times. One could also ask why Socrates was so interested in problems of human relations. It is highly likely that this interest was not purely academic, and that the people of Socrates' times were interested in the subject because human relations were making trouble.

What was there about nineteenth-century culture that made a theory of evolution spread like wildfire over the Western world, that gave special interest to the study of primitive man, and stimulated the birth of a new discipline split off from the long tradition of philosophy—namely psychology?

We can get some clues from the King-and-battle historians, from the economists, and from the historians of ideologies. The nineteenth century was ushered in by the Napoleonic wars. For twenty-five years, until 1815, Europe was in a social, political, and ideological revolution. Some phases of this revolution ended in 1815 with the defeat of Napoleon. A period of "peace" and creativity was ushered in, known generally as the Industrial Revolution. There was also a great ideological and artistic ferment beginning around 1770 and continuing until 1850, commonly known as the Romantic Movement.

Jacques Barzun has described the transition from Classicism to Romanticism from a cultural and adaptational point of view in his book, *Romanticism and the Modern Ego*. He makes it clear that there was nothing fortuitous about these two art forms. Each was the expression of a particular social ethos. The Classical was a mode initiated in the last flush of feudalism—a declining order that believed it had a tenure in perpetuity; the Romantic was the emotional accompaniment of a violent upheaval in the social order.

The high prosperity of the age of Louis XIV was not created by the aristocracy; it was created by the merchant class. The political power of the merchant class, although not manifest, was very great. But such is the power of prestige that the prosperous bourgeoisie imitated the dying feudal caste. According to Barzun, the culture of the feudal caste was codified in principles, attitudes, and conventions. It produced the illusion of stability in the order of things. It emphasized fixity, grandeur, dignity, authority, and high polish. These values were not the creation of man's judgment, which is fallible and changeable, but were rooted in the order of the universe, as the exact sciences of the time were demonstrating. The fixity of this order was determined by reason, and not emotion. Hence intelligence and discipline, renunciations of private desire and impulse, solidarity within a fixed social hierarchy, and punctilious behavior toward members of one's own caste—all these became cherished values. Toward everything else there was a systematically cultivated blindness.[1]

Originally established by force, this tenure of status was maintained by a social machinery of custom that was intended to inspire awe. This it did by formalization of human relationships with regulations of obsessive thoroughness. The ruling clique enforced not only social subordina-

[1] This particular style of taste and convention is not original to the age of Louis XIV. It is characteristic of every social order in which human relations are governed by dominance and submission, by fear of the consequences of insubordination, and awareness of the awards of ingratiation. Feeling is either absent, impounded, or under rigid control; most of all it is subordinated to self-preservation or status interest.

tion but also exercised decisive influence on manners, language, art, and thought. It embarked on territorial conquest and spread its culture by the contagion of snobbery and the force of arms. The image of nature and of reason to which the ruling classes subscribed was the product of the same coercion, selection, and cultivated blindness for unseemly things. Mathematics became the handmaiden of a rigorous social discipline, and was dominated by abstraction and generalization. In the laws of geometry and calculus this culture saw the reflected image of the social order it had brought about by coercion. Government was a branch of applied mathematics, and philosophers of the time, such as Descartes and Spinoza, used the geometric method to arrive at truth.

In this brief description of the highlights of the ethos of this period we have an interesting problem in sequences. We must solve this problem because we must try to understand the place that each factor has in the social process involved. Is this a purely arbitrary system, capriciously decreed and enforced because the power was there to enforce it? If this is the case, we have nothing to study. We must look further.

Some of the productions of the contemporaries of this period give us some clues. It was claimed that the feudal order was a quest for stability and order, and that the restraints it imposed constituted a necessary defense against anarchy. One can agree with this conclusion, for it is almost true. But there are different kinds of restraints: there are those that originate in fear of the police, and those that originate in conscience. In the first, the fear is of an external agency that will punish; in the second, the discipline is internalized, it acts automatically. Conscience is a powerful social cohesive that acts automatically; it is accompanied by highly emotional attachment to the source of conscience. The power of police lasts only as long as it has the power to enforce. This, then, was a society held together by force.

As long as the coercive power remained in the hands of the feudal aristocracy, there was no problem. The values that were devised had the effect of creating what seemed to be an atmosphere of stability and serenity. Among other things, however, the extreme formalization and order in the art forms of this period suggest that those in power were in constant need of reassurance about the stability and serenity of their world. They well knew that this stability was mounted on the shoulders of a caste system that effected a very inequitable distribution of opportunities for the enjoyment of available satisfactions. As long as they could enforce control of hate, rebellion, and misery, they had nothing to fear. To a certain degree they could count on the ability of people to identify themselves with their superiors. But this identification is not a very powerful bulwark because it lasts only as long as the identification pays off in borrowed prestige. When the source of this borrowed pride collapses, the underlying rage emerges.

The use of force as a social agent to insure the dominance of one group over another has insidious consequences on the whole fabric of life. Human relations are governed by rules and not by feeling. Correctness takes the place of truth and maxims of expediency and prudence take the place of wisdom. Spontaneity of feeling is lost, and is replaced by affectation. Human relatedness is controlled entirely by an institutionalized formalism. Men being what they are, however, feeling cannot be contained forever. Given the opportunity men will break the bonds of emotional constriction. The Romantic Movement represented such a breakthrough.

Arnold Hauser, whose book *The Social History of Art* is a remarkable social survey of art, claims that in the Romantic Movement the bourgeoisie came to exalt sentiment (feeling) because the aristocracy valued reserve and control. That is to say, the bourgeois did the opposite of what the aristocrat did, as an expression of rebellion. There is some doubt on this point because for a long time the bourgeoisie sought to emulate the aristocracy. We cannot accept the explanation that this alteration of emphasis was due to perversity or the wish to be different. The roots of this emotionality came from the same source that the Classical ethos came from—the adaptational opportunities of a particular institutional setup.

The way of life of the middle classes (the merchants) had insinuated itself into the feudal organization since the Crusades. This merchant group rendered society a high service by opening channels of communication and by accelerating the speed and range of human relations through the creation of machinery for stimulating and satisfying an ever-enlarging ambit of needs. This was the secret of their success; they pleased everyone and hurt no one. The freedom that they needed to make their rounds became institutionalized. The merchant's calling was originally that of the disfranchised elements in the feudal caste system. A larger and larger number of people could emulate the merchant and establish relations to sell labor or goods under contract, or consent to exchange goods or services for money. The merchants established the whole social machinery for making and distributing things for consumption or ornamentation. They increased in power and significance right under the noses of the landed aristocracy, which neither appreciated them nor could interfere with them. Their activity established a new ethos. Although they did not abolish the need for "salvation" they altered its significance by introducing a rival claim—enjoyment of life here and now. This could only be achieved by altering the secular social organization.

It was only a question of time before this ethos would begin to push against the feudal institutional setup, including the Church. The Church was the first victim, and the result was the Reformation. By dint of slow and continuous pressure the way of life of the merchant class took over the state and finally the culture.

Whereas the fixed hierarchy with its anxieties and its restraints was the key to the Classical ethos, the Romantic ethos was the expression of the new opportunities opened up by the bourgeois way of life.

What were these new opportunities? Suppose we first contrast them with the opportunities of the feudal organization. In feudalism what happened to you in your secular life was decided by the status into which you were born. If you were a serf, you lived in that status until you died. A serf got protection from his lord and also a share of what was produced in his household economy. In return he had to be faithful to his lord. If he gave up the shelter of this position, he became, in a way, free. But this freedom was not what we mean by freedom; it was the equivalent of disfranchisement. There were no institutionalized opportunities except those offered by the Church (monasteries), the army, or the merchant class with all its risks. There was really not much one could do about his secular fate. Responsibility for oneself was limited but concrete. There was a ceiling on aspiration because the choices were very few. Character did not matter because it decided very little in one's life. Ability did not vary much except in the upper echelons, because most people did the same thing. Above all, living was difficult and there was much hostility.

From the Reformation onward the institutional framework of Western culture changed in such a way as to give more opportunity for individual expression. The Reformation proclaimed the direct responsibility of man to God. In the changing institutional framework he had more opportunity for responsibility for himself. He had new opportunities for enterprise, more risk and more choices. With more opportunities for activity and enjoyment, the general level of aspiration became elevated, especially since this aspiration was tied to goals that were concrete and attainable with effort. This increased the individual's sense of responsibility.

Under these conditions fear of failure took precedence over fear of damnation as a motivating force, and enhancement of self-esteem became more important than the promise of salvation in the next life. Worldly well-being and sensual satisfaction became socially approved pursuits. Under these conditions suffering acquired a new interpretation; it acquired the right to social recognition as a social evil. Thus new social opportunities loosened one of the most powerful influences for social stability: recognition of the claims of human misery. Some doubt was cast on the assumption that suffering was really God's will. The feudal accommodation to suffering and misery by means of the "wages of sin" or "fall from grace" doctrines suffered a complete reversal.

It was because of this reversal that the Romanticists were eventually able to expose human suffering and misery, and to press the claim that this was a social responsibility. Need became legitimized; so did the right to feel envy and greed. Competition became legitimate and so did the individual emotions it demands. As Barzun puts it, the factory had become the prelude to citizenship. The issues of freedom could only be waged in the terms of existing opportunities. The Romanticists emphasized risk and venture. They did not want to endorse the evils of a fixed and implacable social hierarchy, and in the light of the newly created opportunities, proclaimed the right of the individual to aspiration, risk, and failure. They denied that society was a fixed order and a law of nature. They advocated a change.

The introduction of manufacture stimulated needs, and there was a social machinery for satisfying them. If one made the requisite effort, he could satisfy these needs. In the feudal ethos this was not possible for the great masses; needs and wants had to be suppressed with the consequence that hatred and aggression (envy) toward those who had what one wanted was inevitable—notwithstanding the ingratiating and submissive attitudes that prevailed. One could not "crash" the aristocracy. It was a closed clique admission to which could only be effected by birth. It is because human needs were unlimited that the bourgeoisie remained an open group, entrance into which required only energy, enterprise, daring, ability, and capital. Business could not, at its inception, become a caste, because human needs were insatiable and the taste of man for variety and new experience appeared inexhaustible. The right to have needs and the creation of a social machinery for satisfying them completed an arrangement that would benefit everyone. It could only lead to more aspiration, action, and productivity.

If we want to look for "psychological" changes that

follow in the wake of institutional changes, this is an excellent illustration. The feudal ethos constricted feeling and emotion and prevented the identification of society's constituents with each other. Romanticism, and the institutions which created it, opened the way for personal identification, for reciprocity of feeling and, consequently, for the inclusion of the lowly and their way of life as a matter of social interest and concern. Their sufferings and discomforts therefore acquired some demonstrative value. Once this suffering and its sources acquired the right to recognition, one could begin to talk about political freedom, which has to do with the institutionalized barriers to human relatedness. Without the emotional component, no political problem could arise.

The Romantic Movement was, therefore, the manifestation of an emotional breakthrough occasioned by the effective alteration of a certain social patterning. Although this was a Western phenomenon, its effects varied in different places. It was different in England from what it was in France. The political setup was different in each place. The French Revolution was not the beginning of a movement, but its end. It liquidated, in a formal way, the political gadgets that had lost effective power a long time before. The Napoleonic wars did much to liquidate the remains of feudalism all over Europe and to spread the new culture.[2]

The crowning achievement of this period was that it liberated vast sources of human energy. Action, the assertion of power, the cult of energy, power over the world, and power over one's own fate became the directives of the nineteenth century. It was in favor of emotion and action and against contemplation and complacency.[3]

Having described some of the institutional alterations

---

[2] Napoleon himself could not have been a very good judge of what his mission in Europe was. For on top of the middle-class culture of which he was the spearhead, he tried to re-establish a modernized version of the old feudal system in his short-lived "empire." Although he was defeated, the social revolution he represented was not.

[3] For an excellent essay on the personality and achievement of a representative of this period see J. Barzun, "Byron" in *The Energies of Art*.

and their effects on man in the early part of the nineteenth century, we now turn our attention to some of the interests he developed during the ensuing decades.

The people of this period saw the fall of dynasties and the rise of a new social order. They were therefore not inclined to place unlimited confidence in the stability of any social order. Moreover, the idea had been planted in the minds of people that they had something to say about the kind of order they wanted. At the very least, they knew that it changed. In addition, they saw the dawn of a new era of the inventiveness of man—the Industrial Revolution. Whatever difficulties and social dislocations it brought with it, this revolution created the techniques for making and distributing goods. Enjoyment here and now was being demonstrated and materialized.

But the greatest of all changes took place in the domain of man's relation to himself. The new order, based on liberalism as a political creed and a way of life, altered the feeling of responsibility for oneself. One's status in life was determined only in part by one's status at birth. It could be altered by will and enterprise. Thus one's fate depended on one's *character* and *ability*, and the latter was influenced by the former. Character became recognized as the implement of social interaction; institutions were not divinely decreed but were created by man.

It is natural that under these circumstances man turned his attention to himself. The manifestations of this interest were many. The poets, first, then the novelists created a renewed interest in character. This was a reflection of the same interest that showed itself in politics, but on a reduced and more intimate scale. The interest of the novelists lasted the entire century and culminated in the remarkable performances of Thackeray, Dickens, Jane Austen, the Brontes, George Eliot, Dostoyevski and Tolstoy.

In 1859 Darwin published his *Origin of Species.* Although the idea of evolution had been publicized for a century through the efforts of Lamarck and Buffon, Darwin's work galvanized the entire Western world. Something about this doctrine had an immediate relevancy for the time. The importance of this work was vested not only in its scientific merits, but also in the fact that it supplied a new frame of reference within which man came to think of himself.

Man had already seen a changing world and had begun to like it and encourage it. Change was now seen as a pattern for improving his worldly position, and was called *progress*. The theory of evolution provided a scientific justification for this optimism; it contained an antidote to the ecclesiastical conception of man's fate. It affirmed man's position in the universe as due to his own will, ingenuity, and dogged persistence. By endorsing this view man merely reaffirmed the responsibilities he had already assumed with liberalism. The idea of evolution also encouraged the tendency—already under way—to conquer nature and to subject it to man's needs. The influence of the supernatural in human affairs was formally conceded; but it was pure lip service, and the observance of religion became a social routine. Man became indifferent to supernatural intervention as his power over nature became confirmed.

The ability of man to survive and to subject the environment to his needs and uses became known as adaptation. This concept underwent some strange transformations during the Victorian age. *Well adapted* became synonymous with good. The idea that only the fittest survived stimulated an endless quest for effective adaptations to the end of still more effective adaptation.

In some ways, the idea that only the fittest survived had implications similar to the Calvinist doctrine that only the elect were saved. In evolution the elect were the successful ones; the unsuccessful had the equivalent of damnation. Failure in adaptation could no longer be blamed on the caprices of Divine Will, nor could it be interpreted as punishment for sin. It could only be interpreted as an indictment of adaptive capacity. The state promoted the welfare of the merchant group according to the principle that society was a self-regulating organism with built-in mechanisms for homeostasis. Responsibility for success was now vested in character and ability, and failure was viewed as biological and social inferiority. Failure that was noble and pathetic in 1820 became a disgrace in 1880. The doctrine of survival of the fittest gave its blessing to social ruthlessness in a free market of competition for commodities and labor. This blessing took out of the reach of moral judgment those perversions of the "instinct of self-preservation" that the business practices of the time encouraged. This does not mean that Darwinism implied business immorality. It does mean that the businessmen found in the slogan of survival of the fittest the scientific justification for the practice of social ruthlessness.

The contingency of philosophy on a prevailing ethos is illustrated by the English utilitarians of the time who believed that enlightened self-interest had the same self-regulating effect morally that laissez faire did politically.

The entire ethos of the nineteenth century made the individual responsible for himself to an unusual degree. Living acquired new hazards in the unexpected form of an increase in the demands the individual had to make on himself in order to maintain his self-esteem. Man had merely changed masters. In place of the fear of losing the support of a feudal superior, he now had to fear the demands of an exacting "superego" based on the cultural norm. This ethos increased man's burdens by increasing the demands for action, change, progress, success. Failure became a cause of anxiety, an anxiety that could no longer be allayed by the conviction that failure was the will of God. The anxiety of failure is not the kind that reduces aspirations —it increases them. In this period increased aspiration was directed toward the goal of social betterment as expressed by the "standard of living." This became the most powerful social incentive. It was not limited to any class or calling, but became the common claim.

The theory of evolution became popular when it did because it was an accurate reflection of the total ethos of the nineteenth century. It was the greatest success story of all time. It was an allegory in which man saw a reflection of his daily struggles. Just as the doctrine of the fall of man was suitable to the feudal ethos in that it put a damper on human aspiration and gave an acceptable interpretation to human suffering, so did the theory of evolution supply the mythology for the ethos of responsibility for oneself, and for ceaseless and restless effort and creativity. We must finally note that the elements who protested against this theory were the clergy. The businessman did not complain; it was good for business.

It was in this atmosphere that the science of man and culture was born. Whereas the eighteenth century had specialized in mathematics and the exact sciences, the nineteenth century specialized in the biological sciences. The functioning organism and its adaptational vicissitudes became the center of scientific interest, and the methods of biology became the prototype for most scientific investigation. Even the physical sciences started to move away from the methods of mathematical mechanics toward more functional and organic concepts.

We are in a position now to see that the intense interest that developed during this period in physiology, anthropology, and psychology was no accident. It was a direct result of man's changed conception of himself. Any great change in man, as in individual men, depends on an alteration of emotional patterns, and these are affected by the actual experiences man has under a specific set of social institutions.

Our special plea for a place for psychodynamics in any comprehensive study of man is based on the claim that the adaptational processes in individual men constitute the fulcrum around which historical events and social institutions—great and small—are delicately balanced. Without this fulcrum as the center of inquiry, historical and social phenomena can only be seen as unrelated and free-floating entities. As such, their interest is only for the collector, the statistician, and the dilettante.

The study of social patterning is a crucial issue. There is great anxiety the world over about the problems of social adaptation. The minimum condition of survival is even in doubt. Some day there may be an opportunity for scientific opinion on the subject of the merits of various types of social patterning. If that day comes, the instrument of investigation known as adaptational psychodynamics will have to be included.

# SELECTED BIBLIOGRAPHY

## Charles Darwin

### BIOGRAPHICAL SOURCES

Darwin, Francis, *The Life and Letters of Charles Darwin,* 1887.
———— *More Letters of Charles Darwin,* 1903.
Huxley, Julian S., "Charles Darwin: The Decisive Years," *Nation,* 157:536-38, 1946.
West, Geoffrey (pseud. Wells, Geoffrey Harry), *Charles Darwin, a Portrait,* 1938.

### PRIMARY SOURCES

Darwin, Charles, *Journal of Researches,* rev. ed., 1845.
———— *The Origin of Species,* 1859.
———— *The Descent of Man,* 1871.

### SECONDARY SOURCES

Barrett, S. A., editor, *Century of Darwin,* 1958.
Eiseley, L. C., *Darwin's Century,* 1958.
*Encyclopedia of Social Sciences,* 1931.
Himmelfarb, G., *Darwin and the Darwinian Revolution,* 1959.
Irvine, William, *Apes, Angels and Victorians,* 1955.
Keith, Arthur, *Darwin Revalued,* 1955.
Moore, R. E., *Charles Darwin,* 1955.
Osborn, H. F., *From the Greeks to Darwin,* 1894.
Thompson, J. A., "The Influence of Darwinism on Thought and Life," in F. S. Marvin, *Science and Civilization,* 1923.
Tripp, N. R., *The Substance of the Descent of Man,* 1926.

# Herbert Spencer

### BIOGRAPHICAL SOURCES

*Dictionary of National Biography,* Supplement 1901-1911.
Duncan, David, *The Life and Letters of Herbert Spencer,* 1908.
Spencer, Herbert, *An Autobiography,* 1904.

### PRIMARY SOURCES

Spencer, Herbert, *Social Statics,* 1855.
———— *The Man Versus the State,* 1884.
———— *Principles of Sociology,* 3rd ed., enlarged, 1885.
———— *Essays,* rev. ed., 3 vols., 1890.
———— *Principles of Biology,* rev. ed., 1898, 1899.
———— *Principles of Psychology,* 4th ed., 1899.
———— *First Principles,* rev. ed., 1900.

### SECONDARY SOURCES

Borraw, J. W., "Herbert Spencer: the Philosopher of Evolution,"
    *History Today,* 8:676-83, Oct., 1958.
Collins, F. Howard, *An Epitome of the Synthetic Philosophy,*
    1889.
Dewey, John, "The Philosophical Work of Herbert Spencer," *The
    Philosophical Review,* 13:159-75, 1904.
Goldenweiser, Alexander, *History, Psychology, and Culture,* 1933.
Royce, Josiah, *Herbert Spencer—An Estimate and Review,* 1904.
Simon, W. M., "Herbert Spencer and the Social Organism,"
    *Journal of the History of Ideas,* 21:294-99, April, 1960.

# Sir James Frazer

### BIOGRAPHICAL SOURCES

Campion, Sarah, "Autumn of an Anthropologist," *New Statesman
    and Nation,* 41:34, January 13, 1951.
Downie, R. Angus, *James George Frazer: The Portrait of a
    Scholar,* 1940.
Fleure, H. J., *Royal Society of London, Obituary Notices of Fel-
    lows,* 1941.
Frazer, J. G., *Gorgon's Head,* 1927.
Jaloux, Edward, "A Visit to Sir James Frazer," *Living Age,*
    348:135-39, 1935.
Malinowski, B., *A Scientific Theory of Culture,* 1944.

Marett, R. R., *Proceedings of the British Academy, Obituary Notices,* 1941.

GENERAL HISTORIES

Lowie, R. H., *History of Ethnological Theory,* 1937.
Penniman, T. K., *A Hundred Years of Anthropology,* revised, 1952.

PRIMARY SOURCES

Frazer, James, *Totemism and Exogamy,* 1910.
———— *The Golden Bough,* abridged ed., 1922.
———— *Garnered Sheaves,* 1931.

SECONDARY SOURCES

Dawson, W. R., editor, *The Frazer Lectures,* 1931.
Downie, R. Angus, (above).
Fleure, H. J., (above).
Goldenweiser, A., *History, Psychology and Culture,* 1933.
———— "Totemism and Exogamy," *Current Anthropological Literature,* 2:199-212, 1913.
Malinowski, B., (above).
Marett, R. R., (above).
Steiner, Franz, "Frazer and his Critic Marett," in *Taboo,* 1956.

## Edward Tylor

BIOGRAPHICAL SOURCES

*Dictionary of National Biography,* Second Supplement, Vol. 24.
Lang, Andrew, Introductory essay in *Anthropological Essays Presented to Edward Burnett Tylor,* 1907.
Marett, R. R., *Tylor,* 1936.

GENERAL HISTORIES

Goldenweiser, A., *History, Psychology and Culture,* 1933.
Haddon, A. C., *History of Anthropology,* 1910.
Lowie, R. H., *History of Ethnological Theory,* 1937.
Penniman, T. K., *A Hundred Years of Anthropology,* 1955.

PRIMARY SOURCES

Tylor, E. B., *Anahuac,* 1861.
———— *Researches Into The Early History of Mankind,* 1865.
———— *Primitive Culture,* 1871.

———— "On a Method of Investigating the Development of Institutions; Applied to Laws of Marriage and Descent," *Journal of the Anthropological Institute*, 18:45, 1888.

SECONDARY SOURCES

Goldenweiser, A., (above).
Haddon, A. C., (above).
Hodgen, M. T., *The Doctrine of Survivals*, 1936.
Lang, Andrew, (above).
Lowie, R. H., (above).
Marett, R. R., (above).
Penniman, T. K., (above).
Wallis, W. D., "Anthropology in England Early in the Present Century," *American Anthropologist*, 51:781-90, Oct., 1957.

## Emile Durkheim

BIOGRAPHICAL SOURCES

Alpert, Harry, *Emile Durkheim and his Sociology*, 1939.
Branford, V. D., "A Brief Memoir," *Sociological Review*, 10:77-82, 1918.

GENERAL HISTORIES

Barnes, H. E., *Introduction to the History of Sociology*, 1948.
Beach, C. G., *Growth of Social Thought*, 1939.
Bristol, L. M., *Social Adaptation*, 1921.
*Encyclopedia of the Social Sciences*, 1937.
Goldenweiser, A., *History, Psychology and Culture*, 1933.
Lowie, R. H., *History of Ethnological Theory*, 1937.

PRIMARY SOURCES

Durkheim, Emile, *Division of Labor*, 1893.
———— *Rules of Sociological Method*, 1895.
———— *Suicide*, 1897.
———— "Individual Representations and Collective Representations," 1899.
———— "The Determination of Moral Facts," 1907.
———— *Elementary Forms of the Religious Life*, 1912.

SECONDARY SOURCES

Alpert, Harry, *Emile Durkheim and his Sociology*, 1939.

——— "Durkheim and Sociologismic Psychology," *American Journal of Sociology*, 45:64-70, 1939.

——— "Emile Durkheim and the Theory of Social Integration," *Journal of Social Philosophy*, Vol. 6, No. 2, Jan., 1941.

*The American Journal of Sociology*, May, 1958. A commemorative issue for Emile Durkheim and Georg Simmel. Papers on Durkheim by P. H. Rossi, K. D. Naegele, K. H. Wolff, H. C. Selvin, L. F. Schnore, M. Gold, H. Alpert.

*The American Sociological Review*, August, 1959. Special papers on Durkheim by R. N. Bellah, H. Alpert, B. P. Dohrenwend.

Barnes, H. E., (above).

Durkheim, Emile, *Education and Sociology,* translation and Introduction by Sherwood D. Fox; Foreword by Talcott Parsons, 1956.

——— *Professional Ethics and Civic Morals,* translation by Cornelia Brookfield; Introduction by H. N. Kubali, 1957.

——— *Sociology and Philosophy,* translation by D. F. Popock; Introduction by J. G. Peristiany, 1953.

Evans-Pritchard, E. E., *Social Anthropology,* 1951.

Gehlke, C. E., *Emile Durkheim's Contributions to Sociological Theory,* 1915.

Goldenweiser, A., (above).

Lowie, R. H., (above).

Merton, R. K., "Durkheim's Division of Labor in Society," *American Journal of Sociology*, 40:319-28, 1934.

——— *Social Theory and Social Structure,* 1949.

Parsons, Talcott, *The Structure of Social Action,* 1937.

# Franz Boas

### BIOGRAPHICAL SOURCES

Benedict, Ruth, "Appreciation," *Science,* 97:60-62, 1943.

Boas, Franz, "An Anthropologist's *Credo,*" *Nation,* 147:201-04.

——— "Response to President's Address at American Anthropological Association," *American Anthropologist,* 9:646 ff., 1907.

——— "Scientists as Spies," *Nation,* 109:797.

*Current Biography,* 1940.

Herskovits, M. J., *Franz Boas: The Science of Man in the Making,* 1953.

Kroeber, A. L., and others, *Franz Boas: 1858-1942.* Memoir series, no. 61, American Anthropological Association, 1943.

Lowie, R. H., "Biographical Memoir of Franz Boas," National

Academy of Science, *Biographical Memoirs,* 24:303-22.

———— "Franz Boas (1858-1942)," *Journal of American Folklore,* 57:59-69.

———— "Franz Boas, his predecessors and his contemporaries; a reply to Ruth Benedict," *Science,* 97:202-03, 1943.

Spier, Leslie, "Franz Boas and Some of His Views," *Acta Americana,* 1:108-27, 1943.

Yampolsky, Helene Boas, "Excerpts From the Letter Diary of Franz Boas On His First Trip To the Northwest Coast," *International Journal of American Linguistics,* Vol. 24, No. 4, Oct., 1958.

### PRIMARY SOURCES

Boas, Franz, *The Mind of Primitive Man,* rev. ed., 1938.

———— *Race, Language and Culture,* 1940.

———— "Recent Anthropology," *Science,* 98:311-14, 1944.

———— *The Central Eskimo,* Smithsonian Institute, Bureau of Ethnology, 6th Annual Report.

———— "Evolution or Diffusion," *American Anthropologist,* N.S. Vol. 26, No. 3:340-44.

———— "Kwakiutl Culture as Reflected in Mythology," *Memoirs of the American Folklore Society,* 28:1-190.

———— "Primitive Custom" (Review of Malinowski's *Crime and Custom in Savage Societies*), *Forum,* 76:791-93.

### SECONDARY SOURCES

Buettner-Janusch, John, "Boas and Mason: Particularism versus Generalization," *American Anthropologist,* 59:318-24, 1957.

Herskovits, (above).

———— "Some Further Notes on Franz Boas' Arctic Expedition," *American Anthropologist,* 59:112-16, 1957.

Kroeber, A. L., and others, (above).

———— "History and Science in Anthropology," *American Anthropologist,* 37:539-69, 1935.

———— "The Place of Boas in Anthropology," *American Anthropologist,* 58:151-59, 1956.

Lowie, R. H., (above).

———— "Boas Once More," *American Anthropologist,* 58:159-63, 1956.

Penniman, T. K., *A Hundred Years of Anthropology,* 1955.

Radin, Paul, "Boas and 'The Mind of Primitive Man,'" in M. Cowley and B. Smith, *Books That Changed Our Minds,* 1939.

Ray, V. F., "Boas Once More. Rejoinder," *American Anthropologist,* 58:164-70, 1956.

——— Review of M. J. Herskovits', *Franz Boas: The Science of Man in the Making, American Anthropologist,* 57:138-40, 1955.


## Bronislaw Malinowski

### BIOGRAPHICAL SOURCES

*Current Biography,* 1941.

Kluckhohn, Clyde, "Bronislaw Malinowski 1884-1942," *Journal of American Folklore,* 56:208-19, 1943.

Lowie, R. H., *History of Ethnological Theory,* 1937.

Montagu, M. F. Ashley, "Bronislaw Malinowski (1884-1942)," *Isis,* 34 Part 2:146-50, 1942.

Murdock, Peter, "Bronislaw Malinowski," *American Anthropologist,* 45:44-51, 1943.

Richards, Audrey I., "Bronislaw Kaspar Malinowski," *Man,* 43: 1-4, 1943.

"Professor Bronislaw Malinowski." An account of the Memorial Meeting held at the Royal Institute of London, July 13, 1943.


### PRIMARY SOURCES

Malinowski, Bronislaw, *Argonauts of the Western Pacific,* 1922.

——— "Psychoanalysis and Anthropology," Letter to the Editor, *Nature,* 112:650-51, 1923.

——— "Psychoanalysis and Anthropology," *Psyche,* 4:293-332, 1924.

——— "Anthropology," *Encyclopaedia Britannica,* 13th ed., Supplemental Vol., No. 1, 1926.

——— *Crime and Custom in Savage Society,* 1926.

——— *The Sexual Life of Savages in Northwestern Melanesia,* 1929.

——— *Sex and Repression in Savage Society,* 1927.

——— "The Foundations of Faith and Morals" (1936), Riddell Memorial Lectures, 7th series, 1934-1935.

——— "Introduction" in Hogbin, H. I., *Law and Order in Polynesia,* 1934.

——— "Culture," *Encyclopaedia of the Social Sciences,* 1937.

——— "Culture as a Determinant of Behavior," in *Harvard Tercentenary Conference of Arts and Sciences,* 1937.

———— "The Group and the Individual in Functional Analysis," *Journal of American Sociology,* 44:938-64, 1939.

———— "The Scientific Approach to the Study of Man," in R. N. Anshen, *Science and Man,* 1942.

———— *A Scientific Theory of Culture and Other Essays,* 1944.

———— *Magic, Science and Religion and Other Essays,* 1948.

———— "Social Anthrolopolgy," *Encyclopaedia Britannica,* 14th ed.

### SECONDARY SOURCES

Firth, Raymond W., editor, *Man and Culture: An Evaluation of the World of Bronislaw Malinowski,* 1957.

Goldstein, L. J., "Logic of Explanation in Malinowskian Anthropology," *Philosophy of Science,* 24:156-66, 1947.

Gluckman, Max, "Malinowski Reassessed," *New Statesman,* 59: 405-06, 1960.

———— *Malinowski's Sociological Theories,* 1949.

Herskovits, M. J., *Man and His Works,* 1950.

Jones, Ernest, "Mother-Right and the Sexual Ignorance of Savages," *International Journal of Psychoanalysis,* Vol. VI, Part 2:109-30, 1925.

Kluckhohn, Clyde, (above).

Lowie, R. H., (above).

Montagu, M. F. Ashley, (above).

Murdock, Peter, (above).

Rex, J. A., "Plural Society in Sociological Theory," *British Journal of Sociology,* 10:114-24, 1959.

Richards, Audrey, (above).

## Alfred Louis Kroeber

### BIOGRAPHICAL SOURCES

Lowie, R. H., editor, *Essays in Anthropology in Honor of Alfred Louis Kroeber,* 1936.

*National Cyclopaedia of American Biography,* 14:120.

### PRIMARY SOURCES

Kroeber, A. L., "The Morals of Uncivilized Peoples," *American Anthropologist,* 12:437-41, 1910.

———— "Eighteen Professions," *American Anthropologist,* 17:283-288, 1915.

———— "The Superorganic," 1917. Republished in *The Nature of Culture,* 1952.

———— "Order in Changes in Fashion," 1919. Republished in
*The Nature of Culture,* 1952.

———— *Handbook of the Indians of California,* 1925.

———— "The Culture-Area and Age-Area Concepts of Clark Wissler," in *Methods in Social Science,* a Case Book, edited by
S. A. Rice, 1931.

———— "Culture Element Distribution," III, *University of California Publications in American Archaeology and Ethnology,*
37:101-16, 1936.

———— "Cultural and Natural Areas of Native North America,"
*University of California Publications in American Archaeology and Ethnology,* 48:1-242, 1939.

———— "Elsie Clews Parsons," *American Anthropologist,* 45:252-255, 1943.

———— *Configurations of Culture Growth,* 1944.

———— *Anthropology,* 1948.

———— "White's View of Culture," *American Anthropologist,* 50:405-15, 1948.

———— "Configurations, Causes and St. Augustine," *American Anthropologist,* 53:279-84, 1951.

———— "Causes in Culture," 1947. Reprinted in *The Nature of Culture,* 1952.

———— "Culture, Events and Individuals," 1946. Republished in
*The Nature of Culture,* 1952.

———— "Three Centuries of Women's Dress Fashions: A Quantitative Analysis," 1940, with Jane Richardson. Republished in
*The Nature of Culture,* 1952.

———— " 'Totem and Taboo: An Ethnologic Psychoanalysis,' 1920
and 'Totem and Taboo in Retrospect,' " 1939, *Culture,* 1952.

———— *Style and Civilizations,* 1957.

———— "History of the Personality of Anthropology," *American Anthropologist,* 61:398-404, 1959.

SECONDARY SOURCES

Goldenweiser, A. A., "The Autonomy of the Social," *American Anthropologist,* 19:447-49, 1917.

Herskovits, M. J., *Man and His Works,* 1948.

Sapir, Edward, "Do We Need a Superorganic," *American Anthropologist,* 19:441-47, 1917.

Sorokin, P. A., *Social Philosophies in an Age of Crisis,* 1950.

Strong, Edward W., "A Question of Interpretation," *American Anthropologist,* 50:216-24, 1948.

Tax, Sol, editor, *An Appraisal of Anthropology Today,* 1953.
White, Leslie A., "Kroeber's 'Configurations of Culture Growth,'"
  *American Anthropologist,* 48:79-93, 1946.

## Ruth Benedict

### BIOGRAPHICAL SOURCES

Barnouw, Victor, "Ruth Benedict: Apollonian and Dionysian,"
  *University of Toronto Quarterly,* April, 1949.
*Current Biography,* 1941.
Hutchinson, G. E., *The Itinerant Ivory Tower,* 1953.
Mead, Margaret, *An Anthropologist at Work: Writings of Ruth
  Benedict,* 1959.
——— "Ruth Fulton Benedict: 1887-1948," *American Anthropol-
  ogist,* 51:457-68, 1949.
*The National Cyclopedia of American Biography.*
*Poetry,* 31:192-95, 1928; 35:304-07, 1930.
"Ruth Fulton Benedict—A Memorial," 1949, Viking Fund, No-
  vember 4, 1949.

### PRIMARY SOURCES

Benedict, Ruth, "Psychological Types in the Cultures of the South-
  west." Proceedings: *Twenty-third International Congress of
  Americanists,* pp. 572-81, 1928.
——— "Configurations of Culture in North America," *American
  Anthropologist,* 34:1-27, 1932.
——— "Anthropology and the Abnormal," *Journal of General
  Psychology,* 10:59-82, 1934.
——— *Patterns of Culture,* 1934.
——— *The Chrysanthemum and the Sword, Patterns of Japanese
  Culture,* 1946.

## Sigmund Freud

### BIOGRAPHICAL SOURCES

Jones, Ernest, *Life and Work of Sigmund Freud,* 3 vols., 1953,
  1955, 1957.

### PRIMARY SOURCES

Breuer, J., and Freud, S., "On the Psychical Mechanism of Hysterical Phenomena," 1893. In Collected Papers of Sigmund
  Freud, Vol. I.

———— Studies on Hysteria, 1895.

Freud, Sigmund, "Freud's Psycho-Analytic Method," 1904. In Collected Papers of Sigmund Freud, Vol. I.

———— *The Interpretation of Dreams,* 1913.

———— *Totem and Taboo,* 1913.

———— "On the History of the Psycho-Analytic Movement," 1914. In Collected Papers of Sigmund Freud, Vol. I.

———— *Group Psychology and the Analysis of the Ego,* 1921.

———— Two Encyclopedia Articles, 1922. "Psycho-Analysis," "The Libido Theory." In Collected Papers of Sigmund Freud, Vol. V.

———— *The Future of an Illusion,* 1928.

———— *Civilization and Its Discontents,* 1930.

———— *Moses and Monotheism,* 1939.


SECONDARY SOURCES

Erikson, Erik, *Childhood and Society,* 1951.

Kardiner, Abram, *The Individual and His Society,* 1939.

———— and others, *The Psychological Frontiers of Society,* 1945.

———— with Ovesey, L., *The Mark of Oppression,* 1951.

———— *Sex and Morality,* 1954.

Roheim, Geza, *Psychoanalysis and Anthropology,* 1952.

# INDEX

## ABOUT THE AUTHORS

ABRAM KARDINER was born in New York City in 1891 and is a graduate of the College of the City of New York. He received his M.D. degree from Cornell University in 1917 and four years later he went to Austria where he studied psychiatry under Sigmund Freud. Returning to this country in 1922, Dr. Kardiner served on the faculty of the New York Psychoanalytic Institute, became Clinical Professor of Psychiatry at Columbia University, and Director of Columbia University's Psychoanalytic Clinic, a post that he relinquished in 1957.

Currently Research Professor of Psychiatry at Emory University, Dr. Kardiner continues his work as a practicing psychiatrist. The author of many well-known books, including *The Individual and His Society, The Psychological Frontiers of Society,* and *Sex and Morality,* Dr. Kardiner makes his home with his wife in New York City.

EDWARD PREBLE was born in Portland, Oregon, in 1922. After military service with the army in both France and Germany during the Second World War, he became a student at Lewis and Clark College. Between 1950 and 1956 he attended the Columbia University Graduate School, studying first law, and then philosophy and anthropology. During this same period he was also a high school science teacher and worked as a professional tennis player during the summers.

From 1955 to 1958 Edward Preble engaged in anthropological field work with delinquent youths in New York City. And since 1958 he has been Assistant Professor of Anthropology at The New York School of Psychiatry. Mr. Preble makes his home in Suffern, New York, where he lives with his wife and six children.